FLORIDA HOME GROWN: LANDSCAPING

FLORIDA HOME GROWN: LANDSCAPING

by
Tom MacCubbin

Illustrations by Mike Wright,
Gerald Masters and Garth Schweizer

A publication of The Orlando Sentinel

Sentinel Communications Company

Orlando/1987

Edited by Becky Slavis and Lynn O'Meara
Designed by Mike Wright
Illustrations by Mike Wright, Gerald Masters and Garth Schweizer
Cover illustration by Mike Wright
Insect illustrations by members of The Orlando Sentinel Editorial Graphics Department
Back cover photograph by Dennis Wall

Printed in the United States

First Edition: March 1987
Second Printing: July 1988

Library of Congress Cataloging-in Publication Data

MacCubbin, Tom, 1944-
  Florida home grown.

  "A publication of The Orlando Sentinel."
  1. Landscape gardening--Florida.   I. Title.
II. Title: Landscaping.
SB473.M19 1987   635.9'51'759   86-33909
ISBN 0-941263-00-2 (pbk.)

About the author

A NATIVE OF MARYLAND and horticulture graduate of the University of Maryland, Tom MacCubbin has been Orange County's urban horticulturist since 1972.

In 1980 Mr. MacCubbin started the weekly television program *Florida Home Grown*, produced by WMFE-Orlando. His name and face have also become familiar to Florida gardeners through columns written for *The Orlando Sentinel*, talks on local radio programs, and frequent appearances at gardening clubs and civic organizations.

Throughout his career, Mr. MacCubbin has earned numerous accolades, including The Garden Communicator's Award from the American Association of Nurserymen. He has also been named Best Horticulture Writer and Best Garden Editor by the Florida Nurserymen and Growers Association.

When he is not busy advising Central Floridians on their horticultural problems, Mr. MacCubbin can be found cultivating his Seminole County garden with his wife, Joan, and their five children.

Dedication

THIS BOOK IS DEDICATED to the people of Florida, especially to the residents of Orange County, who years ago put their trust in a fledgling horticulturist and with encouragement and support allowed him to help cultivate their gardens.

It's a tribute to the staff members of *The Orlando Sentinel*, who through the years have nurtured an immature but willing writer.

Most of all, it is dedicated to my devoted wife, Joan, whose love and support in the garden as well as the home make my life as a horticulturist possible.

Acknowledgements

THIS BOOK IS NOW IN YOUR gardening library thanks to the assistance of many.

There is no way to completely express an author's gratitude to *The Orlando Sentinel* staff members Becky Slavis and Lynn O'Meara for their editorial expertise, patience and belief in this Florida gardener. Special thanks also to Bethany Mott who inspired and supervised the progress of this book from concept to completion. Their hours of work and frustrations can only be compensated by your beautiful and productive gardens.

Thanks to Mike Wright, also of the *Sentinel*, whose inspired illustrations and book design bring gardening to life as we turn the pages. His devotion to completing this work, often under considerable pressure, is deeply appreciated.

Thanks also to Jerry Masters for the many lifelike and excellent plant illustrations that grace the pages and tempt gardeners to plant.

A special thank you to Garth Schweizer of Integrated Design Group for the clear, step-by-step landscape designs as well as his expertise and guidance as a landscape architect.

All gardeners, including this author, owe a debt of gratitude to the Institute of Food and Agriculture Sciences (IFAS) at the University of Florida, Gainesville. Its researchers, teaching professors and extension agents provide invaluable information for home gardeners.

Thanks to the IFAS Florida Cooperative Extension Service for the many charts and other information contained in this book.

Thanks to the staff of WMFE-Orlando who have made the television program *Florida Home Grown* a household phrase and offer its name for this book's title.

Appreciation is also expressed to the American Rose Society for contributing illustrations to the section on rose culture.

Last but not least, thanks to my wife, Joan, for typing the original manuscript that hopefully will help you produce your landscape and gardens.

Contents

Introduction

I GREW UP WITH MANURE IN my pockets. As a young boy it was the easiest way to bring home the fertilizer for a grandmother's rose bed. It must have been good stuff because most of those roses survived transplanting and produced flowers for more than 30 years.

Many of those early years were spent in the vegetable patch. An early memory was my first experience of weeding. I was given the chore of weeding out beets and that is exactly what happened. Those colorful red-topped vegetables were oh, so obvious to a boy of about 4 and each was plucked gingerly from the row.

Well, the career was off to a rough start and my garden was moved to the back forty. Most vegetables grew like weeds in our fertile Maryland soil, even from the year-old seeds given to me for planting.

Luckily, my parents also enjoyed flowers, and words like delphinium, zinnia and gladiolus became part of my vocabulary. I was spoon-fed the knowledge of how to grow plants and I grew up appreciating the land and its bounty.

This farm boy had many loves and it was hard to pick between the cows and the garden. I was educated to care for each, but for financial reasons I decided to make horticulture my career.

I went off to the University of Maryland to obtain two degrees, followed by a short term of college teaching and then the long happy career with the Extension Service that is still enjoyed today.

Having experienced Northern life makes one appreciate Florida that much more. It was a great move to a horticultural paradise where plants grow year-round.

The transition is easy. Soil is soil; some just needs a little more water and fertilizer. Plants that grow as houseplants in the North are landscape ornamentals in Florida. It takes just a little time to readjust to four gardening seasons.

All that's needed is a guide to reorient a new resident's thinking and that is what lies ahead in this book. The chapters are packed with information to make the homesite a great Florida garden.

I know how most "transplants" think and this book will ease the adjustment. It first helps to organize your land with simplified but sound landscape principles, then carries you through the fun and rewards of cultivating the crops, flowers and lawns of Florida.

For the native it offers information on both the traditional and the less common plants for your garden. It also provides the benefits of the most recent scientific research and cultural techniques that help you make the home landscape beautiful and productive.

Garden along with me and enjoy the best life this great state has to offer.

1

Florida gardening — a year-round affair

FLORIDA CAN BE A YEAR-round paradise for gardeners. The growing seasons are long and the weather prompts luxuriant plant growth.

The pleasant climate invites outdoor living, allows four seasons of gardening, and encourages non-stop flowers with the proper selection of plants.

Many newcomers assume Florida is a tropical paradise. However, freezes do occur consistently in the northern regions and from time to time in the southernmost extremities. In those years when freezes are not severe such tropical plants as bananas and crotons can flourish.

Not every plant will succeed however. Some plants familiar to Northern gardeners, such as rhubarb and daffodils, require a period of winter cold. Other favorite plants, such as strawberries and delphiniums, burn out in the Florida sun and are best treated as annuals.

While temperatures vary significantly from north to south, Florida gardens share these similarities:

- Sandy soil.
- Subtropical plants.
- Prevalent pests.

- Heavy summer rainfall.
- Dry periods fall through spring.
- Saltwater intrusion in coastal regions.

There are, of course, regional differences.

North Florida has a hilly, rolling landscape. The region has four distinct seasons and freezes are expected each winter. The soil ranges from pure sand to sandy clay. It is possible to grow many deciduous fruits and a few hardy varieties of citrus. Walnut and pecan trees are popular, and bulbs and flowers of northern states are likely to flourish.

In South Florida the land is flat and frequently swampy. The seasons are indistinct, and while light frosts may occur, freezes are rare. In sand to limestone aggregate soils it is possible to grow true tropicals year-round. Vegetation is lush. Citrus and exotic fruits are cultivated here.

Central Florida is relatively flat and the soil is predominantly sand. Spring and fall are enjoyable gardening times, when temperatures generally range from 60 to 85, but these seasons are often very short. Ninety-degree days can begin in June and last well into September.

Forty- to 50-degree nights begin as early as November. The first killing frost can be expected as early as mid-December, but by the end of February winter is usually over.

From late September through May — the times of least frequent rainfall — 2 to 3 inches of rain a month are all a gardener can expect. During the warmer months of spring and fall irrigation is essential. An average lawn may require a quarter inch of water per day to stay green.

June through September is the rainy season, with thunderstorms arriving on most afternoons. Expect seven inches or more of rain each month to create a rich green landscape.

The Florida landscape is divided into U.S. Department of Agriculture Zones 9 and 10. This means that gardeners have a huge variety of plants from which to select.

A word of caution: Not all plants that catalogs suggest for Zone 9 will flourish in Florida. For many plants, summer weather will be too hot.

Purchases from garden centers are almost always smart buys, as local businesses offer trees, shrubs and flowers that thrive in their geographic area.

Save leaves for the compost pile

Don't let your bags of "brown gold" be hauled away. Those leaves and other easily decomposable material can be invested in the compost pile.

Compost piles are a vital resource for home gardeners. The decomposed organic material builds soil particles needed to hold moisture and nutrients in Florida sand. Compost incorporated into soil reduces compaction, improves aeration and helps maintain a uniform root temperature.

Leaves are a good beginning for compost piles. Grass clippings, stems and stalks from harvested vegetables, dropped citrus fruits, small twigs and eggshells and other kitchen waste can be added.

Cement blocks, wood fencing and even old bed springs can be used to contain compost piles. The piles can be hidden behind a fence, encircled with shrubs or otherwise concealed. Many gardeners like to build two piles side by side so the organic matter can be turned from one to the other, speeding decomposition.

A basic approach to composting involves forming layers of organic material 12 inches thick, each topped with an inch of microorganism-rich soil from the garden.

To encourage faster decomposition, sprinkle 6-6-6 fertilizer over the soil layer at the rate of a half cup per 4-foot-square surface area. Compost is normally ready to use in three to four months but a thorough mixing of the layers speeds this process.

Work in large quantities of compost when preparing a garden site. Compost should also be incorporated into the planting holes of new trees and shrubs, applied as a mulch for landscape plantings and used when formulating soils for potting houseplants.

In the garden, spread compost around plants to supply many of the nutrients needed for flower and fruit production.

Cement block construction with corner pipes to hold blocks in place.

Fertilizer layer

Organics layer   Soil layer

When in doubt check your County Extension Service plant lists before ordering. Remember: If it's not seen growing in your community, it probably won't.

Sand in your shoes is also your topsoil

All Floridians have sand in their shoes. Some homesites can boast a clay base or high organic content but most landscapes consist of well-drained sands.

The new gardener will be shocked to discover his topsoil is simply fine-grained sand.

Ordering topsoil is not recommended because Florida's sands can be suprisingly productive. Water and fertilizer are all it takes to grow sky-high produce, green lawns and bouquets of flowers. However, the addition of organic matter is always welcome.

Good, rich compost is your Florida gold. It helps the soil retain water and nutrients, keeps the soil at a uniform temperature and maintains a loose, well-drained garden site.

Other forms of organic matter are also useful. These include manures laden with sawdust or straw, old hay, grass clippings and peat moss. Few Floridians will ever have a completely organic garden, but the practices of returning vegetable matter to the soil can greatly improve plant culture.

Sandy soil is sterile and needs the nutrients supplied by manures or fertilizers. Regular feedings are essential for plant growth. Get accustomed to frequent feedings to keep the foliage green or the crops productive.

Do not plant a garden or landscape without a pH test. Florida soil ranges from very acid to extremely alkaline. Lime leaches readily from buildings and sidewalks, making azaleas, camellias, philodendrons and blueberries difficult to grow unless gardeners accordingly adjust the pH.

The pH range for bahia grass is about 5.5 to 6, but for St. Augustine it ranges from 6 to 6.5. A simple test — and adjustment, if needed — could mean the difference between success or failure.

Perspective of completed landscape for entrance area.
Step-by-step instructions for designing
landscapes, Chapters 2-4.

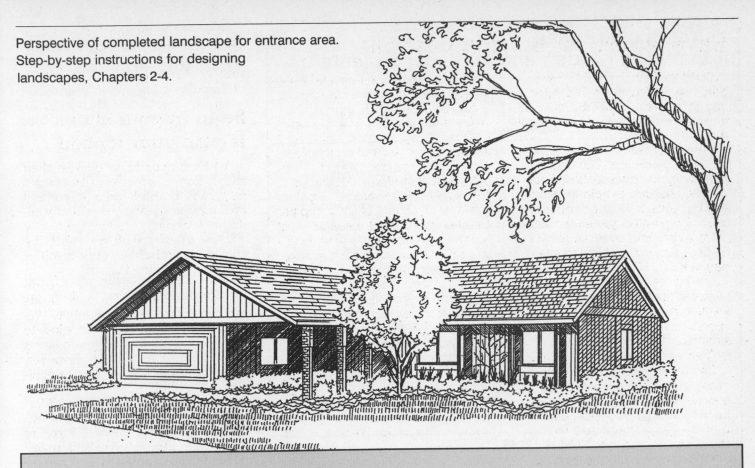

How to test your soil's pH

What's all the fuss about a pH test?

It's a simple test to determine — through chemical dyes and a colormetric reading — the acidity or alkalinity of soil.

So why a pH test?

Because pH is the single most important factor gardeners can regulate in the soil that affects plant growth. Among chemists pH is just shorthand — numbers from 0 to 14 — that describes acidity levels. But to plants the proper pH means nutrient availability, good growth and resistance to problems.

Readings below 7 indicate an acid soil, right at 7 is neutral, and readings above 7 indicate an alkaline soil. The numbers follow a geometric progression, so that a small difference in numbers can mean a big difference in acidity.

The pH test can be performed at home but the kits commonly marketed tend to confound the beginning gardener.

Most garden centers will do a pH test, County Extension Services often perform the analysis during clinics, and samples for testing can be sent to the Extension Service lab in Gainesville. Your County Extension Service office has the kits that make this chore almost effortless.

The accuracy of a pH test will depend on you. Only a small sample of soil is required, but it should be representative of the planting site.

Remove samples of soil from the surface to the 6-inch level of the planting site. Take several samples and mix them together in a pail to make sure the composite represents the entire planting. Collect a pint of soil from the pail for testing by your County Extension Service.

Where different types of plants are to be grown you may want to make separate samples. Label each container with your name, address and crop to be grown.

You will receive a pH reading and a recommendation. Lime is suggested when a soil is too acid and will raise the pH to a better level for growth. Sulfur can drop an alkaline pH to suit the acid-loving plants.

Lime comes in many forms but the dolomitic type is recommended. It's slow to act but gives a uniform and consistent adjustment of pH levels.

Gardeners should avoid hydrated or pickling limes. They react fast and

pH values for common substances

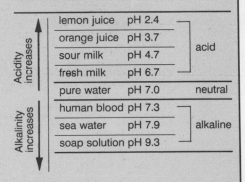

Acidity increases			
	lemon juice	pH 2.4	acid
	orange juice	pH 3.7	
	sour milk	pH 4.7	
	fresh milk	pH 6.7	
	pure water	pH 7.0	neutral
Alkalinity increases	human blood	pH 7.3	alkaline
	sea water	pH 7.9	
	soap solution	pH 9.3	

often burn roots.

Sulfur is available as either a fine, dusty powder or as a coarse agricultural grade product. Either way it effectively increases soil acidity over a given period of time.

Where soil pH *does* require adjusting, it's usually not necessary to recheck the soil more than once or twice a year. The reason: both lime and sulfur are slow to react.

Where soil pH does *not* need adjusting, a test every few years is adequate.

Desirable pH ranges
for common garden and landscape plants

Strongly acid below pH 5.4	Moderately to strongly acid pH 5.5-5.9	Moderately acid pH 6.0-6.4	Slightly acid pH6.5-6.9
Woody ornamentals			
Azalea	Allamanda	Allamanda	Arborvitae
Bougainvillea	American redbud	American redbud	Butterfly bush
Crape myrtle	Arborvitae	Arborvitae	Crape myrtle
Croton	Azalea	Bougainvillea	Croton
Feijoa	Bougainvillea	Butterfly bush	Feijoa
Firethorn	Camellia	Camellia	(also to pH 7.5)
Flowering dogwood	Citrus	Citrus	Firethorn
Gardenia	Crape myrtle	Crape myrtle	Pink hydrangea
Hibiscus	Croton	Croton	(also to pH 7.5)
American holly	Feijoa	Feijoa	Oleander
Blue hydrangea	Firethorn	Firethorn	Palms
Ligustrum	Flowering dogwood	Flowering dogwood	Red cedar
Magnolia	Gardenia	Gardenia	Sycamore
Oleander	Glossy abelia	Glossy abelia	Yucca
Pittosporum	Hibiscus	Hibiscus	
Podocarpus	American holly	Ligustrum	
Yaupon	Ligustrum	Magnolia	
	Magnolia	Oleander	
	Oleander	Palms	
	Palms	Pittosporum	
	Podocarpus	Red cedar	
	Shrimp plant	Shrimp plant	
	Wisteria	Sycamore	
	Yaupon	Wisteria	
		Yaupon	
		Yucca	
Garden flowers and bulbs			
Blue lupine	Amaryllis	Amaryllis	Begonia
China aster	Begonia	Begonia	Carnation
Coreopsis	Blue lupine	Calendula	China aster
Pansy	Calendula	Carnation	Daylily
Phlox	China aster	China aster	Marigold
	Chrysanthemum	Chrysanthemum	Nasturtium
	Coreopsis	Daylily	Petunia
	Gladiolus	Gladiolus	Poinsettia
	Lycoris	Easter lily	Rose
	Marigold	Lycoris	Snapdragon
	Moraea	Marigold	Zinnia
	Narcissus	Moraea	
	Nasturtium	Narcissus	
	Pansy	Nasturtium	
	Petunia	Pansy	
	Phlox	Petunia	
	Rose	Poinsettia	
	Snapdragon	Rose	
	Zinnia	Snapdragon	
		Zinnia	
Lawn grasses			
Carpet	Carpet	Bermuda	Bermuda
Centipede	Centipede	Fescue	Fescue
Bahia	Bahia	Italian rye	St. Augustine
	Italian rye	St. Augustine	Zoysia
		Zoysia	

Gardens change with the seasons

To enjoy your garden year-round, establish a schedule that will have flowers and greenery flourishing every month.

As the seasons change, so must the plants. Pansies, petunias, snapdragons and dianthus thrive in the cool season while marigolds, salvia and torenia flourish during the warmer months. Tomatoes and peppers grow spring and fall but lettuce will head only during the winter.

Many northern bulbs will have to be grown in pots but Florida gardeners can grow the amaryllis, blood lily and agapanthus outdoors.

Insects also have their seasons. Summer and fall are the real pest-prevalent times of year. The bugs like the sun and rains just as much as the plants. Winter and spring tend to be less pest prone. By becoming familar with your plants and their pests, you can predict when problems are about to arrive and take preventive action.

Caterpillars and 3-inch grasshoppers are among the pests prevalent in the Sunshine State. The aphid, mealybug, scale and thrip also reside in Florida. Handpicking and, where needed, spraying will control most problems.

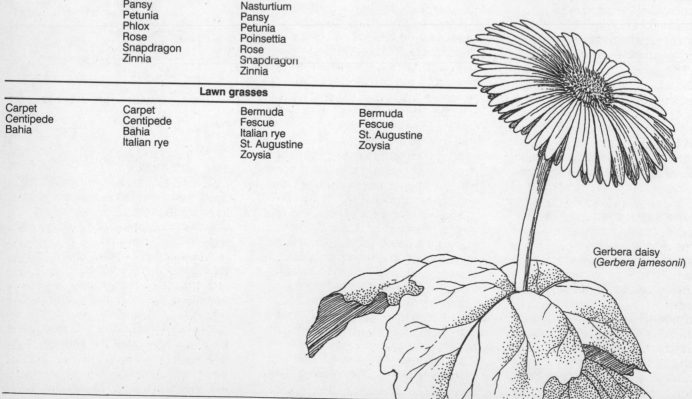

Gerbera daisy
(Gerbera jamesonii)

2

Landscaping part 1 — thinking it through on paper

WHETHER A GARDENER keeps his present home or sells it within a few years, a well-designed landscape is worth the investment.

According to a *Money* magazine report, the dollars spent on quality landscaping have between 100 percent and 200 percent recovery value when the house is sold.

But reasons for landscaping go beyond the potential financial payback. They include:

• Landscaping turns simple flower gardens into real showoffs, supplying the backdrop and framing needed to make annuals and perennials featured attractions.

• The planned design organizes the homesite so all space is well used.

• Plantings create interest and intrigue as you move from one well-defined living area to another.

• Trees, shrubs and flowers properly spaced and clustered create a harmony that is yours to enjoy.

Think of landscaping as a way of connecting the house to its surroundings. Landscape architects call this developing an indoor-outdoor relationship and refer to landscaping as a process of adding rooms. One might be a workroom; another, a swimming room; and another, a game room.

Difficult as it may sound, try not to think of an oak, azalea, ligustrum or annual bed in the early stages of design. Instead concentrate on a wall to block a view, an accent to draw attention or a covering to hide the ground. Remember all these items have height and occupy space. They may be curved, upright or horizontal.

Good landscapes can be made without ever knowing a plant's name. Picking the plants to accomplish an objective such as giving red flowers in spring and staying green all summer is the last step in completing a design.

Modern landscaping should reflect the lifestyle of the family. For this reason it is important to gather the family together to plan these outdoor rooms. Designated features may include:

• Children's play area.
• Vegetable garden.
• Space to work on a car or boat.
• Clothesline.
• Storage site.
• Outdoor eating area.
• Swimming pool.
• Tennis court.
• Greenhouse.

Remember to plan for the future, keeping in mind that the needs of

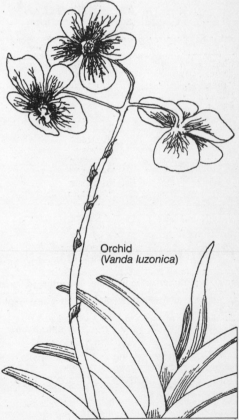

Orchid
(*Vanda luzonica*)

the family will change. A sandbox may eventually give way to a playhouse and the work area may be expanded to house a sports car. Specifically, note the areas you believe will change as the number of family members grows or decreases.

Before redesigning the landscape on paper spend time outdoors. Walk the property line, taking note of trees, shrubs, lake views, sunsets, existing gardens or plants you want

Existing conditions

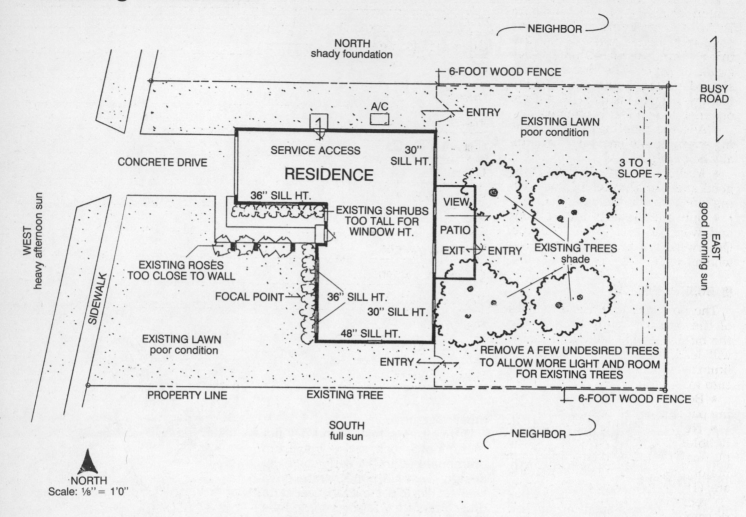

NEIGHBOR

NORTH
shady foundation

6-FOOT WOOD FENCE

BUSY
ROAD

A/C

ENTRY

EXISTING LAWN
poor condition

CONCRETE DRIVE

SERVICE ACCESS

30"
SILL HT.

3 TO 1
SLOPE

RESIDENCE

36" SILL HT.

VIEW

WEST
heavy afternoon sun

EXISTING SHRUBS
TOO TALL FOR
WINDOW HT.

PATIO

EAST
good morning sun

SIDEWALK

EXIT

ENTRY

EXISTING TREES
shade

EXISTING ROSES
TOO CLOSE TO WALL

FOCAL POINT

36" SILL HT.

30" SILL HT.

EXISTING LAWN
poor condition

48" SILL HT.

REMOVE A FEW UNDESIRED TREES
TO ALLOW MORE LIGHT AND ROOM
FOR EXISTING TREES

ENTRY

PROPERTY LINE

EXISTING TREE

6-FOOT WOOD FENCE

SOUTH
full sun

NEIGHBOR

NORTH
Scale: ⅛" = 1'0"

Planning a landscape — checkpoints to note

1. Draw the homesite to scale. Make the scale large; let 1 inch equal 5 feet.

2. Include all existing plants — even if they might be removed. Sketch plants in clusters rather than individually.

3. Draw plants to mature size. An oak, for example, may eventually have a spread of 60 feet in diameter.

4. Have a family meeting to consider needs. Discuss areas for dog runs, tree houses, rest areas, barbecue and boat storage.

5. Use tracing paper to make quick sketches. Don't erase. Add another sheet of tracing paper, and retrace what you like.

6. Study the sun's movement to determine shade patterns. Ths sun is overhead in summer, deep in the south during the winter.

7. Pick best views to emphasize, poor views to conceal.

8. Screen your landscape from neighbors with trees, shrubs and fencing.

9. Work with one area of the yard at a time. Attempts to design the entire landscape at a sitting will boggle the mind.

10. Study books on landscape design. Drive through local neighborhoods to get ideas. Borrow from good designs.

to keep. Eyesores and service areas also must be taken into consideration.

Mapping out a landscape

There are two basic steps to mapping out a landscape — drawing a sketch to scale, then creating a bubble design. An optional third step, the thumbnail sketch, is designed to help the would-be landscape designer who is having a difficult time getting started.

■ SKETCHING TO SCALE

For a sketch to scale, begin with an existing inventory of home and plant features plotted to scale on paper. Plan for the future by drawing all existing plants to their approximate mature sizes. Then follow these steps to complete a base plan:

● Create a plot plan, a simple scaled drawing of the homesite without landscaping. This base plan, with house and existing features, should be placed on a heavy grade of paper. The drawing scale should be large enough to make features easy to visualize. A scale of one inch to five feet is often used.

● Add the plantings to the drawing even though some may eventually be eliminated.

● Make note of all important good and bad features of the existing landscape on the base plan.

● Split the property into sections and work on one area at a time. Otherwise, the project can be overwhelming.

■ **BUBBLE DESIGN**

The next step is to visualize uses of the outdoor living area. Apply the bubble design technique and it will lead you to a completed preliminary landscape. The bubble design works this way:

● Begin by laying a piece of tracing paper over the base plan.

● Next, draw big circles — or bubbles, on your paper to define the major outdoor areas. The three major areas you need to include are: (1) general entrance; (2) service; (3) recreation or entertainment. A private garden is a fourth option.

● Designate specific use areas by dividing bubbles into smaller bubbles. For example, the service area could have one bubble for storage and trash near the house and another for an outbuilding and car service location in the rear of the yard.

● Be realistic when allocating space. The bubbles should represent the space you want to devote to the activity.

● The outline of the bubbles defines the landscape. Inside the bubbles are work or play spaces; outside are areas to be planted.

● Smooth out landscape boundaries to create a free-flowing completed preliminary design.

■ **THUMBNAIL SKETCH**

The thumbnail sketch works this way: When thoughts are evasive, pick up a pencil and just make lots of squiggly lines across a tracing of the base plan.

Study the drawing. There may be

Evaluating your property

	What's good	What's bad
House		
Orientation (sun exposure)		
Garage		
Driveway		
Walks		
Soil		
Grass		
Shade trees		
Shrubs		
Vegetable garden		
Cut flower garden		
Service area		
Play area		
Utility lines		
Retaining walls		

Chrysanthemum

Bubble design

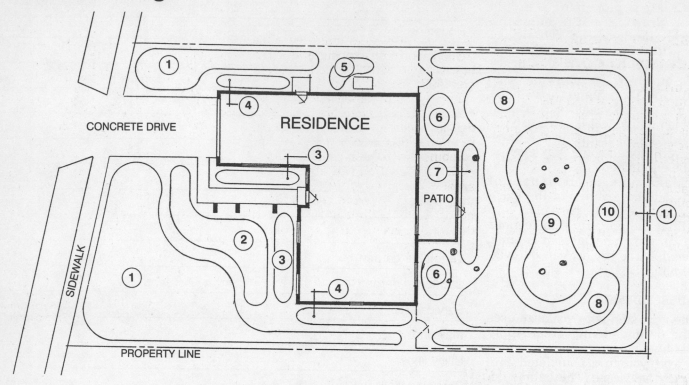

CONCRETE DRIVE

RESIDENCE

PATIO

SIDEWALK

PROPERTY LINE

NORTH
Scale: ⅛" = 1'0"

1. Open lawn area with access to rear yard
2. Single variety plant material to provide continuity
3. Medium to low plantings
4. Foundation plantings
5. Buffer air conditioner
6. Low foundation plants
7. Dwarf foundation plants
8. Open lawn for access and activities
9. Children's play area
10. Rose garden
11. Buffer fence with plantings

some lines that catch the eye — the beginnings of the outline of the landscape. Go back to your original concept of creating outdoor living areas. Trace in the lines you want to keep and let the big, open areas created be the locations for work or play and the outlying portion, the landscape to be planted.

Walkways serve as outdoor hallways

When the outdoor living areas are defined, decide where the walkways will be built. Just as there are hallways in a house, there are routes leading to and from outdoor areas via paths, stepping stones and gates.

Sketch the walkways and keep in mind where shade will be needed or a screen planted. Do not let your drawings hug the property line if plantings will be needed.

In general, the trees should be kept to the back of the home and not in the middle of an outdoor area. One large tree at maturity has a spread of about 60 feet; a medium size tree, 35 feet; and a small tree, 15 feet. Trees can be clustered for a massive shade planting but generally they are kept to the side of an outdoor activity area.

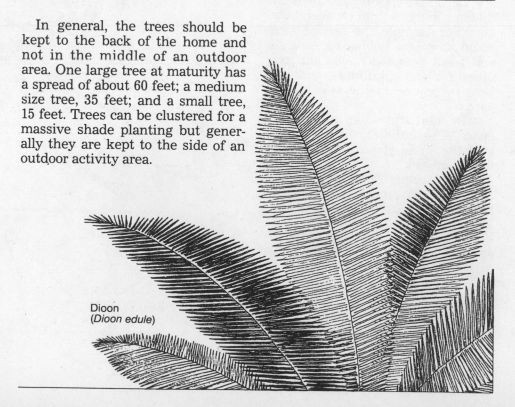

Dioon
(*Dioon edule*)

8

Pitfalls to avoid, concepts to consider

Beginning designers often put too much emphasis on the front yard or entrance area. The front yard is a passageway and does not require elaborate plantings.

Service areas for storing trash, fixing the boat, etc. should be closely related to the kitchen, garage or outbuildings.

Children should have their own space in the recreation area — a place where they can dig holes, swing on a rope and maybe climb a tree. Give them a swing set, sandbox and tree house in their own corner of the recreation area.

Finally, some landscapes can accommodate a private area — a garden in which to relax. Where space is limited this area will have to be combined with the recreation area.

Remember: Don't be afraid to try several designs before settling on the one best suited to your family's needs. Take the time to think about the design, even setting it aside for a day or two.

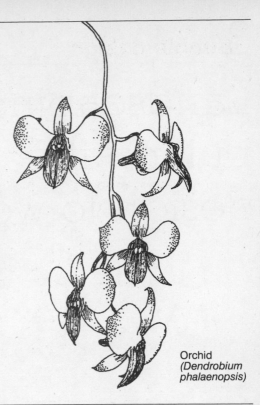

Orchid
(*Dendrobium phalaenopsis*)

Completed thumbnail sketch

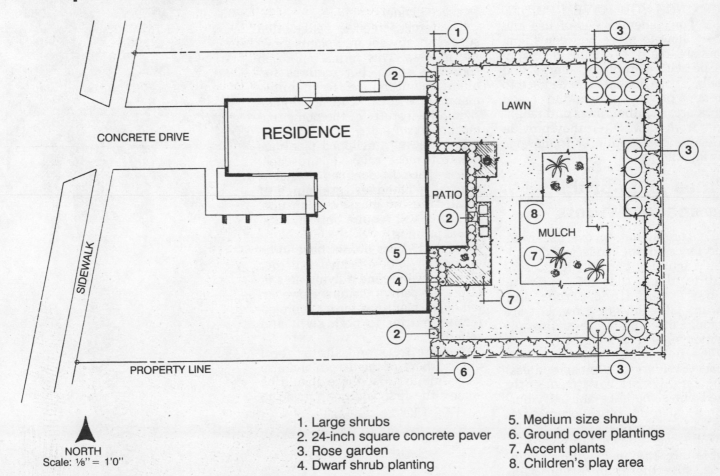

NORTH
Scale: ⅛'' = 1'0''

1. Large shrubs
2. 24-inch square concrete paver
3. Rose garden
4. Dwarf shrub planting
5. Medium size shrub
6. Ground cover plantings
7. Accent plants
8. Children's play area

Landscaping part 2 — putting the design to work

ONCE YOU HAVE DECIDED on general areas of use and how to move between them, you are ready to divide the landscape with shrubbery, fences and walls. These dividers can be used to create a private space and to screen work areas, outbuildings and neighbors from view. Often they provide effective background or framework for favorite plants.

Trees and shrubs as space dividers

Be careful not to overuse walls and fences in the landscape design. When building barriers, try to substitute plants that soften strong construction lines. Trees and shrubs take time to grow, but are equally effective at reducing unwanted sights and sounds.

The list of plants suitable for space dividers is almost endless. You might start with frequently used but sometimes abused viburnum, ligustrum, pittosporum, juniper and podocarpus.

Not as well known, but just as reliable, are Indian hawthorn, photinia, silverthorn, anise and bamboo.

Azalea, camellia, jasmine, plumbago and feijoa plantings add seasonal color to the design when used as space dividers.

The terms screen or hedge often suggest neatly sheared plants growing in rows. This formal approach conserves space, but requires frequent maintenance. Regimented plantings also can end up emphasizing the features of the home that most need softening.

Free-flowing unclipped plantings create a more relaxed landscape. These space dividers can consist of naturalized hedges, groupings of small trees or masses of shrubs. Plantings will require only an occasional pruning.

Space dividers do not have to be tall or long to be effective. A border planting will define a living area or direct the path of visitors. However, tall dense plantings form a more effective barrier to both sight and sound.

Because trees and shrubs form the backbone of the design and also take time to grow, these should be among the first additions made to the landscape.

Canary Island date palm
(*Phoenix canariensis*)

Forming spaces

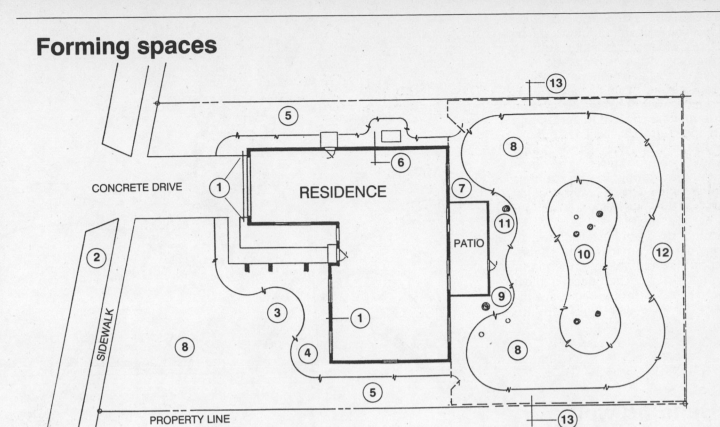

CONCRETE DRIVE

RESIDENCE

PATIO

SIDEWALK

PROPERTY LINE

NORTH
Scale: ⅛" = 1'0"

1. Space for accent plants
2. Space to define property lines
3. Define space with an interesting bed line
4. Space to allow for small, medium and tall plantings
5. Provide space for access to rear yard
6. Space to buffer air conditioner
7. Provide transition space from medium plantings to dwarf plantings
8. Open lawn space
9. Provide transition space from dwarf plants to ground covers
10. Children's play area
11. Define space to allow trees in bed areas
12. Rose garden space
13. Buffer space for hedge plantings

How to plan a home landscape

DO:
- Draw every plant, fence, pool and patio to scale.
- Try several different designs.
- Plan plenty of lawn and shade.
- Create screens for privacy.
- Group plants together for dramatic effect.
- Leave room for future additions such as a pool or greenhouse.
- Study the characteristics of plants.
- Use low-maintenance plants.
- Get ideas from books and neighborhood walks.
- Plan for irrigation.
- Space plants for mature growth.

DON'T:
- Plant trees within 15 feet of the house or septic tank.
- Scatter individual plants throughout the landscape.
- Place near the houseplants with either a severe upright or rounded shape.
- Use tall-growing plants in front of windows.
- Plan to shear plants to keep them in bounds.
- Use too many plants.

Accents — from plants to works of art

Accent plantings add pizazz to the landscape. They create interest by contrasting with the space dividers.

Living accents may be flowering trees, showy shrubs, plants with interesting bark or a bed of flowers. They should be positioned to frame a view, draw attention or guide the visitor through the landscape. For example, place big, bold flowers against a screen of fine green foliage.

Use accent plantings sparingly to maximize their impact. A rule of thumb is 10 percent to 20 percent of the plantings in any one view should be accents. Any more and the design may be too busy.

As with space dividers, plants are not the only material that may be used as accents. Consider statues, fountains or other works of art.

Some accents stand out only at certain times of the year. Plants such as azalea, tabebuia or banana shrub may be colorful in spring and then fade into the background for the rest of the year. Other plants have year-round interest. The crape myrtle, for example, sports summer blooms, bark with pleasing color and texture, and an attractive shape.

A plant does not have to flower to be exciting. Consider leaf shape, color and overall shape of the plant. Bright crotons never need a blossom to offset a dark green space divider. The sago palm with fernlike

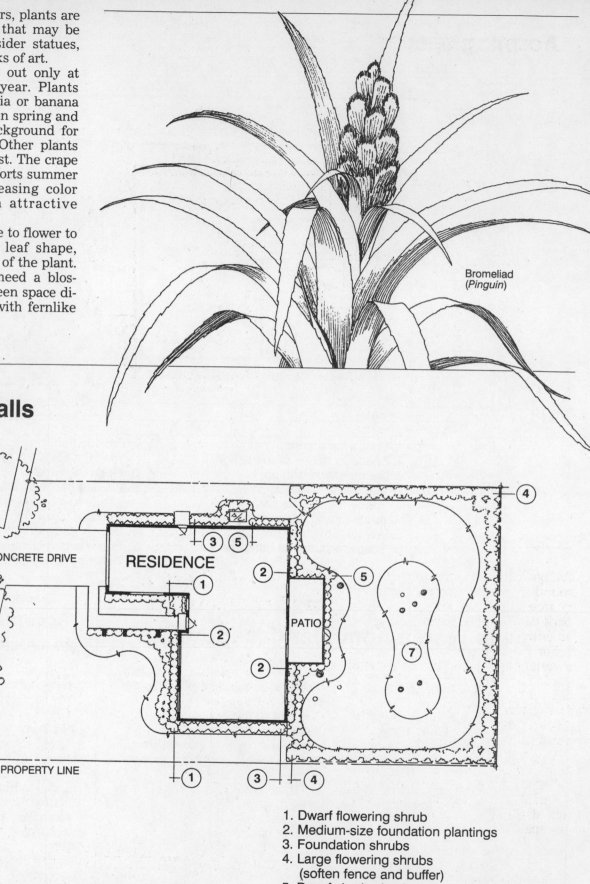

Bromeliad (*Pinguin*)

Building walls

NORTH
Scale: 1/8" = 1'0"

1. Dwarf flowering shrub
2. Medium-size foundation plantings
3. Foundation shrubs
4. Large flowering shrubs
   (soften fence and buffer)
5. Dwarf shrub plantings
6. Street trees (afternoon shade
   and define property)
7. Children's mulched play area

12

Accent plants

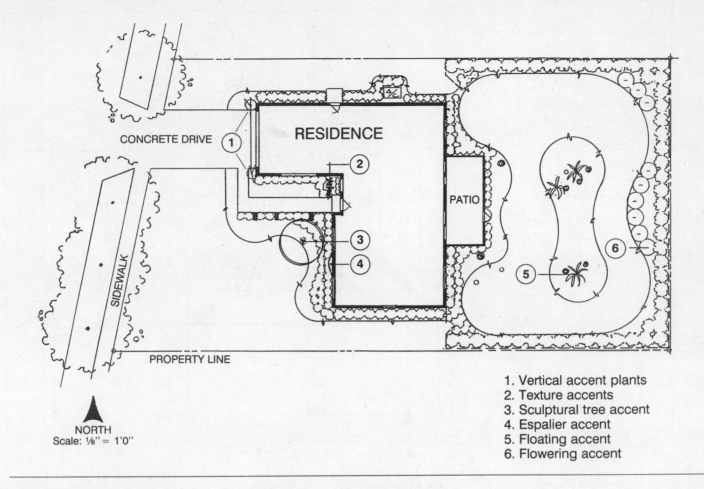

CONCRETE DRIVE

RESIDENCE

SIDEWALK

PATIO

PROPERTY LINE

NORTH
Scale: ⅛" = 1'0"

1. Vertical accent plants
2. Texture accents
3. Sculptural tree accent
4. Espalier accent
5. Floating accent
6. Flowering accent

foliage contrasts greatly with the rounded-leaf pittosporum. A shapely tree ligustrum with its exposed bark could be the accent plant near an entrance.

For gardeners who like to collect a variety of flowers, try a perennial garden as the accent feature. In this case it is acceptable to have one, two or three of an individual plant. Avoid scattering single flowering shrubs throughout the landscape.

Vegetable gardens can also be accent features. In fact, vegetables and flowers are often intermingled.

Other accents might be well-positioned planters, pots of annuals or an espalier.

Making the best use of filler plants

Transition plants form connections between space dividers and accents or between the home and the land. They should share characteristics of the plantings found in the space dividers and accents. A similar leaf shape or shade of green brings harmony to the design.

Bromeliad
(*Cryptanthus spp.*)

13

How to irrigate

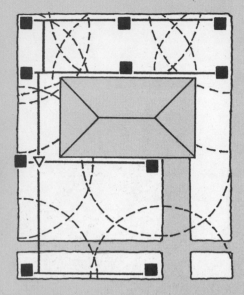

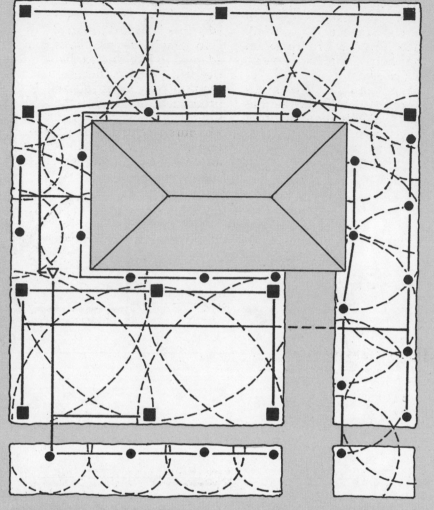

Water lines	——————
Large spray heads	■
Small spray heads	●
On/off valves	△

Basic irrigation system (above) gives adequate coverage, but there is some overlap and some waste where water sprays on the house, drive and sidewalk.

Advanced irrigation system (right) is developed by adding more pipes and a variety of sprinkler heads to the basic system. It delivers a balanced water supply to planted areas only.

Although Central Florida's monthly rainfall averages appear adequate to sustain plants, just a few hot days without moisture can lead to permanent wilt. An in-ground irrigation system can be designed to simplify watering when rainfall is erratic.

Good irrigation systems begin on paper. Publications to help do-it-yourselfers are available at book stores, garden shops and from irrigation supply dealers.

Costs will vary depending on whether you plan to install a manually or electronically controlled system and how many options you select.

Be sure to check for rules governing installation and permits required.

To get the most from your system:
- Schedule watering for pre-dawn hours.
- Water only when needed: twice a week for lawns and gardens; once a week for trees and shrubs.
- Set the system to operate for 30 to 45 minutes.
- Apply no more than an inch of water per week.
- Curtail irrigation during rainy weather.
- Check heads frequently; clean when clogged and cut away obstructing grass or limbs.

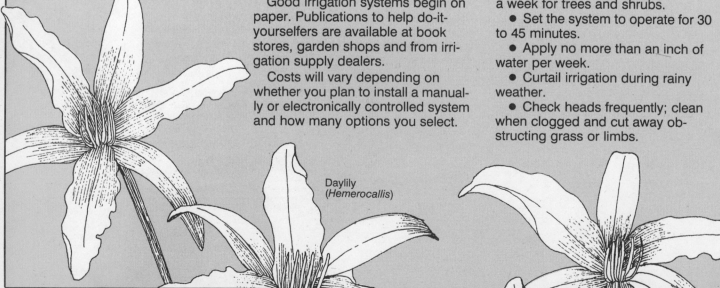

Daylily
(Hemerocallis)

Transition plants, sometimes called fillers, give added greenery to help unify the design and soften architectural lines of the home. Foundation plantings are transition plants that help blend the home to the open spaces.

Transition plants at times become accents. An azalea hedge that functions as a transition planting most of the year becomes an accent when it bursts into bloom in the spring.

Among plants that serve as good transitions are Indian hawthorn, yaupon holly, dwarf pyracantha, anise, viburnum and jasmine.

In general, select plants that are adapted to Florida and that at maturity will produce the desired landscape effects. Plant selection is covered in detail in later chapters. County Extension Services, libraries, nurseries and local garden centers provide instruction and guidance for the beginning gardener.

Saw palmetto
(*Serenoa repens*)

Filling spaces

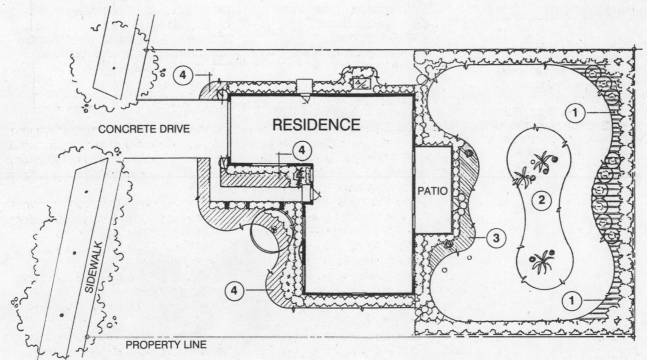

CONCRETE DRIVE

RESIDENCE

PATIO

SIDEWALK

PROPERTY LINE

NORTH
Scale: ⅛'' = 1'0''

1. Flowering ground cover with full sun
2. Mulched play area
3. Low ground cover with shade
4. Low ground cover with full sun

Final landscape plan

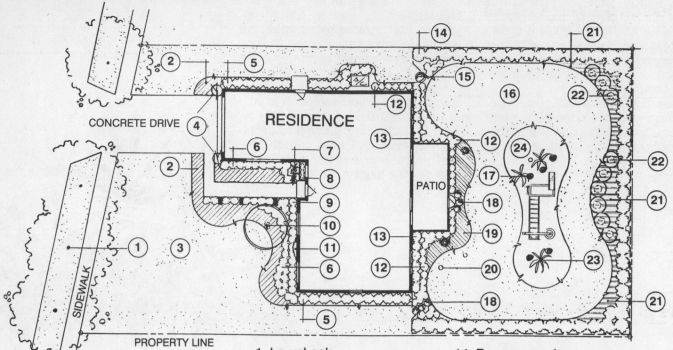

CONCRETE DRIVE

RESIDENCE

PATIO

SIDEWALK

PROPERTY LINE

NORTH
Scale: ⅛'' = 1'0''

1. Laurel oak
2. Dwarf shore juniper
3. St. Augustine sod (Floratam)
4. Nandina
5. Variegated pittosporum
6. Indian hawthorn
7. Cast iron plant
8. Impatiens in planter
9. African iris
10. Ligustrum tree
11. Pyracantha (espalier)
12. *Liriope* Evergreen Giant
13. Duc de Rohan azaleas

14. Formosa azaleas
15. 36-inch round concrete paver
16. St. Augustine (Bitterblue)
17. Existing trees to remain
18. 24-inch round concrete pavers
19. English ivy
20. Remove undesired trees to allow
    additional light and room for
    existing trees to grow
21. Daylilies
22. Rose garden
23. Crinum lily
24. Mulched children's play area

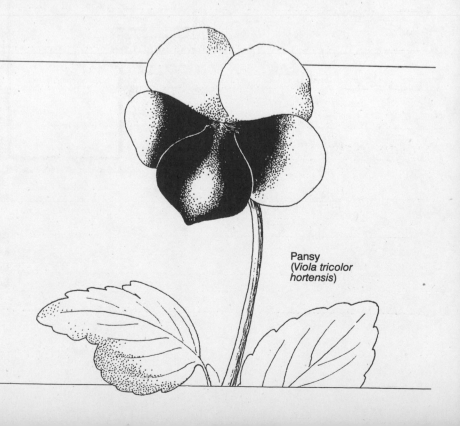

Pansy
(*Viola tricolor
hortensis*)

Landscape worksheet

Features to include

_____

_____

_____

_____

_____

_____

Views to screen

_____

_____

_____

Views to emphasize

_____

_____

_____

Accents to add

_____

_____

_____

_____

4

Living outdoors — more room than you think

Daylily
(*Hemerocallis*)

MILD FLORIDA WEATHER invites gardeners to spend as much leisure time outside as they do inside the home. An appealing landscape makes time spent outdoors more enjoyable.

It's up to the designer to make each area of the landscape functional and enjoyable. Trips through well-planned landscapes will illustrate how these areas work.

Entrance areas — life in full view

In most landscapes front footages or entrance areas are open to view. Consequently, they often do not lend themselves to family activities.

The entrance area is the place where guests gain first impressions of the home and family. Landscaping here can be kept simple. Select plants that invite interest. Use plantings to guide visitors to the door.

Concentrate landscaping efforts on blending the home with the immediate surroundings. Frame the best view of the house with trees, soften hard edges with greenery and roll out a carpet of lawn.

Small- to medium-sized trees are usually selected for the public area as they are more in proportion with the size of modern homes. Keep the trees at least 15 feet from the foundation. In most designs, larger trees provide shade for the general living area.

Shrubs positioned near the home are often referred to as foundation plantings. An original intent was to hide unattractive building supports. Modern architecture has eliminated that need.

A contemporary use of shrubs is to form a gentle transition from the lines of the house to the surrounding landscape. Use similar shrubs in foundation plantings. Too much diversity confuses the eye and competes with the home for a position of prominence.

Be conscious of size when buying new shrubs. Plants can quickly increase in size, creating the need for frequent pruning. Select dwarf varieties that at maturity will be in scale with the home.

Accent plants attract attention and guide visitors to the front entrance. Shrubs with multiseason appeal that are often used in public areas include crape myrtle, oleander, ligustrum and small palms.

Flower beds are welcome additions to the public living area. Many residents create entrance displays that combine potted plants, rock displays and wood features.

Save the best plantings for the general living area where you will be spending most of your at-home time.

Recreation areas — outdoor living rooms

A recreation area should be a part of every landscape. Devoted to family outdoor living, it often includes gardens, a sand box, pool, patio and barbecue. Keep this area light, lively and full of color.

Imagine this outdoor living area as an extension of the family room. A patio or deck may serve as a natural transition from the home to the planted surroundings.

Patios are commonly constructed of concrete. Many are less-than-imaginative squares or rectangles

that repeat the blockiness of the home. Create interest with circular, curved or flowing patterns. Investigate materials such as wood, brick, tile and stone that can add another dimension to the patio.

Decks have become popular additions to the Florida landscape. The natural look of wood decks fulfills the landscape objective of blending the home with surrounding plantings.

Even when elevated just a few inches off the ground, decks break the monotony of flat landscapes. Cypress and redwood are popular building materials, but the less expensive yet durable treated pine is commonly selected.

Deck designs can be varied to suit the landscape. Squares and rectangles are popular and easy to construct. Circular and curved decks

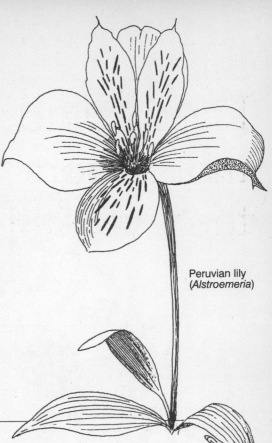

Peruvian lily
(*Alstroemeria*)

Entrance

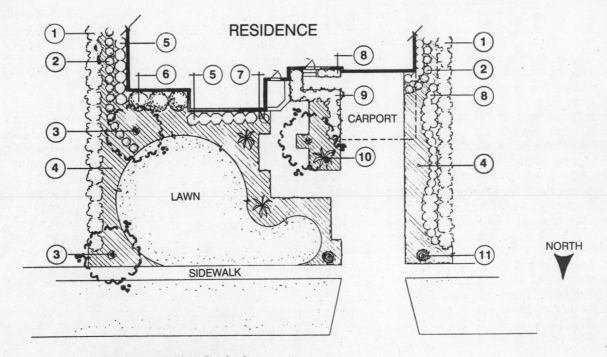

RESIDENCE

CARPORT

LAWN

SIDEWALK

NORTH

1. Formosa azalea (hedge)
2. 24-inch round concrete pavers
3. Ligustrum tree (multistem specimen)
4. Dwarf shore juniper (ground cover)
5. Indian hawthorn (foundation planting)
6. Camellia japonica (accent)
7. Nandina (vertical accent)
8. *Liriope* Evergreen Giant (dwarf plantings)
9. Lady palms (buffer carport)
10. Crinum lily (accents)
11. Existing pine trees

Patio landscape

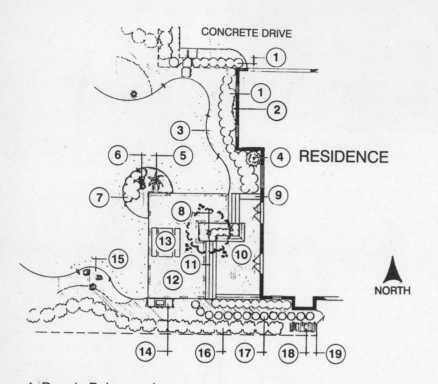

1. Duc de Rohan azaleas
2. Tree ivy
3. *Liriope* Evergreen Giant
4. Lady palm
5. Sago palm
6. Existing tree
7. Red Ruffle azaleas
8. Ligustrum tree with accent lighting
9. Cedar bench
10. Cedar deck with pressure-treated pine frames
11. Cedar steps with step lights
12. Concrete deck with a rock-salt finish and brick edging to match house
13. Cedar picnic table
14. Brick gas grill
15. Variegated Algerian ivy
16. Southern Charm azaleas
17. 24-inch round concrete pavers
18. Wood pile
19. 6-foot privacy fence

emphasize the natural flowing lines of the landscape.

Because of Florida's hot summer days, position patios or decks where at least a portion will always be in the shade. In the absence of suitable shade, a northern or eastern side of the home is second best. Where trees are still small, use an overhead lathe or wooden-beam structure to provide screening.

Plants in pots, tubs and boxes are welcome additions to the patio. Display colorful annuals and fancy foliage plants. In the shade, use coleus, impatiens, ferns, orchids and other plants with striking leaf patterns. Give marigolds, petunias, salvia, torenia and edible figs a try in full sun locations.

Use shrubs to soften the lines of the building, provide focal points and screen out undesirable views.

Choose shrubs that have dramatic color, form and texture. For accents pick from palms, crape myrtle, azaleas, camellias, thryallis and others with seasonal interest. Transition plants with contrasting green color and interesting foliage include anise, pittosporum, viburnum and ligustrum.

Queen sago
(*Cycas circinalis*)

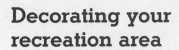
Bleeding heart
(*Dicentra spectabilis*)

Private rear yard

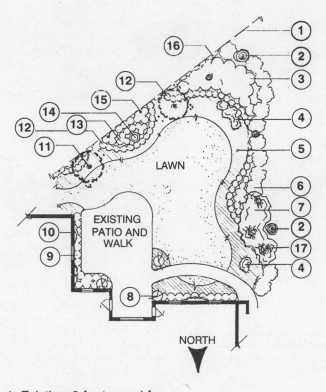

LAWN

EXISTING PATIO AND WALK

NORTH

1. Existing 6-foot wood fence
2. Existing trees
3. Duc de Rohan azaleas (color accent)
4. Landscape boulder (accent existing boulders)
5. *Liriope muscari* (ground cover)
6. George Gerbing azaleas (buffer and color)
7. Existing boulder feature
8. Nandina (vertical accents)
9. *Liriope* Evergreen Giant (low foundation plants)
10. Pyracantha (espalier)
11. Existing camellias
12. Cuphea (colorful border)
13. Red Ruffle azalea (dwarf color accent)
14. Garden statue (focal point)
15. Existing Hollywood juniper (frame)
16. Carolina jasmine (soften fence)
17. Fireball bromeliads (soften boulder feature)

Decorating your recreation area

Locate trees to shade your home and patio. They can also be positioned near property lines and space dividers.

Small trees with interesting trunks, bark, leaf shapes or seasonal flowers are the best choices for backyard plantings. Grouping several together is often more desirable than a random spacing throughout the yard.

Choose evergreens such as oak, cherry laurel, ligustrum, holly and magnolia. For deciduous specimens that let in winter warmth select maple, sweet gum, Chinese tallow, golden-rain, tabebuia and elm.

Use space dividers and fences as backgrounds for showy shrub displays. Cluster plantings of azaleas, camellias, thryallis and plumbago to enjoy from the patio and home.

Create year-round color with flower beds. Tough, permanent perennials include daylilies, Stokes' aster, bromeliads, society garlic and moraea.

Pick annuals for their seasonal beauty. A warm-season selection might include marigolds, celosia, zinnias, portulaca and torenia. Gardeners with shady living areas can enjoy impatiens, coleus, caladiums, begonias, plus attractive foliage plants as warm-season residents of the garden.

A private area — just for you

A secluded niche can become your private living area. It is just the right place to read a book, commune with nature or ponder the new day.

Locate the private area out of the main traffic flow, possibly to the side or rear of the home. In a small yard, a secluded section of the patio or garden may serve this purpose.

Block out neighboring landscape activities with a wooden fence, ornamental hedges or thickets of plant growth.

Keep landscape plantings simple but intriguing. Choose shrubs with curious foliage such as the small finely cut palm fronds or a plant with a number of interesting features such as the wax myrtle.

Accent plants should not be overpowering in a private garden. This is also a good location for a statue or fountain.

Poolside — the summertime escape

The pool area offers a welcome escape during hot Florida days. Although the recreational aspect is what makes a pool a welcome addition to the home, carefully selected plants, trees, and even grass, can add to its pleasure.

Despite popular notions, chlorine in the pool water is not responsible for damage to nearby plantings. Rather, most plant damage results from constant soakings caused by splashing pool water or from hosing down the pool decking.

Where possible, slightly slope planting beds away from the pool to aid drainage. If the landscape setting permits, raise beds near the pool to promote a drier root system.

Petunia

General living

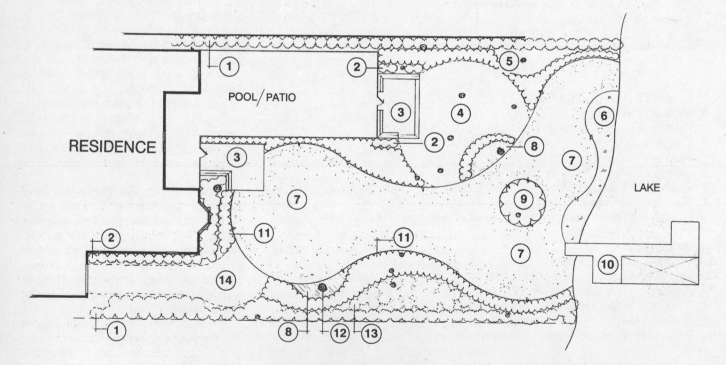

1. Formosa azaleas (buffer)
2. Indian hawthorn (foundation plantings)
3. Cedar deck with benches
4. Mulched activity area
5. Small vegetable garden
6. White sand beach
7. St. Augustine lawn area

8. Impatiens (multicolor)
9. Rose garden
10. Dock and boat house
11. *Liriope* Evergreen Giant
12. Existing trees
13. Camellia garden
14. Mulched service access

Pool landscape

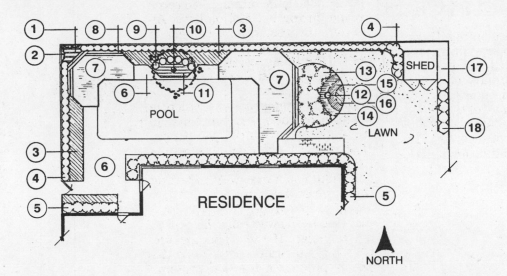

1. Shasta daisy (color accent)
2. Yellow allamanda (espalier)
3. Blue Pacific juniper (ground cover)
4. African iris
5. Duc de Rohan azaleas (foundation plantings)
6. Pool deck
7. Cedar deck with bench
8. Bench
9. 24-inch round concrete pavers
10. Ligustrum tree (small canopy tree)
11. Begonias (color poolside garden)
12. Bird bath in cut flower garden
13. Long stem roses
14. Salvia (high)
15. Gerbera daisy (medium)
16. Bachelor button (low)
17. Black weed cloth with cypress mulch
18. *Viburnum suspensum* (hedge)

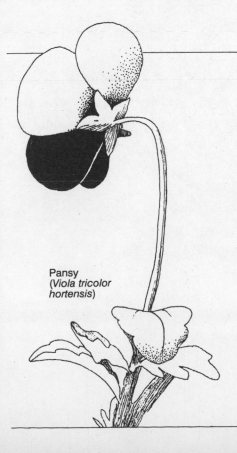

Pansy
(*Viola tricolor hortensis*)

Select poolside ornamentals that can tolerate moist soil. Examples are nandina, plumbago, yaupon holly, Japanese ligustrum, coontie and lantana. For the tropical look select medium growing palms.

Poolside ground covers are easy to maintain and provide coverage for the soil that can blow or wash into the water. Many gardeners cluster taller shrubs further away from the pool to give privacy and protection from chilling winds. Try several arrangements on paper until you have one that suits your needs.

Trees should be kept a minimum of 15 to 20 feet from the pool. Select trees that drop most of their leaves at the same time to help simplify pool maintenance.

Potted plants are useful on pool patios. Tropical plants that withstand hot summer sun — including ficus, Norfolk Island pine and schefflera — can be used for shade and screening. In shady areas plants such as dracaenas, palms and philodendrons can complete the tropical setting.

It's not necessary to have a pool completely enclosed with ornamentals. Grass grown next to the concrete edging produces a good walk area and a buffer zone against sand and dirt. Most grass can survive the constant splashing of pool water and hosing down of walks if drainage is adequate.

5

Trees and shrubs — the components of a good landscape

ONE LANDSCAPE ARCHItect said, "I first plant the forest, then cut out the design." It's an oversimplification but it does indicate the value of trees — givers of shade for the home and shelter for much of the outdoor area.

Trees and shrubs are the building blocks of outdoor designs. They occupy a big portion of your yard — and consume a large share of your landscape budget. Take time to review charts and visit nurseries.

Today's busy homeowner wants every plant to be flowering, evergreen, pest free and low maintenance. Such a plant doesn't exist, but many have attributes worth considering.

Ornamentals may be deciduous or evergreen. All, however, drop leaves. Some lose foliage all at once during fall or early spring while others drop a few leaves throughout the year.

Trees and shrubs grow to a variety of heights, widths and shapes. Consider all of these factors when selecting plants. Junipers, for example, may be cute when planted but can grow quickly to unmanageable proportions.

There are trees and shrubs that flower, ones that bear attractive

Live oak
(Quercus
virginiana)

How to fertilize a tree

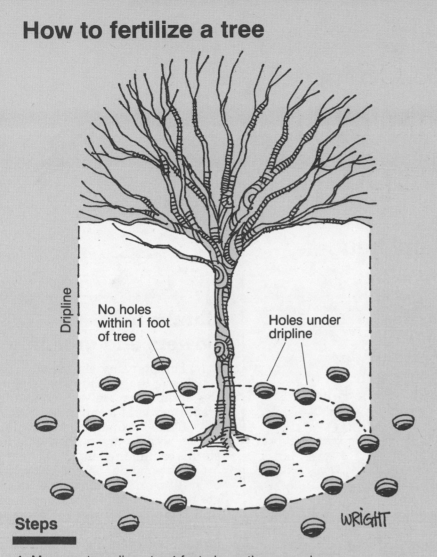

Dripline

No holes within 1 foot of tree

Holes under dripline

WRIGHT

Steps

1. Measure tree diameter 4 feet above the ground.

2. Use 6-6-6 fertilizer. The best product will contain minor nutrients, plus 25 percent of its total nitrogen in a water-insoluble form.

3. Weigh out fertilizer. Amounts are for twice a year (winter and summer) feedings.

 • Small trees (less than 6 inches in diameter): Use 1 pound for each inch of diameter.

 • Large trees (more than 6 inches in diameter): Use 2 pounds for each inch of diameter.

4. Punch holes 12 inches deep into soil. Space holes 2 to 3 feet apart from trunk to drip line. Where turf will not be affected, simply scatter fertilizer under spread of tree and water in, thus skipping steps 4, 5 and 6.

5. Divide fertilizer up into the holes.

6. Fill holes with soil or press closed with foot and water entire area.

Other techniques using liquid fertilizers and fertilizer spikes are available. Consult product labels when using these feeding practices.

fruit and some that have peeling bark. Other variables to consider are soil preference, rate of growth, salt tolerance and fragrance.

Don't settle for less than you want and the landscape demands without exhausting all resources.

Shade trees

Gardeners who can't take the heat better plan for summer shade. Shade trees are selected for their longevity, limb strength and shape. Flowers aren't a major concern when shade is the main objective. However, some trees also double as accents. In addition, shade trees may form the background for ornamental plantings and function as space dividers.

Where gardeners desire shade during the summer but warmth from the sun in winter, a deciduous tree is recommended. These specimens will lose their leaves during the fall and regain their canopy in the spring.

Consider planting several kinds of trees. The Federal Forestry Service cautions against overplanting a single species that could be devastated by disease or pests. Epidemics have claimed many elms, chestnuts and coconut palms. Florida oaks, which now account for up to 60 percent of some community plantings, could be vulnerable to a similar plight.

When selecting a tree, consider the planting site. Are there overhead obstacles, sewers or buildings that may eventually interfere with growth? Should the tree provide shade, serve as a flowering accent or both? Trees are long-term investments that should be among your first landscape plantings.

Some popular tree varieties are listed in the chart on Page 31.

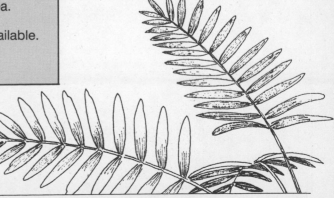

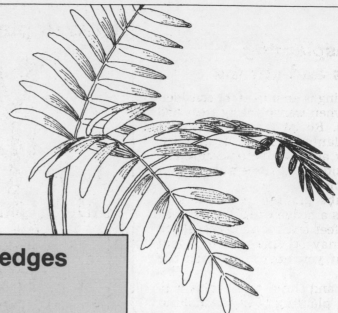

How to fertilize shrubs and hedges

This plant covers
50 square feet
(5 feet X 10 feet =
50 square feet).
It needs ½ to
1 pound of
fertilizer.

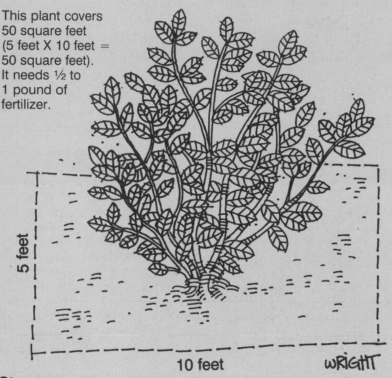

5 feet

10 feet

WRIGHT

Steps

1. Measure area under shrub or hedge; calculate square footage.
2. Use 6-6-6 fertilizer. *
3. Weigh out fertilizer.
Use 1 to 2 pounds for each 100 square feet of soil surface under shrub or hedge.
4. Spread fertilizer under shrub or hedge on soil surface.
5. Fertilize once in:
   ● Middle February
   ● Early May
   ● Middle July
   ● Early October

* For maximum efficiency 25 percent of the fertilizer's total nitrogen should be in a water-insoluble form. This information may be obtained by reading the product's label.

Shrubs for flowers and greenery

In Florida many shrubs add seasonal color to the landscape. Among the shrubs are azaleas for spring, crape myrtles for summer, cassias for fall and camellias for winter. Where accents are needed colorful shrubs can fill the bill.

Check potential height and width of shrubs to determine how many are needed to fill a landscape function. One large bright-red crape myrtle may be all that is needed to form an eye-catching accent, but a single petite azalea is hardly an attention getter, even in full bloom. In general, plant small shrubs in clusters to form splashes of color.

Plain green shrubs cover the ground to form transitions and build barriers. Use just a few types in any one design and again think of a group planting. Traditional favorites have included the yaupon holly, viburnum and ligustrum.

Shrubs once considered the cornerstone of Florida landscapes have crumbled in the wake of the 1983 and 1985 freezes. Formerly reliable ligustrum, pittosporum and viburnum, besieged with consecutive killing freezes, are now planted with caution.

Hardiness is on the minds of many landscapers and shrubs once little-known are now becoming popular. Hardy plants that withstand temperatures plummeting into the teens include photinia, silverthorn, anise, Indian hawthorn and banana shrub.

Transplanting trees and shrubs

Spacing is an important consideration when transplanting trees and shrubs. Resist cramming young transplants together. They grow quickly and may become crowded, competitive and susceptible to pest problems.

Shrubs planted in clusters or lined as a hedge usually are spaced 2 to 3 feet apart for a quick effect. They may be spaced 3 to 4 feet apart if you need to stretch the budget.

Tree and shrub care begins with proper planting. Dig the hole at least a foot deeper and wider than the root ball. Save the soil in a wheelbarrow or tarp to refill the hole when planting.

Many gardeners like to improve the fill soil before planting. Mix in additions such as peat moss, compost or similar forms of decomposed organic matter. These amendments to the soil should not exceed a third of the volume. Do not add fertilizer at this time to avoid root burn.

Fill the transplant hole with enough prepared soil to allow the ornamental to rest at the same level as it was growing in the field or container. Firmly pack the soil then position the plant so the trunk sits straight in the hole. Begin filling in around the ball, watering thoroughly as new soil is added to ensure good root-to-soil contact.

Facilitate future watering by forming a saucerlike basin of soil 4 to 6 inches high and 2 to 3 feet from the trunk. Add a 2- to 3-inch mulch layer to the basin to conserve water and keep soil uniformly moist. In massive plantings skip the individual saucers but pay special attention to water needs.

How to plant a tree

1. Dig the hole a foot deeper than the height of the roots, and twice as wide as the root span. Loosen soil at the bottom of the hole to facilitate drainage.

2. Add soil to the hole and build a mound under the plant. The plant should rest about the same depth as before it was moved.

3. Fill ¾ of the hole with soil, then water.

4. Finish filling in soil. For small plants, drive in stakes to secure. Use guy wires to secure larger plants.

Many trees will need to be staked or guyed because leafy tops can catch the wind and rock the plant. Even slight rocking can break new roots and slow plant establishment. Stakes also form a partial barrier around the trees and protect the trunks from mechanical injury.

Trees with trunks less than 2 inches across can usually be anchored by a sturdy wooden stake or metal rod. Young trees more than 2 inches in diameter may require two or three supports. The stakes should be positioned a few inches beyond the root ball and driven 2 feet into the ground.

Ensure the success of transplants by watering frequently. Soak the soil twice weekly until plants are well established. The first feeding should begin in four to six weeks with a light scattering of a 6-6-6 fertilizer, about one pound for each 100 square feet of planted area.

New leaf growth will be the first sign a tree or shrub has been successfully transplanted. Most plants will need frequent irrigation and continued fertilization to look their best.

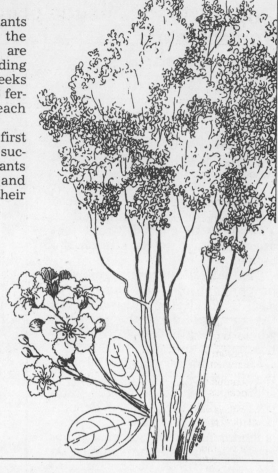

Crape myrtle
(*Lagerstroemia indica*)

Hedges provide privacy

Privacy can be achieved quickly with a properly pruned and maintained hedge. Whether the hedge is young or old it can be stimulated to form a physical and visual barrier. Where total privacy is required the ultimate goal should be a hedge 6 feet or higher. Lower plantings may form a barrier, but will not obstruct sight.

Hedges are dense plantings of trees and shrubs. Individual plants need extra good conditions including fertile, well-drained soil, to compete with one another and to withstand the stress of pruning while maintaining attractive growth. In Florida this usually means improving the soil through addition of organic matter.

Trimming and training should start when the hedge is very young. With privet, viburnum, cherry laurel, holly or similar ornamentals prune off approximately half of the previous season's growth at planting. This may seem drastic, but it stimulates new shoots to fill in basal areas and voids. As branches begin to grow upward, clip their tips at least once during the growing season.

All hedges need water and fertilizer. A 6-6-6 fertilizer may be applied once each season at the rate of 1 to 2 pounds for each 100 square feet of soil under the planting. Water the fertilizer into the soil to start immediate feeding of the plants.

Irrigation should keep the soil moist. Hedges that suffer drought become stunted and sparsely foliated. Water is needed at least once, and probably twice, a week. Mulch will help maintain even soil moisture. Check water needs by digging into the ground periodically; it may not be as moist as you think.

When 4 to 6 inches of new growth accumulate, the hedge needs trimming. At least once, stretch string the length of the hedge at the desired height to ensure uniformity. Trim only those branches that extend beyond the string. Never shear a hedge to its original size. Always allow approximately 1 to 2 inches of new growth to remain.

Keeping the hedge green to the ground means shaping it properly. Make sure the plantings are wide at the bottom and narrow at the top. When standing at the end of the planting you should see an obvious increase in width from the bottom to the top. (See sketch, facing page.)

Proper pruning techniques allow your hedge to grow in height and width. After several years, renovation is required to keep the hedge within its boundaries.

A neglected or overgrown hedge needs severe pruning. Early spring is the preferred time, but healthy plants pruned in summer also recover quickly. Prune overgrown specimens to 10 to 12 inches below desired height and width.

Prune a hedge with big spaces at the bottom to within 1 to 2 feet of the gaps.

Narrow-leaf evergreens, including junipers and arborvitae, should never be sheared beyond the area of existing needles. Better yet, do not formalize these ornamentals. Let them assume a natural shape and selectively hand cut overgrowth.

Popular Florida hedge plants

Name	Light	Planting distance	Hedge height	Comments
Anise (*Illicium anisatum*)	shade, full sun	30-36 inches	6+ feet	Broad dark green leaf; fragrant foliage when crushed.
Boxthorn (*Severinia buxifolia*)	partial shade, full sun	30-36 inches	4-5 feet	A thorny citrus relative; a very impermeable hedge.
Cherry laurel (*Prunus caroliniana*)	full sun	36-48 inches	6+ feet	Very rapid growth; suckers freely; also grows as tree.
Elaeagnus, silverthorn (*Elaeagnus pungens*)	full sun	30-36 inches	4-6 feet	Silvery foliage; fragrant but small fall flowers.
Feijoa (*Feijoa sellowiana*)	partial shade, full sun	30-36 inches	4-6 feet	Flowers white with red stamens; edible fruits; gray-green foliage.
Indian hawthorn (*Rhaphiolepis indica*)	partial shade, full sun	24-30 inches	3-4 feet	Dwarf spreading shrub with dark green foliage; white flowers borne in early spring.
Juniper (*Juniperus chinensis*)	full sun	24-48 inches	2-6 feet	Narrow-leaf evergreens; many varieties available for planting.
Ligustrum (*Ligustrum japonicum*)	partial shade, full sun	30-36 inches	5+ feet	Very popular, rapid growing; dark green leaf; some recent winter injury.
Photinia, red top (*Phontinia glabra*)	full sun	30-36 inches	4-6 feet	New growth bright red; eventually fades to green.
Pittosporum (*Pittosporum tobira*)	shade, full sun	30-36 inches	4-6 feet	Dark green and variegated leaf forms; dwarf form available.
Podocarpus (*Podocarpus macrophylla*)	shade, full sun	24-36 inches	6+ feet	Narrow dark green foliage; bears edible purple-fleshed fruit.
Sandankwa viburnum (*Viburnum suspensum*)	shade, full sun	30-36 inches	4-6 feet	Leaves bold with slightly scalloped margin; white flowers in spring; some winter injury.
Sweet viburnum (*Viburnum odoratissimum*)	full sun	36-48 inches	6+ feet	Popular large-leafed hedge; white springtime flowers; recent severe winter injury.
Schellings holly (*Ilex vomitoria* Schellings Dwarf)	shade, full sun	24-30 inches	2-3 feet	Excellent dwarf hedge; resembles boxwood; little pruning needed.

How to prune hedges

The method of pruning hedges depends on the type desired. Informal hedges generally consist of a row of closely planted shrubs which are allowed to develop into their natural shape. Annual pruning consists of cutting just enough to maintain desired height and width.

Formal or clipped hedges require a specialized pruning which may become a continuous job during the growing season. The desired appearance of a formal hedge is a soft outline of continuous foliage from the ground up.

Two important factors to remember when pruning formal hedges are: (1) hedges should be clipped while the new growth is green and succulent; (2) plants should be trimmed so the base of the hedge is wider than the top.

Hedges pruned with a narrow base will lose lower leaves and branches because of insufficient light. This condition will worsen with age. It results in sparse growth at ground level and an unattractive hedge which does not give desired privacy.

Formal flowering hedges should be sheared after they have bloomed since more frequent shearing reduces the number of blooms. The blooms, however, are considered of secondary importance, since a mass of foliage is the primary objective.

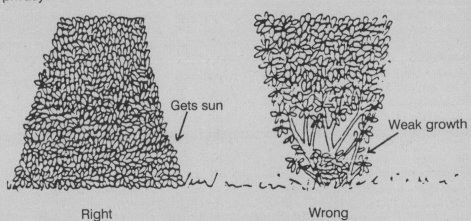

Right

Wrong

Gets sun

Weak growth

Air layering — sure way to get new plant

Air layering, practiced for centuries, is still an important technique to modern propagators. It is an almost foolproof method of rooting limbs while they remain attached to the parent tree or shrub.

Hard-to-root or valuable plants are selected frequently for propagation by air layering. The technique is often used where a large, mature specimen will be needed for the landscape. Air layers can be formed on limbs of almost any size or length. Unless a project calls for a large mature specimen it is best to select a young branch with recently hardened wood.

Start by removing the leaves from the limb at a point where the layer is to be constructed, usually 12 or more inches back from the tip. Clear leaves from a 4- to 6-inch segment to provide plenty of working space.

Rooting is stimulated by wounding a leaf-free portion of the stem. One way to create the wound is to make a long, slanting but shallow cut upward under the bark. Keep this incision from healing by placing a bark chip or toothpick in the wound.

A second method is to make two shallow cuts an inch apart that completely girdle the limb. Make a downward slit in the bark and remove the segment between the two cuts. Immediately apply a rooting powder to the exposed plant tissue using a fine brush or the tip of a knife to lightly coat the wounds. Too much powder can delay rooting.

Before the wound has a chance to dry, enclose the area in a ball of moist sphagnum moss. Garden centers often market small bags of this water-absorbent, stringy material. The ball is made by taking two handfuls of damp sphagnum moss and placing them on each side of the wounded stem.

Enclose the moss in plastic film or aluminum foil. Sandwich, newspaper or bread bags make ideal wrappings. Extend the wrap above and below the moss ball to seal in moisture. To complete the air layer, tie off both ends of the wrap with twine, rubber bands or twist-ties.

The rate of rooting inside the moss ball will depend on the plant type, time of the year and age of the tissue. Most houseplants will root within two months, while trees and shrubs may take longer. Check the air layer periodically for roots. With plastic, the entire ball surface can be seen without unwrapping. Foils will have to be removed from time to time to detect root growth.

When five or six strong roots are evident on the ball surface, remove the new plant. Make a cut below the moss ball and roots. Do not remove or disturb the moss ball. Plant the new ornamental in a pot or a prepared bed. Air layers can be planted as deep in the soil as needed to give the trunk adequate support.

1. Make a long, slanting cut upward and insert a toothpick or bark chip.

2. Apply rooting powder to the cut and wrap with moist sphagnum moss. Enclose with plastic or aluminum foil.

3. After rooting takes place, cut just below the moss ball. Do not disturb the moss ball. Plant the new ornamental in a pot or prepared bed.

WRIGHT

Recommended trees for Florida

This list of select trees is recommended to residents for planting in Central Florida by the Beautification Committee of the Greater Orlando Chamber of Commerce. Information for this list was prepared by the Orange County Extension Service and the Florida Division of Forestry.

Commom name	Height	Light	Flower/season	Accent	Shade	Street	Patio	Framing	Comments
American holly	30 feet	sun, partial shade	inconspicuous	X		X		X	A broadleaf native evergreen holly with attractive red berries. Varieties East Palatka or Savannah are preferred.
Bald cypress	80 feet	sun	inconspicuous		X			X	A deciduous conifer that grows near or away from water. It's a medium to rapid growing tree.
Bottlebrush	15 feet	sun	red/spring	X			X		An evergreen that grows into a small tree. Few pest problems.
Camphor	50 feet	sun	yellow/spring		X				Popular broadleaf evergreen with slow to medium growth rate. Fruit is often objectionable due to staining when crushed. May have mite problem.
Cherry laurel	35 feet	sun	white/spring		X	X		X	Broadleaf evergreen with berries that attract birds. Subject to boring insect damage.
Chickasaw plum	20 feet	partial shade	white/spring	X			X		Small native tree with showy white flowers in spring.
Chinese elm	40 feet	sun	inconspicuous	X		X	X		Preferred species in elm family. Tree tends to lose leaves in winter.
Chinese tallow	40 feet	sun	inconspicuous		X	X			Rapid growing, deciduous tree. One of few trees that show fall color. Few pest problems.
Crape myrtle	20 feet	sun	varied/summer	X			X		Deciduous large shrub to small tree. Drops leaves in late fall and has smooth cream-colored bark. Has aphid, sooty mold problems.
Dahoon holly	40 feet	sun, partial shade	inconspicuous	X		X		X	Native evergreen holly with red berries. Prefers moist soils. Few pest problems.
Dogwood	30 feet	partial shade	white/spring	X			X		Native tree with showy white flower, bracts in spring. Boring insects can be problem.
Golden-rain tree	30 feet	sun, partial shade	yellow/fall		X	X			Excellent rapid growing deciduous tree. Few pests.
Jerusalem thorn	25 feet	sun, partial shade	yellow/summer	X			X		Open crown small tree, useful in small areas. Thorns are prickly. Few pest problems.
Laurel oak	60 feet	sun, partial shade	inconspicuous		X	X		X	Semi-evergreen oak. Few pest problems.
Ligustrum	40 feet	sun, partial shade	white/spring	X			X		Evergreen that grows rapidly.
Live oak	60 feet	sun, partial	inconspicuous		X	X		X	Popular, long-lived broadleaf evergreen. Few pest problems.
Magnolia	90 feet	sun, partial shade	white/summer		X	X		X	Broadleaf, native evergreen. Problems with white scale.
Redbud	30 feet	partial shade	red/spring	X	X	X			Deciduous native; small tree with great potential for use in home landscapes.
Red maple	40 feet	sun, partial shade	red/spring		X	X		X	Rapid growing, native deciduous tree. Few pest problems. Red flowers, fruit in spring; red or yellow foliage in fall before leaves drop.
Slash pine	60 feet	sun	inconspicuous		X	X		X	Fast growing deciduous tree. Should be planted in clumps for good shade.
Sweet gum	80 feet	sun, partial shade	inconspicuous		X	X		X	Rapid growing deciduous tree. Spiny seed ball can be problem. Few pest problems.
Sycamore	90 feet	sun	inconspicuous		X	X		X	Rapid growing deciduous tree. Foliage subject to non-fatal insect, disease problems. Showy cream- and brown-colored bark.
Tabebuia	25 feet	sun, partial shade	yellow/spring	X			X		Open deciduous tree also referred to as trumpet tree due to flower shape. Attention getter when in flower.
Wax myrtle	15 feet	sun, partial shade	inconspicuous				X		Native evergreen that grows well in most soils. No pest problems.
Yellow poinciana	70 feet	sun	yellow/summer	X					Also referred to as scrambled egg tree because of its summer flowers. Fast growing deciduous tree that needs plenty of room to grow.

Selected shrubs for Central Florida

Small shrubs

Common/scientific name	Growth habit	Common height	Flower color/season	Light conditions	Soil type	Salt spray tolerance	Comments
Coral ardisia (*Ardisia crenata*)	upright, multistems	3-4 feet	inconspicuous	shade	fertile, acid	no	Coral red berries in winter; Alba is white fruited cultivar.
Dwarf schefflera (*Brassaia arboricola*)	spreading, compact	2-4 feet	inconspicuous	partial shade	fertile	moderate	Sensitive to cold.
Japanese boxwood (*Buxus microphylla*)	globose, compact	3-4 feet	inconspicuous	partial shade, shade	fertile, acid	no	Tolerates shearing. Nematodes, mites, leaf miners are problems.
Dwarf natal plum (*Carissa grandiflora* Nana)	spreading	3-4 feet	white/warm season	full sun	sandy	yes	Attractive scarlet fruit. Other dwarf cultivars are Emerald Blanket, Boxwood Beauty.
Cuphea (*Cuphea hyssopifolia*)	spreading, compact	3-4 feet	red to white/summer	full sun	fertile	no	Susceptible to frost.
Crown-of-thorns (*Euphorbia milii*)	spreading	3 feet	inconspicuous; showy bracts	full sun	very well drained	yes	Showy red, pink or cream bracts. Susceptible to frost.
Prostrate gardenia (*Gardenia jasminoides* Prostrata)	spreading, compact	1-2 feet	white/spring	partial shade	fertile	no	Sensitive to nematodes, white fly, sooty mold.
Dwarf Chinese holly (*Ilex cornuta* Rotunda)	spreading	3-4 feet	inconspicuous	full sun, partial shade	well drained, acid	no	Multispined leaves. Best in groups.
Dwarf yaupon holly (*Ilex vomitoria* Nana)	spreading	3-4 feet	inconspicuous	full sun, shade	variety	yes	Other cultivars include Stokes Dwarf, Schellings.
Chinese juniper (*Juniperus chinensis*)	broad spreading	2-3 feet	inconspicuous	full sun	fertile, well drained	moderate	Cultivars include Parsonii, Parsonii Variegata.
Shore juniper (*Juniperus conferta*)	broad spreading	1-2 feet	inconspicuous	full sun	fertile, well drained	moderate	Superior cultivars include Blue Pacific, Compacta.
Fortune's Mahonia (*Mahonia fortunei*)	upright, multistems	3-4 feet	yellow/early spring	partial shade	well drained	no	Thick mounded shrub. Good as specimen plant.
Dwarf Nandina (*Nandina domestica compacta*)	spreading, compact	2-3 feet	inconspicuous	full sun, partial shade	fertile	no	Cultivars include Purpurea Dwarf, Harbour Dwarf.
Kurume hybrid azaleas (*Rhododendron obtusum*)	spreading	4 feet	variable/spring	partial shade	acidic	no	Variety of colors, growth habits.
Serissa (*Serissa foetida*)	spreading	2 feet	white/warm season	partial shade	fertile, moist	no	Used as edging, foundation plant.

Medium shrubs

Common/scientific name	Growth habit	Common height	Flower color/season	Light conditions	Soil type	Salt spray tolerance	Comments
Century plant (*Agave americana*)	globose	5-6 feet	flowers only once, then dies	full sun	well drained	yes	Tolerates poor sandy soil. Marginata has yellow-white marginal stripes.
Golden trumpet (*Allamanda cathartica*)	broad spreading, climbing	8-10 feet	yellow/warm season	full sun	variety	no	Trained to shrub or vine; poisonous.
Aucuba (*Aucuba japonica*)	upright	5-6 feet	inconspicuous	shade	fertile, organic	no	Multistems; variegated cultivars common.
Snow bush (*Breynia disticha*)	spreading, open	5-6 feet	inconspicuous	full sun	light, sandy	no	Brightly variegated foliage in several colors. Susceptible to frost.
Beauty berry (*Callicarpa americana*)	spreading, compact	5-6 feet	lilac/spring	partial shade	fertile, moist	no	Showy magenta fruit in autumn. White fruited selection available.
Natal plum (*Carissa grandiflora*)	spreading, compact	5-6 feet	white/warm season	full sun	sandy	yes	Attractive scarlet fruit; milky sap.
Candle bush (*Cassia alata*)	spreading	8 feet	yellow/fall	full sun	variety	moderate	Susceptible to freeze injury.
Croton (*Codiaeum variegatum*)	spreading, open	5-6 feet	inconspicuous	full sun, partial shade	variety	moderate	Multicolored leaves, color differs with variety; cold sensitive.
Cherokee bean (*Erythrina herbacea*)	upright	5-6 feet	red/spring	partial shade	fertile	no	Deciduous; showy flowers; bright scarlet seed.
Poinsettia (*Euphorbia pulcherrima*)	upright, multistems	8 feet	inconspicuous	full sun	well drained	no	Showy red bracts at Christmas.
Fatsia (*Fatsia japonica*)	upright	5-6 feet	inconspicuous	partial shade	fertile, acid	moderate	Does well in landscape containers.
Gardenia (*Gardenia jasminoides*)	spreading, compact	5-6 feet	white/spring	partial shade	fertile, acid	no	Susceptible to nematodes, whitefly, sooty mold. Showy spring color.
Thryallis (*Galphimia glauca*)	spreading, compact	8 feet	yellow/warm season	full sun, partial shade	variety	no	Plant injured by 28°F (2°C).
Chinese hibiscus (*Hibiscus rosa-sinensis*)	upright, multistems	6-8 feet	variable/warm season	full sun, partial shade	moist, fertile	no	Many selections, hybrids available.
Hydrangea (*Hydrangea macrophylla*)	spreading	5-6 feet	blue to pink to white/late spring	shade	fertile, well drained	no	Flower color varies with soil pH.
Dwarf Burford holly (*Ilex cornuta* Burfordii Compacta)	spreading	5-6 feet	inconspicuous	full sun, partial shade	well drained, acid	no	Not readily infested by scale insects.
Primrose jasmine (*Jasminum mesnyi*)	broad spreading	5-6 feet	yellow/late winter	full sun	variety	no	Mounding growth habit.
Downy jasmine (*Jasminum multiflorum*)	broad spreading, sprawling	5-6 feet	white/warm season	full sun, partial shade	variety	no	Downy leaf surface; often used as clipped hedges.
Shining jasmine (*Jasminum nitidum*)	spreading, sprawling	5-6 feet	white/warm season	full sun, partial shade	variety	no	Shiny leaf surface; often used as clipped hedges.

33

Medium shrubs (continued)

Common/scientific name	Growth habit	Common height	Flower color/season	Light conditions	Soil type	Salt spray tolerance	Comments
Chinese juniper (Juniperus chinensis)	spreading	6-8 feet	inconspicuous	full sun	fertile, well drained	moderate	Varieties include Mint Julep, Hetzii, Blue Vase.
Lantana (Lantana camara)	upright, multistems	5-6 feet	red, pink, orange or yellow/summer	full sun	variety	yes	Susceptible to frost.
Texas sage (Leucophyllum frutescens)	spreading, compact	5-6 feet	lavender/summer	full sun	well drained, sandy	moderate	Good for hot, dry locations.
Loropetalum (Loropetalum chinese)	spreading, compact	6-8 feet	cream to yellow/early spring	partial shade	fertile, well drained	no	Horizontal branching; needs frequent watering.
Chinese holly grape (Mahonia lomarifolia)	upright, multistems	6-8 feet	yellow/early spring	partial shade	fertile, well drained	no	Good as border plant in formal garden. Interesting grapelike fruit.
Turks cap (Malvaviscus arboreus)	spreading	6-8 feet	red to white/warm season	full sun	variety	no	Susceptible to freeze.
Myrtle (Myrtus communis)	spreading, open	5-6 feet	white/spring	partial shade	fertile, well drained	no	Microphylla, Variegata are superior selections.
Nandina (Nandina domestica)	upright, multistems, unbranched	5-6 feet	white/spring	partial shade	fertile	no	Red fruit in winter.
Indian hybrid azaleas (Rhododendron simsii)	spreading	5-6 feet	variable/spring	partial shade	fertile, acid well drained	no	Evergreen.
Fire cracker plant (Russelia equisetiformis)	spreading, weeping	5-6 feet	red/summer	full sun	variety	no	Also called coral plant.
Boxthorn (Severina buxifolia)	spreading, compact	5-6 feet	white/spring	full sun, partial shade	well drained	no	Black berries.
Crape jasmine (Tabernaemontana divaricata)	spreading, symmetrical	6-8 feet	white/warm season	full sun, partial shade	variety	no	Fragrant waxy flowers. Susceptible to hard freezes.
Rice-paper plant (Tetrapanax papyriferus)	upright	8 feet	yellow to white/warm season	full sun, partial shade	variety	no	Produces suckers. Susceptible to freezing temperatures.
Sandankwa viburnum (Viburnum suspensum)	spreading	6-8 feet	white/spring	full sun, shade	fertile	no	Easily maintained at smaller size.
Spanish dagger (Yucca gloriosa)	upright	6-8 feet	white/summer	full sun	well drained	moderate	Good for hot, dry locations.

Large shrubs

Common/ scientific name	Growth habit	Common height	Flower color/ season	Light conditions	Soil type	Salt spray tolerance	Comments
Bougainvillea (*Bougainvillea spp.*)	spreading	10-12 feet	red to white showy bracts/ warm season	full sun	variety, non-alkaline	no	Aggressive grower, informal character.
Butterfly bush (*Buddleia officinalis*)	spreading	12-15 feet	lilac/ midwinter	full sun	light, sandy	moderate	Fragrant flowers, good border plant. Susceptible to frost.
Powderpuff (*Calliandra haematocephala*)	spreading, open	12-15 feet	red to white/ summer	full sun	variety	no	Vigorous; popular flowering shrub.
Lemon bottlebrush (*Callistemon citrinus*)	upright, spreading	12-15 feet	red/ late spring	full sun	well drained	moderate	Good specimen or accent plant.
Bottlebrush (*Callistemon rigidus*)	upright	8-10 feet	red/ late spring	full sun	well drained	moderate	Leaves are quite stiff.
Camellia (*Camellia japonica*)	upright, dense	10-12 feet	variable/ winter	full sun, partial shade	well drained, acid	no	Many cultivars available.
Sasanqua (*Camellia sasanqua*)	upright	10-12 feet	variable/ winter	full sun, broken shade	well drained, acid	no	Many cultivars available.
Butterfly bush (*Cassia bicapsularis*)	upright, spreading	10-12 feet	bright yellow/ fall	full sun	variety	moderate	Specimen shrub.
Cocculus (*Cocculus laurifolius*)	spreading, weeping	12-15 feet	inconspicuous	full sun, partial shade	variety	no	May be injured by cold. Coarse texture.
Angel's trumpet (*Datura arborea*)	upright	12-15 feet	white/ summer	full sun, partial shade	variety	no	Large fragrant flowers; poisonous.
Golden-dewdrop (*Duranta repens*)	spreading	12-15 feet	blue/ warm season	full sun	variety	no	Yellow fruit is poisonous.
Silverthorn (*Elaeagnus pungens*)	spreading	12-15 feet	inconspicuous	full sun	variety	yes	Vigorous growth; long sweeping shoots.
Surinam cherry (*Eugenia uniflora*)	spreading, compact	12-15 feet	white	full sun	variety	no	Edible ribbed black or red berry. Good clipped hedge.
Feijoa (*Feijoa sellowiana*)	spreading, compact	8-10 feet	white with red stamens/ spring	full sun, partial shade	variety	moderate	Edible fruit. Good clipped hedge.
Kumquat (*Fortunella japonica*)	spreading	12-15 feet	white/ spring	full sun	variety	yes	Attractive, fragrant edible fruit.
Chinese holly (*Ilex cornuta*)	spreading	12-15 feet	inconspicuous	full sun, partial shade	well drained, acid	no	Scarlet or red berries; good cut foliage. Burfordii is popular cultivar.
Yaupon holly (*Ilex vomitoria*)	spreading	12-15 feet	inconspicuous	full sun, shade	variety	yes	Excellent large shrub.
Anise (*Illicium anisatum*)	spreading	8-10 feet	inconspicuous	full sun, shade	variety	no	Easily maintained at smaller size. Foliage fragrant when crushed.
Ixora (*Ixora coccinea*)	spreading, compact	8-10 feet	red, yellow or orange/ warm season	full sun	fertile, slightly acidic, well drained	moderate	Many hybrids. Sensitive to cold.
Chinese juniper (*Junperus chinensis*)	upright, columnar	12-15 feet	inconspicuous	full sun	fertile, well drained	moderate	Cultivars include Sylvestris, Torulosa.
Crape myrtle (*Lagerstroemia indica*)	upright	12-15 feet	white, pink, red or purple/ summer	full sun	variety	no	Deciduous; susceptible to powdery mildew. Often used as small tree.

Large shrubs (continued)

Common/scientific name	Growth habit	Common height	Flower color/season	Light conditions	Soil type	Salt spray tolerance	Comments
Japanese privet (*Ligustrum japonicum*)	upright spreading	12-15 feet	white/spring	full sun, partial shade	variety	no	Fragrant flowers. Excellent screen or barrier.
Chinese privet (*Ligustrum sinense*)	upright	8-10 feet	white/spring	full sun, partial shade	variety	no	Variegated form. Often used as clipped hedge.
Orange jasmine (*Murraya paniculata*)	upright	8-10 feet	white/spring	full sun, partial shade	well drained	no	Fragrant citruslike flowers; red attractive fruit.
Southern wax myrtle (*Myrica cerifera*)	upright spreading, clumping	12-15 feet	inconspicuous	full sun, partial shade	variety	yes	Excellent, vigorous growing plant. Often used as small tree.
Oleander (*Nerium oleander*)	upright	12-15 feet	red, pink, cream or white/summer	full sun	variety	yes	Showy flowers. Excellent seaside species.
Pittosporum (*Pittosporum tobira*)	spreading, compact	8-10 feet	white/spring	full sun, shade	fertile, acid	yes	Easily maintained at smaller sizes. Variegated selections available.
Oriental arborvitae (*Platycladus orientalis*) (*Thuja orientalis*)	globose, densely foliated	15-20 feet	inconspicuous	full sun	variety	no	Often misused; not a foundation plant.
Weeping podocarpus (*Podocarpus gracilior*)	spreading	20-30 feet	inconspicuous	full sun, shade	variety	none	Susceptible to hard freezes.
Yew podocarpus (*Podocarpus macrophyllus*)	upright, compact	20-25 feet	inconspicuous	full sun, shade	variety	moderate	Easily maintained at smaller size.
Nagi podocarpus (*Podocarpus nagi*)	upright	20-25 feet	inconspicuous	full sun, shade	variety	moderate	Strong accent plant. Good cut foliage.
Cherry laurel (*Prunus caroliniana*)	spreading	20-25 feet	white/spring	full sun, shade	fertile	no	Easily trained to small tree or clipped hedge. Messy fruit.
Cattleya guava (*Psidium littorale*)	spreading, compact	15-20 feet	white/spring	full sun	variety	no	Red or yellow edible fruit in summer. Interesting trunk character.
Firethorn (*Pyracantha coccinea*)	spreading	15-20 feet	white/spring	full sun	variety	no	Often trained as espalier. Bright fruit in fall.
Japanese cleyera (*Ternstroemia gymnanthera*)	upright	12-15 feet	white	partial shade, shade	fertile, well drained	no	Reddish midribs in leaves.
Lucky nut (*Thevetia peruviana*)	upright, compact	12-15 feet	yellow to peach/warm season	full sun	variety	no	Susceptible to frost. Angular fruit; poisonous.
Princess flower (*Tibouchina urvilleana*)	spreading, open	12-15 feet	purple/warm season	full sun	well drained	no	Flowers showy. Good border shrub.
Sweet viburnum (*Viburnum odoratissimum*)	spreading, dense	15-20 feet	white/spring	full sun	variety	no	Not a foundation plant. Regular pruning required.
Chaste tree (*Vitex trifolia*)	spreading	10-12 feet	lavender to blue/summer	full sun	sandy	moderate	Vigorous shrub. Variegated cultivar most common.
Spanish bayonet (*Yucca aloifolia*)	upright, clumping	12-15 feet	white/summer	full sun, shade	well drained	yes	Excellent seaside plant; accent plant.
Spineless yucca (*Yucca elephantipes*)	upright, clumping	15-20 feet	white/summer	full sun, shade	well drained	yes	Harmless leaf tips. Some selections with striped foliage.

6
Palms add the Florida look

P ALMS ARE AN EXPECTED feature of picturesque Florida. Their tropical look promises lush growth and balmy weather.

Often called trees, palms are related botanically to the family of grasses. Unlike trees, one main bud in a palm's trunk produces all upward growth. Once mature, palm trunks do not continue to enlarge like those of trees. Without this increasing diameter and bark formation, palms cannot heal their wounds and the injured tissue simply hardens. The feathery or fan-shaped palm foliage is also quite different from trees.

Most palms native to the United States are found growing in Florida. They range in size from the 3- to 4-foot dwarf palmetto and saw palmetto to the 60-foot cabbage palm, the state tree. Twelve palms are native to Florida but about half, including the coconut and royal palms, need the warmth of South Florida to survive.

Small palms may be used in border plantings, as screens or for garden greenery. Some serve as in-home or patio plants when grown in containers.

Large palms are ideal for streetside planting because they are able to survive with minimal care. Landscapers suggest clustering large palms in odd-numbered groups of three, five or more where they can create a visual barrier and offer shade for underneath plantings.

Many of Central Florida's common palms have succumbed to recent freezes. Queen palms, once heavily planted along streets and in landscapes, have been severely injured. Palms that appear to be recovering from frost may develop butt rot. The disease enters the wounds and deteriorates the trunks.

Hardy substitutes include the cabbage, Canary Island date, Washington and Chinese fan palms. These can grow from 30 to 60 feet tall, so plan for mature heights.

Where smaller specimens are needed, the European fan and windmill palms can be used. At maturity, heights can range from 5 to 10 feet, making these good substitutes for the much-planted but cold-sensitive pygmy date palm.

The butia is a most graceful broad-spreading palm, but must be planted where there is ample room for growth. Blue-green foliage and exceptionally colorful deep orange fruits make the butia a good accent plant.

The lady palm produces a dense

Lady palm
(*Rhapis*)

cluster of growth and is excellent in a protected location as a screen or patio accent.

Dwarf and saw palmettos are durable palms resistant to drought and cold. Developers once cleared these trees from homesites, but now many native stands are being left as weather-resistant beds or screens. Because these palms are difficult to transplant from the wild, many gardeners will not be able to add them to existing landscapes.

Most other palms are easy to transplant. Potted specimens are often available at garden centers and many palms are sold by tree companies in an almost bare-root form. The root balls are often much smaller than many gardeners expect for the size of the specimens.

The best time to transplant a palm is during the warm, rainy season, May through September. The palm is one ornamental that can be planted a little deeper than it was growing in the field or container because new roots often form along the trunk.

Follow general tree planting procedures when positioning a new palm in the landscape. Dig a hole twice the size of the root ball and add an improved fill soil if you desire.

Palms are not particular and many are set in sandy soils with no improvements. It is important to bank soil in a circle around the base to form a water basin that can be filled daily for the first 10 to 14 days

after transplanting. After that, palms will need watering about twice a week during hot, dry weather. During cooler months little additional water will be needed.

Many gardeners like to bunch and tie the fronds of newly transplanted fan palms over the bud to protect from drying. Use a cord that will deteriorate in a month or so, letting the leaves spread open.

Large palms should be staked when transplanted. The root systems often are small and the bulky trunks and foliage can catch brisk winds and topple over. Brace palms with boards that have been padded to protect the trunk. Inclining planks can be nailed to the padded portions but never to the trunks.

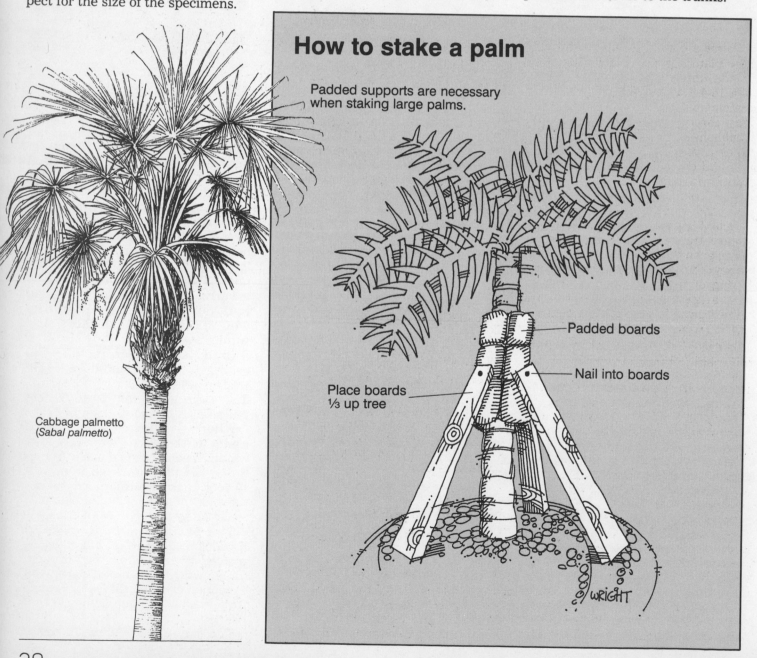

Cabbage palmetto
(*Sabal palmetto*)

How to stake a palm

Padded supports are necessary when staking large palms.

Padded boards

Nail into boards

Place boards ⅓ up tree

WRIGHT

Saw palmetto
(*Serenoa repens*)

Canary Island date palm
(*Phoenix canariensis*)

Palms are heavy feeders. Fertilize new plantings as soon as the first fronds unfurl. Use a turf fertilizer of a 16-4-8 or similar analysis. New transplants should be fed monthly May through August. Older, well-established palms can be fed three times a year: late winter, midsummer and early fall. The fall application is important because it increases cold tolerance.

Central Florida palms are often deficient in magnesium and manganese, trace elements important to palm growth. A magnesium deficiency shows up as a gradual yellowing of the oldest leaves. A lack of manganese also affects the newest growth, producing a disease called frizzle top that is indicated by misshapen new shoots that are often a yellow to brown color.

Both deficiencies are easily corrected with applications to the foliage or soil of missing nutrients.

Palms are relatively carefree additions to the landscape. Some older drying fronds periodically may need removal, but as they hang many form characteristic skirts that are attractive and aid in identifying the species.

Palm boots — the base of cut or deteriorated fronds — may also create interesting criss-crossing bark patterns. Many gardeners prefer to leave these in place until rot causes major deterioration.

When arctic gusts freeze home collections, don't give up. As the extent of cold damage is detected, re- move the browned leaves back to the trunk. Where palms are severely frozen, remove all dead or decaying tissue covering the bud so that it can dry out. Apply a copper fungicide spray and make a repeat application in 10 days to prevent further decay.

This prompt treatment of freeze-damaged palms and replanting with cold-hardy species can help preserve a bit ot the tropics growing in home landscapes.

Ancient cycads have look of palms

Cycads may look like palms but at best are very distant relatives. More than 180 million years ago when dinosaurs and giant reptiles dominated the earth, cycads' palm-like foliage was prevalent. The once widely distributed order now comprises nine genera restricted to tropical and subtropical regions.

Native cycads along with introduced species are some of the most valued plants for the Florida landscape.

The genera *Zamia*, which includes the common Florida coontie, is the largest group of cycads. Native stands frequently inhabit the state's pinelands and coastal regions, forming clumps of vegetation up to 3 feet high. The thick, stocky roots have been an important source of arrowroot starch, a yellowish white flour used by early Florida inhabitants.

Introduced cycads often cultivated for home planting include the genus *Cycas*, the sago palms and the little-known *Dioon*. All are durable, easy-to-grow landscape plants. Historically, cycads have been kept in the background, the dark pinnate foliage blending with other greenery. However, they have potential as accent, foundation and border plantings.

The king and queen sagos, species *Cycas*, are the tallest growing of the frequently planted cycads. The king predominates not because it's bigger but because it's hardier. Identification is often the source of much confusion. The queen sago is the taller, growing to 20 feet. Every-

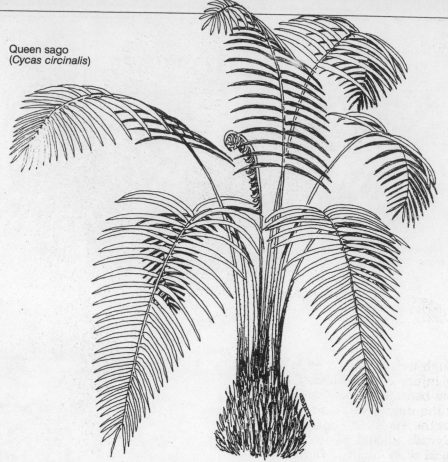

Queen sago
(*Cycas circinalis*)

thing is bigger about this species, but its graceful arching foliage possibly led to the more feminine name. Old king sagos may grow to 15 feet and live to be more than 100 years old. The foliage is more rigid, with leaves and leaflets just half the size of the queen's.

The *Dioon* is the least known of the cycad genera. It's not hardy and should be protected when temperatures drop below 35 degrees. The long fronds are stiff, standing semi-erect from a short, stout trunk. A plant 30 years old may be only 3 feet tall, but older specimens will grow to 6 to 8 feet in height. Even

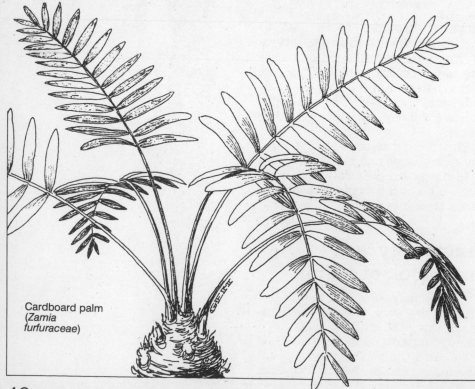

Cardboard palm
(*Zamia
furfuraceae*)

though the *Dioon* and other cycads are injured by cold they usually grow back from the trunk, renewing the injured plant portions soon after the weather warms.

Cycads do not produce flowers typical of many garden plants, but do have male and female reproductive structures and just a single sex per plant. The male pollen is produced in large conelike growths from which it is blown or carried by insects to a flattened wide-spreading female cone on a separate plant. One female plant may yield more than 100 usually orange-to-scarlet-colored seeds.

Most native cycads produce a flush of foliage and a reproductive structure each year. Only the female king sago differs, producing foliage one year and reproductive structure the next. It's not necessary to remove the old brown and fuzzy reproductive portions because they shatter when seed or pollen production is complete.

Seed germination has been difficult for many Florida growers and contributes to the scarcity of cycads at nurseries.

Gardeners with maturing *Cycas* and *Dioon* species will often notice new offshoots called pups forming near the base. Remove these new shoots with a smooth cut near the trunk to start additional plants. Treat the cut end with captan, a fungicide, and let the new shoot sit one week before planting. Then pot in a loose mix and expect a rooted growing plant within six months.

Zamias growing in clumps can also be divided to form new plants.

Cycads are carefree plants that grow in sandy or well-drained soils. A light fertilization several times a year will meet their nutrient needs. Use products that contain ammonium, such as ammonium sulfate or urea. Avoid nitrate nitrogen sources. Cycads like a slightly acid soil and additional organic matter frequently is mixed with planting soil.

The biggest obstacles to planting cycads in home landscapes are speed of plant production and price. When compared to other ornamentals their growth is slow. Because it takes four to five years to raise a transplant for home culture, the price is higher than for most trees and shrubs. But it is well worth the wait to have this unusual, time-tested and attractive link with the past growing in the landscape.

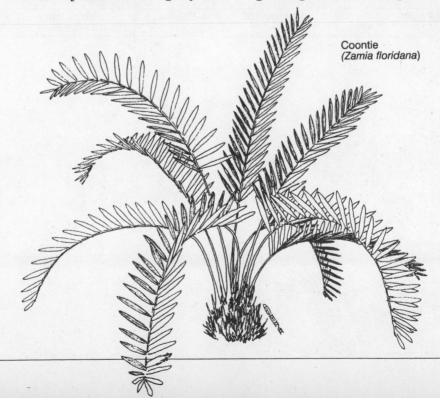

Coontie
(*Zamia floridana*)

Common cycads of Florida

Name	Height	Growth habit	Use	Remarks
Queen sago (*Cycas circinalis*)	20 feet	graceful, arching 5-foot to 8-foot pinnate leaves arise from palmlike trunk	accent, specimen plant	Not reliably cold hardy. Freeze damaged plants usually recover. Leaflets thin, flexible to 12 inches in length.
King sago (*Cycas revoluta*)	15 feet	ridged 2-foot to 5-foot slightly recurved pinnate leaves arise from palmlike trunk	accent, specimen plant	Most common of sagos. Cold hardy. Leaflets very stiff to 6 inches in length.
Dioon (*Dioon edule*)	6-8 feet	stiff, more than 3-foot-long pinnate leaves arise on thickened trunk near or below the ground	accent, specimen plant	Not reliably cold hardy. Freeze damaged plants usually recover.
Florida coontie (*Zamia floridana*)	2-3 feet	clump forming pinnate leaves arise from thickened trunk near or below the ground	ground cover, accent, foundation plant	Cold hardy. Leaflets slightly twisted. *Zamia umbrosa* a similar species with straight leaflets.
Cardboard palm (*Zamia furfuracea*)	4 feet	clump forming pinnate leaves arise from thickened trunk near or below the ground	ground cover, accent, foundation plant	Not reliably cold hardy. Freeze damaged plants usually recover. Leaflets thick like cardboard; hairy beneath.

Hardy palms for Florida

Common name	Leaves	Height	Growth	Remarks
Lady palm	fan shaped	8-10 feet	low-growing, shrub type	Slow grower. Excellent patio or container palm.
Butia palm	feather shaped	10-20 feet	heavy trunks, bluish-gray leaves	Slow grower. Needs space to develop spreading habit.
Cabbage palm	fan shaped	30-60 feet	erect tree, heavy trunk	Florida's official state tree. Excellent native palm; transplants easily.
Canary Island date palm	feather shaped	30-60 feet	stocky, single massive trunk	Large for residential plantings. Often shows magnesium deficiency.
Washington palm	fan shaped	50-60 feet	tall, stiff, erect tree	Good for street plantings.
Chinese fan palm	fan shaped	30-40 feet	heavy trunk	Slow grower until trunk well formed. Cold sensitive.
Dwarf palmetto	fan shaped	3-6 feet	stemless shrub	Seldom used. Native palm with bluish color. Difficult to transplant.
European fan palm	fan shaped	2-5 feet	clump-growing, gray-green	Slow grower. Excellent small palm for homes.
Saw palmetto	fan shaped	3-4 feet	shrubs, twisted, reclining trunk	Excellent small native palm but very difficult to transplant.
Windmill palm	fan shaped	5-10 feet	slender, erect solitary trunk	Very cold hardy; excellent palm.

7

Vines and ground covers — nature's camouflage

Confederate jasmine
(Trachelospermum jasminoides)

VINES AND GROUND COVers smooth rough edges in the landscape. The bright green foliage and showy flowers are invaluable at concealing stark brick, wood or concrete walls, while ground-hugging ornamentals cover steep slopes unsuitable for other cultivation.

Vines and creeping shrubs are the best wall hangings to send climbing up and over vertical surfaces. These coverings add beauty, texture, seasonal interest and privacy.

Most vines require full sun to develop strong stems and flower freely. Young plants usually need a trellis or similar support to begin their climb. Plants will grow in the ground or large containers. Plastic tubs and half whiskey barrels are especially appropriate for the cold-sensitive species. Affix a trellis to the container so you can move the plant when a freeze threatens.

Vines don't require much care but unruly growth needs redirection. Train vines and do not be afraid to prune the stems. Pruning produces new branching that keeps plants full and compact.

Plant vines against the south and west walls of a home to save air-conditioning dollars. The thick leaf covering deflects the summer sun and cooling air circulates between the walls and the vine's trellis.

Some of the prettiest vines have been introduced from the tropics. Many are not hardy, so provide freeze protection or expect some winter dieback. Prettily flowering but tender vines are the mandevilla, Paraguayan night shade, clitoria, flame vine and clock vine.

A few Florida vines are hardy. One exceptionally reliable plant is the Japanese clematis. It's a beautiful midsummer bloomer with small white flowers that contrast with

dark evergreen foliage. Equally hardy is the Carolina yellow jasmine, which offers bright yellow, fragrant flowers for the winter. It continues its cool-season flowering even during winter freezes.

A number of vines can be started from seed to provide quick cover for barren walls and fences. Most gardeners are familiar with the morning glory, which bears clusters of blue, red, pink or white flowers in spring and summer.

The cypress vine is especially attractive with fernlike finely cut foliage and small scarlet or white trumpet-shaped blossoms.

Another rapid grower is the black-eyed Susan vine, also called thunbergia, which produces dense green foliage and orange flowers with shiny black eyes. Start from seed in spring for flowering summer through fall.

Ground covers are ideal in shade and for plots too small to mow. They also can be used as a transition in the landscape. Their lush green growth offers flowers to accent a garden. The ground cover selection for Florida is limited. A variety of plants, including vines, perennials and woody ornamentals, have to be used.

Some of the fastest growing ground covers are familiar as indoor foliage but are not cold hardy. The quick-dividing spider plant, for example, has been a strong survivor in landscapes where nothing else will grow. When frozen during winter it often recovers.

Other houseplants that can double as ground covers include wandering jew, setcreasea, purple queen, oyster plant, Swedish ivy, pothos and aluminum plant. These rampant growers require little care. Maintenance consists mainly of restricting plant growth by clipping meandering foliage out of trees and shrubs.

Proper plant spacing varies dramatically among ground covers. Slow-to-spread mondo grass and liriope may be spaced 6 inches apart; quick-creeping wedelia, 2 feet; and a woody juniper, 3 feet. Get information on growth and spacing from your garden center.

Transplant vines using the procedure recommended for shrubs, but ground covers should have the planting site prepared as you would for perennials. (See Chapters 5, 9.)

Regular feeding encourages growth. Monthly feedings are recommended in the beginning. Use a half pound of a 6-6-6 for each 100 square feet of bedding area.

When the plants near maturity, feed vines like shrubs. Feed ground covers spring, summer and early fall with 6-6-6 at the rate of one or two pounds per 100 square feet of bed. Water to keep soil moist. Mulch is always beneficial.

Confederate jasmine
(Trachelospermum jasminoides)

Training espaliers

Artistic espaliers turn barren walls into landscape displays. Espalier is a French word derived from the Italian *spalliera*, which means a place to rest the *spalla* or shoulder. The Roman gardeners originated the technique of training plants against walls, fences or trellises, but Europeans perfected the rewarding art form.

Classical espaliers often require hours of maintenance, particularly if a complex pattern is undertaken. The simplest is the single cordon design, a one stem plant with shortened lateral branches. Other cordon designs may be trained in tiers or braided to form more intricate patterns. Formal designs also include the U-shaped and palmette patterns.

Informal espaliers are more carefree and free-flowing. Plant limbs may be left to wander until they fill a space, weaving a dense network of foliage against a wall. In the landscape they could be trained as a pyramid or rectangular design to mimic some architectural feature.

Select plants that have flexible limbs and a strong root system. Trees and shrubs about 3 feet tall to start are usually ideal because the twigs bend easily.

Prepare the soil and plant the ornamental with the main branches or trunk 6 inches from the wall or trellis on which it will be trained. Begin the training program immediately by removing all unwanted growth.

If a branching or U-pattern is desired, remove the central leader at a point where the lower limbs are needed for the design. This produces several branches of new growth that can be trained on the wall or prepared scaffolding. If the young branches are stiff and breakage is possible, tie the twig to a heavy gauge wire and slowly bend it over a period of several weeks.

As growth continues, maintain the training program. Unwanted buds or growth should be removed so they do not rob the plant of food. When additional branching is required, simply remove the growing tip from that branch.

Firmly anchoring the plants to the wall is important. Young plants can be held in place using a trellis or special wall ties sold at garden centers.

As the espalier grows, the limbs get heavy and need additional support. Anchoring devices such as masonry staples, concrete nails or lead expansion shields fitted with screw eyes may be placed in the walls to carry the extra weight.

The beauty of many espaliers depends on the exposure of wall or open space. Branches should be kept at least 16 inches apart. Exact spacing is very important with formal designs; approximations will prove unsightly.

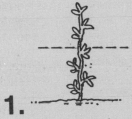

1. Cut main leader at or near where first set of branches is desired.

2. During the first year, let buds or branches develop into long shoots.

3. Train two shoots horizontally and one vertically. Remove all other shoots.

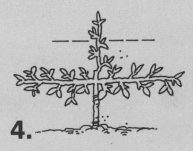

4. During the winter, cut main leader at or near where second set of branches is desired.

5. Let buds develop into shoots.

6. Train two shoots horizontally and one vertically. Repeat process of training new shoots until the desired height is reached.

Popular vines

Name	Section of state to which adapted	Height	Shape of plant	Flower color/season	Light	Soil	Salt spray tolerance	Trellis	Wall & fence	Specimen	Tree trunk
Allamanda (P) (*Allamanda spp.*)	CS	variable	vine	yellow/all year	partial shade	average	+ +	X	—	X	—
Coral vine (*Antigonon lepopus*)	C	30-40 feet	vine	pink & white/spring, summer	sun	any	—	X	X	X	—
Bougainvillea (*Bougainvillea spp.*)	CS	20 feet	vine	various/all year	sun	any	+ + +	X	X	X	—
Trumpet creeper (N) (*Campsis radicans*)	NCS	30 feet	vine	orange/spring, summer	sun or shade	any	—	X	X	X	X
Painted trumpet (*Clytostoma callistegiodes*)	NCS	20 feet	vine	lavender/spring	sun	average	—	X	X	—	—
Showy combretum (*Combretum grandiflorum*)	CS	20 feet	vine	pink-red/winter-spring	sun	dry	—	X	X	X	—
Garlic vine (*Cydista aequinoctialis*)	CS	40 feet	vine	pink & lavender/all year	sun, partial shade	fertile & moist	—	X	X	—	—
Carolina yellow-jasmine (N) (*Gelsemium sempervirens*) (P)	NC	20 feet	vine	yellow/spring	sun or shade	dry	—	X	—	X	—
Jasminum nitidum (*J. amplexicaule*)	CS	20 feet	spreading	white & pink/all year	sun, partial shade	any	—	X	X	—	—
Downy jasmine (*Jasminum multiflorum*)	CS	20 feet	spreading	white/summer, fall	sun, partial shade	average	+ +	X	—	X	X
Ceriman (*Monstera deliciosa*)	S	30 feet	vine	white/all year	partial shade	moist	—	X	—	X	X
Purple wreath (*Petrea volubilis*)	S	35 feet	vine	purple/all year	sun, partial shade	well drained	—	X	X	X	—
Philodendron (*Philodendron spp.*)	CS	variable	vine	none	partial shade	moist	—	X	X	X	X
Pandorea (*Podranea ricasoliana*)	CS	30 feet	vine	pink/all year	sun	average	—	X	X	—	X
Flame vine (*Pyrostegia ignea*)	CS	50 feet	vine	orange/winter, spring	sun	average	+ + +	X	X	—	X
Hunter's robe (*Scindapsus aureus*)	CS	40 feet	vine	none	shade	average	+ +	X	—	—	X
Mexican flame vine (P) (*Senecio confusus*)	CS	25 feet	vine	orange & red/summer	sun, partial shade	any	—	—	X	—	X
Cape honeysuckle (*Tecomaria capensis*)	CS	6-10 feet	vine	orange to red/spring, summer	sun	average	—	X	—	—	—
Confederate jasmine (*Trachelospermum jasminoides*)	NCS	20 feet	vine	white/spring	sun or shade	any	+	X	X	—	—
Chinese wisteria (*Wisteria sinensis*)	NC	60 feet	vine	white, pink, lavender/spring	sun, partial shade	average	—	X	X	X	—

Abbreviations, designations and terms used in table:
1. General designations: (N), native; (P), part of plant poisonous; "X," adapted for listed use; — does not apply or not known.
2. Section of state to which adapted:
   a. N, North Florida — Pensacola to Jacksonville and south to Ocala.
   b. C, Central Florida — Leesburg south to Punta Gorda and Fort Pierce.
   c. S, South Florida — Stuart to Fort Myers and south to Homestead.
   d. NCS, entire state.
3. Salt spray tolerance: +, slightly tolerant; + +, moderately tolerant; + + +, highly tolerant.
4. Hedge and screen: Plants adapted for clipping indicated by "X."

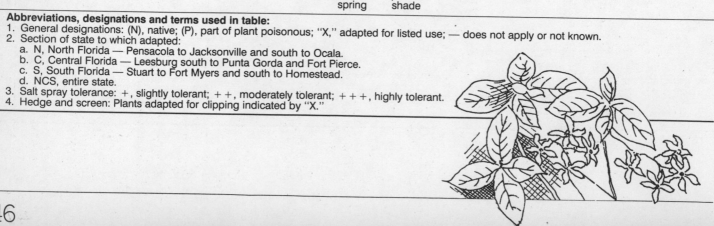

Florida ground covers

Name	Height	Light[1]	Zone[2]	Soil	Salt[3] tolerance	Color	Season	Under trees	Banks & slopes	Edging	Seaside	Open areas	Rock gardens	Remarks
Aloe (Aloe spp.)	12 inches	S,PS	C,S	any	H	red, orange, yellow	late winter		X		X	X	X	An unusual medicinal plant. Spectacular flowers.
Artillery plant (Pilea microphylla)	12 inches	S,PS	S	any	?	inconspicuous		X	X	X		X	X	Grows vigorously with proper care. Excellent cover for patios, terraces.
Asparagus fern (Asparagus densiflorus Sprengeri)	12 inches	S,PS	C,S	well drained	M	whitish-pink	early summer	X	X	X		X	X	Also useful in window boxes, hanging baskets. Cannot stand foot traffic.
Beach morning glory* (Ipomoea pes-caprae)	4 inches	S	C,S	well drained	H	pink	summer		X		X	X		Grows wild on Florida beaches. Will grow to a length of 50 feet and climb a trellis.
Bromeliads (Bromeliaceae)	2-36 inches	S,Sh	C,S	well drained	L-M	some are very colorful	summer	X		X			X	Not tolerant of dune conditions. Members of genus Cryptanthus are often used as ground covers.
Bugle weed (Ajuga reptans)	2 inches; 12 inches at flower	S,PS	N,C,S	well drained	L	violet-blue, red & white	early summer	X	X	X				Does not do well on sandy soils in Central, South Florida. Sensitive to nematodes.
Cape-weed (Phyla nodiflora)	3 inches	S,Sh	N,C,S	any	H	rose-purple, white	all year	X	X		X	X		Easy to establish by sprigs or plugs. Tolerates some foot traffic.
Carolina yellow jasmine (Gelsemium sempervirens)	6 inches	S,PS	N,C	moist	N	bright yellow	late winter to early spring	X	X			X		Highly recommended for slopes, banks, open areas. Slow growing. All parts are poisonous.
Common periwinkle (Vinca minor)	8 inches	S,PS	N,C	well drained	L	blue, violet-blue, white	spring & early summer	X	X	X		X		One of the best covers for North Florida.
Bigleaf periwinkle (Vinca major)	12 inches	S,PS	N,C	well drained	L	blue, violet-blue, white	spring & early summer	X	X	X		X		Bigleaf periwinkle is especially useful for areas where perennial bulbs are grown.
Confederate jasmine (Trachelospermum jasminoides)	6-12 inches	S,Sh	N,C,S	any	H	white	April & May		X			X		Long vine that cannot be trampled. Good for slopes and banks. Not recommended around trees and shrubs.
Coontie* (Zamia integrifolia)	12-36 inches	S,Sh	N,C,S	any	H	none		X	X	X	X	X	X	Palmlike. Prefers dense shade. Very heat, drought resistant. Cannot be sheared or mowed.
Creeping charlie (Pilea nummulariifolia)	1-2 inches	S,Sh	S	well drained	?	inconspicuous		X		X		X	X	Can become weed problem.
Cuphea (Cuphea hyssopifolia)	12-24 inches	S,PS	C,S	fertile soil	N	red, white, purple	all year			X	X			Good pot specimen. Adapted to bright sunny areas. Not drought tolerant.
Daylily (Hemerocallis spp.)	12-36 inches			well drained	M	many	late spring, summer		X			X		Colorful flowers for borders.

Name	Adaptability					Flowers		Uses						Remarks
	Height	Light[1]	Zone[2]	Soil	Salt[3] tolerance	Color	Season	Under trees	Banks & slopes	Edging	Seaside	Open areas	Rock gardens	
Dichondra* (Dichondra carolinensis)	1-2 inches	S,Sh	N,C,S	moist	H	inconspicuous		X		X	X	X		Will withstand some foot traffic. Mowing or shearing not necessary. Susceptible to fungus infection.
Ferns (Polypodiaceae)	12-36 inches	Sh	N,C,S	well drained	L-M	none		X		X				Holly, Boston, Leatherleaf and Sword ferns are recommended for ground covers.
Figs (Ficus montana) (Ficus pumila) (Ficus sagittata)	12 inches	S,PS	N,C,S	any	M-H	inconspicuous		X	X	X	X	X	X	Creeping fig (Ficus pumila), oak-leaf fig (Ficus montana) are good specimens that also can be used as climbing plants.
Fig marigold (Glottiphyllum depressum)	6 inches	S	C,S	well drained	H	yellow	late spring to early summer			X	X	X	X	Withstands dry sandy soils and salt spray.
Hottentot fig (Carpobrotus edulis)	6 inches	S	C,S	well drained	H	yellow, rose-purple	summer			X	X	X		For covering sandy expanses, especially at the seashore. Very salt tolerant.
Ivy (Hedera canariensis) (Hedera helix)	6 inches	Sh	N,C,S	moist	H	inconspicuous		X	X	X				English ivy (Hedera helix) has somewhat smaller leaves than Algerian ivy (Hedera canariensis) and provides finer textured planting.
Junipers (Juniperus spp.)	6-15 inches	S,PS	N,C	well drained	M-H	inconspicuous			X	X	X	X	X	Slow growing. Shore (Juniperus conferta), creeping junipers (Juniperus horizontalis) are recommended for cover plants. Shore juniper excellent for banks, slopes.
Kalanchoe (Kalanchoe spp.)	6-18 inches	S,PS	S	well drained	M	many	summer-fall			X	X	X	X	Best used only in frostless locations. Easily propagated.
Lantana, trailing or weeping (Lantana montevidensis)	36 inches	S,Sh	C,S	any	M-H	red, purple	all year		X	X	X	X	X	Good for combination with junipers or jasmine. Subject to injury below 30°F. Fruit is poisonous.
Lilyturf (Liriope muscari)	12 inches	Sh	N,C,S	any	M	blue	spring & summer	X	X	X	X			Creeping lilyturf (Liriope spicata) is spreading form with purple to white flowers that covers faster than the common type.
Madagascar periwinkle (Catharanthus roseus)	12-24 inches	S,Sh	C,S	well drained	H	red, blue, white	summer		X	X	X	X	X	Excellent flowering plant that thrives with little care.
Mondo grass (Ophiopogon japonicus)	6-12 inches	S,Sh	N,C,S	any	H	lilac	summer	X	X	X	X	X	X	Flowers are usually hidden by foliage. Excellent plant for full shade locations.
Oyster plant (Rhoeo spathacea)	24 inches	S,Sh	C,S	any	M-H	inconspicuous		X	X	X	X		X	Cold sensitive. Leaves are green and purple.
Partridgeberry* (Mitchella repens)	1-2 inches	Sh	N,C	moist	N	white	spring	X	X	X				Grows best in acid soils in shade. Can stand some foot traffic. No mowing required.
Peperomia* (Peperomia obtusifolia)	18-20 inches	PS,Sh	S	moist	N	inconspicuous				X				Will root along nodes. Should be cut back once or twice a year. Also makes good houseplant.

Name	Adaptability					Flowers		Uses						Remarks
	Height	Light[1]	Zone[2]	Soil	Salt[3] tolerance	Color	Season	Under trees	Banks & slopes	Edging	Seaside	Open areas	Rock gardens	
Purple queen (Setcreasea pallida)	14 inches	S,PS	N,C,S	well drained	H	pink	summer	X	X	X	X	X	X	Especially adapted under trees. Leaves are purple.
Selaginella (Selaginella spp.)	12 inches	Sh	N,C,S	moist	?	none		X	X	X	X			Erect selaginella (Selaginella caulesceus) is good for covers around trees. Blue Selaginella (Selaginella uncinata) is vigorous grower, good for slopes.
Small leaf confederate jasmine (Trachelospermum asiaticum)	8-12 inches	S,Sh	N,C,S	any	H	inconspicuous		X	X			X		Among most elite of all ground covers. Forms thick mat that eliminates weeds.
Wandering jew (Zebrina pendula)	4-10 inches	Sh	C,S	well drained	N	red, purple	summer	X	X	X		X	X	Attractive leaves striped with purple, white and green. Excellent for frostless locations. Also makes good houseplant.
Wedelia (Wedelia trilobata)	6-8 inches	S,PS	C,S	moist	H	yellow	summer	X	X	X	X	X	X	Flowers are daisylike. Particularly useful for dune plantings.
Winter creeper (Euonymus fortunei radicans)	24 inches	S,PS	N	moist	L	inconspicuous		X	X			X		Shearing may be required from time to time. Will not stand foot traffic.

*Plants native to Florida

[1]Light:
S — Sun
Sh — Shade
PS — Partial shade

[2]Zone:
N — North Florida
C — Central Florida
S — South Florida

[3]Salt tolerance:
L — Low
M — Moderate
H — High
N — Not tolerant
? — Tolerance unknown

Confederate jasmine
(Trachelospermum jasminoides)

49

8

Annuals make the landscape sparkle

ANNUAL FLOWERS CAN PROvide year-round garden color. The trick, however, is to replant three or four times a year, choosing from the diverse selection of warm- and cool-season varieties.

Prepare the flower bed by improving the soil with organic matter. Mix into the sandy soil liberal amounts of peat moss, compost or stable manure. The best manures include straw or sawdust to develop soil structure.

Help the soil feed the new planting with the addition of composted manure plus a 6-6-6 fertilizer. Scatter only about one pound per 100 square feet to avoid burning developing roots. Add lime if a soil test indicates the pH is too low. Apply lime and fertilizer separately and till the soil between treatments. The site will then be ready for planting.

Flowering plants are susceptible to root-destroying nematodes, microscopic roundworms that live in the soil. Check the roots of previous plantings. Knotted, swollen roots indicate nematode damage and mean special soil treatments are needed to eliminate the pests. Follow fumigation treatments or soil solarization techniques as suggest-ed for vegetable gardens in Chapter 13.

Cutworms can also be a problem and can often be spotted during soil preparation. To eliminate the pests, use a fumigant or insecticide.

Review of a warm season

Springlike weather can arrive in late February. That's the earliest time to plant warm-season flowers. Some varieties will fade when the rainy season arrives. Others can be replanted during the summer season.

Put marigolds at the top of the

Zinnia

list for warm-season plantings. Marigolds tolerate heat, drought and pests and offer compact mounds of bright color. They make excellent cut flowers and are ideal for the beginner to start from seed.

The zinnia is also popular in the spring because it, too, is a sure bloomer. Plantings tolerate heat and survive most soil conditions when grown in bright sun. Zinnias are available in a variety of colors and range in shapes from ruffled- and cactus-flower types to petite pompons.

Start zinnias early in the season to beat the summer rains that stimulate leaf spot problems. Copper fungicide sprays may be needed when the rainy season arrives.

Portulaca or moss rose is a favorite for borders, rock gardens and window boxes. The small plants form a ground cover of bright single or double flowers in white, yellow, orange, rose and red.

Purslane, a closely related family member, is a widespreading succulent suitable for covering a bank or filling a basket.

Plant portulaca or purslane on a well-drained site in full sun and do not overwater. The plants flower in

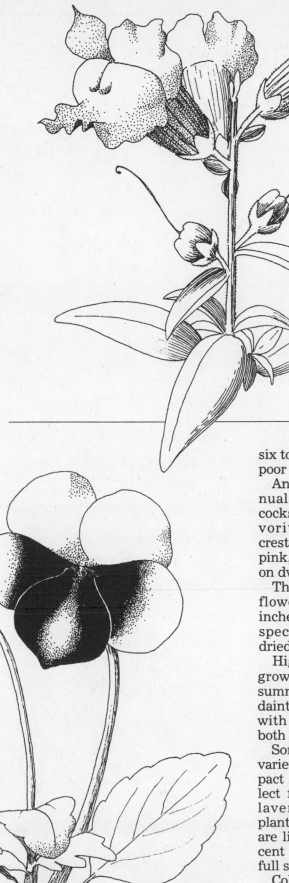

Snapdragon
(*Antirrhinum*)

Pansy
(*Viola tricolor hortensis*)

six to eight weeks and thrive in dry, poor soil.

Another hardy warm-season annual is celosia, commonly called cockscomb. This old-fashioned favorite comes in two forms — crested and plumed. Colors include pink, purple, orange, yellow and red on dwarf or tall plants.

The large-crested varieties have flower heads measuring 6 to 10 inches across. Plumed varieties are spectacular as cut flowers or in dried bouquets.

Highly recommended but seldom grown is the torenia, also called summer pansy. Gardeners love the dainty lavender to purplish flowers with yellow throats. Plants grow both in full sun and light shade.

Some annuals prefer shade. New varieties of impatiens produce compact plants laden with blooms. Select from bright pink, red, purple, lavender and white. Impatiens planted at the beginning of the year are likely to last three seasons. Recent introductions grow in all but full sun locations.

Coleus offer a spectrum of color with many leaf variations. Plant in

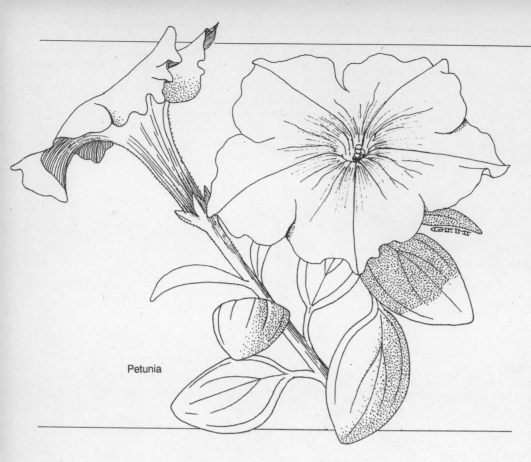

Petunia

hanging baskets. During the coldest days petunias may suffer some leaf burn, but normally recover quickly.

Even when temperatures dip below the freezing mark, the colorful pansy holds its head high. From November through early spring this popular annual blooms in shades of orange, red and purple.

Pansies flourish in full sun. The flowers are large at first, often with blossoms 3 inches in diameter. As the season progresses the flower size decreases, but the number of opening buds may double or triple.

Dianthus is another cold-resistant flower that blooms almost continually. Resembling its close cousin the carnation, the blossoms appear in white and shades of red. Many are striped or bicolored. Dianthus grows as a spreading clump with attractive blue-green foliage. This annual lasts into late spring.

The snapdragon is a great annual for use in bouquets. Throughout the cool season towering spikes grow profusely from rosettes of dark green stems. Colors include bright yellows, deep reds, light pinks and snow whites, plus a selection of bicolors. In addition to the traditional tall varieties there are petite, compact snaps.

The calendula is an easy-to-grow annual. The plant's charming double flowers, in shades of yellow and orange, make an excellent garden display and are also unsurpassed as cut flowers. The calendula will stand considerable cold. If blossoms are blasted by heavy frost, others will quickly open as the weather warms.

The list of popular cool-season annuals is extensive and includes alyssum, cornflower, lobelia and verbena. (See chart, Pages 54-55.)

filtered sun to full shade locations and occasionally pinch out the tips.

Begonias offer flowers and foliage for the shady garden. Blossoms range from white to deep pink and contrast with the waxy bright green to deep red foliage.

The brighter the planting site, the more intense the color will be. Many varieties tolerate full sun, but perform best in filtered shade. Begonias can give several seasons of color in the garden.

Color for the cool season

During fall only a few trees and shrubs present a colorful display. Gardeners rely on flowering annuals for color that lasts through the winter months.

Few flowers surpass the petunia for fall planting. Petunias grow quickly to create a carpet of blossoms. Blooms open in shades of red, yellow, purple and white. Varieties include single and ruffled styles.

Cascading petunias are great for

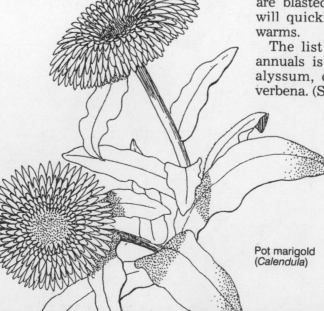

Pot marigold
(*Calendula*)

Planting and continual care

Sowing seeds directly into fine, sandy quick-draining soil is challenging and may produce disappointing results. Thus many gardeners choose to transplant flowers into prepared beds. Transplants can be purchased from garden centers or raised from seeds sown in pots.

If you have given up growing annuals because of soil problems, try growing annuals in pots. Put bedding plants in 6-inch containers filled with potting soil. Sink the pots into the problem planting site. The pots protect plants from nematodes, competitive roots and other soil problems for at least a season. Mulch around the plantings and no one will know your secret to success.

All annuals need special attention when first planted. Water daily for about a week or until the roots become established. Then water when the soil begins to dry.

Mulch extends the time between waterings and improves the growing conditions. Feed plants in sterile sands with a 6-6-6 or similar fertilizer every two to three weeks. Where soils have been improved wait a week or two longer between feedings.

Extend the flowering of annuals by pinching off faded flowers and seed pods. The best way to extend the enjoyment is to cut and use annual blooms indoors.

Grow your own transplants

To have transplants for the flower garden try starting plants from seeds.

Almost any container can be used for seed propagation. Flats, flower pots and trays are commonly used. Egg or milk cartons, cottage cheese bowls or other food storage containers also will work. Make sure each container has drainage holes punched in the bottom.

Use a commercially prepared growing medium or mix your own by combining equal parts of peat moss and vermiculite. These pest-free soil substitutes help ensure success.

To start seedlings:
• Fill a container with growing medium to within an inch of the lip; water until moist.
• Sparingly sow the seeds across the surface. Too heavy a sowing means trouble transplanting. If the seeds are small they will not need a covering of soil. Larger seeds, however, should have a thin layer of growing medium scattered over the top. Check information on seed packet for specific instructions.
• Start the germination process by misting the surface soil. Cover the container with plastic, wet newspaper or a pane of glass to keep the seeds moist. Check seed packet for recommended light and temperature conditions.

Normally, there is no need to rewater if you have created the ideal germination environment. It is all right to peek, however, and check for the first sprouts.

To care for emerging seedlings:
• When the first seedling appears remove the cover and move the container to a location that meets the plant's light requirements.
• The seedlings will now need normal care to develop into transplants. Water as the soil just begins to dry and start fertilizing weekly with a diluted houseplant solution.
• Seedlings grow fast and should be transplanted to individual containers when three or four true leaves have developed.
• In four to six weeks transplants should be ready to add to the garden.

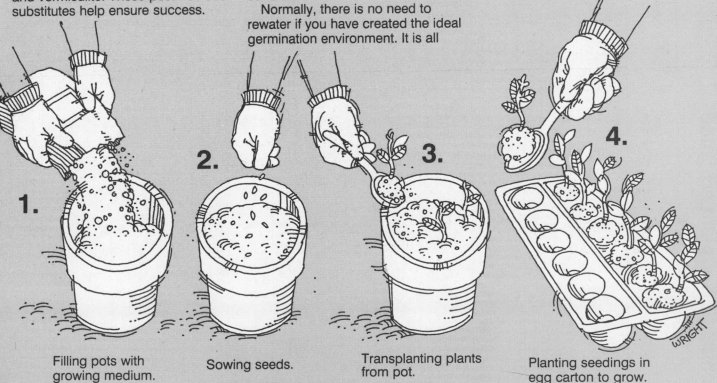

1. Filling pots with growing medium.

2. Sowing seeds.

3. Transplanting plants from pot.

4. Planting seedings in egg carton to grow.

Annual flower planting guide

Name	†Exposure			Cold tolerance	North Florida		Central Florida		South Florida		Spacing (inches)
	Full sun	Sun — a.m. or p.m.	No direct sun		Planting date	Removal date	Planting date	Removal date	Planting date	Removal date	
Ageratum	XX			tender	March 1-15	Aug.	Feb. 15-March 15	July	Feb. 1-March 1	June	10-12
Alyssum	XX			tender	March 1-15	July	Feb. 15-March 15	July	Oct. 1-15, Feb. 1-March 1	March, June	6
Amaranthus	XX			tender	March 15-30	Sept.	March 15-30	July	July-Aug., March 1-5	first frost, July	14-18
Aster	XX			tender	March 1-15	July	Feb. 15-28	June	Oct.-Feb.	June	12
Baby's breath	XX	X		hardy	Feb. 15-March 15	June	Feb.-March	June	Aug.-Dec.	March-April	12
Balsam	XX	X		tender	March 15-30	Aug.	March 1-30	July	March 1-30	June-July	8-12
Begonia (nonstop)		XX	X	tender	March 1-15	June	Feb. 15-28	May	Nov.-March	May	12-14
Begonia (tuberous)		X	XX	tender	March 1-15	June	Feb. 15-28	May	Oct.-Jan.	April	12-14
Begonia (wax)	XX	X		tender	March 15-30	Sept.-Oct.	Feb. 15-28	Sept.	Sept.-Nov.	Aug.	12-14
Browallia	XX	X		hardy	March 1-15	Aug.	Feb. 15-28	Aug.	Oct.-Feb.	Aug.	12
Calendula	XX			hardy	Feb.-March	June	Nov.-Feb.	June	Jan.-March	May	8-10
Carnation (China doll)	XX	X		hardy	Nov.-Feb. 28	June	Nov.-Feb. 28	May	Oct.-Jan.15	April	8-10
Celosia	XX			tender	March 15-July	seed set	March-July	seed set	Feb.-Sept.	seed set	14
Coleus	X	XX		tender	April-Aug.	Oct.	April-Aug.	Oct.-Nov.	March-Sept.	first frost	18-24
Calliopsis	XX	X		hardy	March-May	first frost	March-May	first frost	Feb.-June	first frost	12
Cosmos	XX			tender	March 15	Aug.	Feb.	July	Nov.-Feb.	June	12-14
Crossandra		XX	XX	tender	May-July	Oct.	April-July	Oct.	March-Aug.	Nov.	8-12
Dahlia	X	XX		tender	March 15-30	Aug.	March 1-15	Aug.	Sept.-Dec.	July	18-20
Dianthus	XX			hardy	Feb.	July-Aug.	Feb.	July	Oct.-Feb.	June	10-12
Digitalis (Foxglove)	XX	X		hardy	Sept.-Dec.	July	Sept.-Dec.	July	not recommended		12
Dusty miller	XX	X		tender	Feb.-April	Sept.	Feb.-April	Aug.	Oct.-March	Aug.	12
Exacum	XX	XX		tender	March-July	when overgrown	March-July	when overgrown	Feb.-Oct.	when overgrown	12
Gaillardia	XX	X		semi-hardy	March-May	Aug.	March-May	Aug.	Feb.-May	Aug.	12-18
Gazania	XX			tender	March-May	Nov.	Feb. 15-May	Nov.	Nov.-May	Nov.	8
Geranium	XX	X		tender	March-April	July	Feb.-March	July	Oct.-March	June	16-30
Hollyhock	XX	X		hardy	March 15-June	first frost	Feb. 15-July	first frost	Aug.-Sept.	first frost	12
Impatiens		XX	X	tender	March 15-July	first frost	March 1-July	first frost	Sept.-June	first frost	8-12
Kalanchoe	XX	X		tender	May-July	first frost	May-Sept.	first frost	Sept.-Dec.	first frost	12
Lobelia	XX	X		tender	March 15-April	Aug.	Feb. 15-April	Aug.	Sept.-Feb.	July	6-8
Marguerite daisy	XX			tender	Feb. 15-April	June-July	Feb.-April	June-July	Oct.-Feb.	July	12-14
Marigold	XX			tender	March 15-May	3-4 months after planting	March-April	3-4 months after planting	Feb.-Dec.	3-4 months after planting	8-24

Planting guide (continued)

Name	‡Exposure			Cold tolerance	North Florida		Central Florida		South Florida		Spacing (inches)
	Full sun	Sun — a.m. or p.m.	No direct sun		Planting date	Removal date	Planting date	Removal date	Planting date	Removal date	
Nicotiana	XX			tender	March 15-July	Aug.-Sept.	March 1-July	Aug.-Sept.	Feb.-May, Aug.-Sept.	July-Aug., April-May	16-24
Ornamental pepper	XX			tender	March-July	Oct.	March-July	Oct.	March-Aug.	Nov.	8-10
Pansy	XX			hardy	Oct.-Feb.	June	Oct.-Feb.	May	Oct.-Jan.	April	10-14
Penta	XX	X		tender	March-May	first frost	March-May	first frost	all year	first frost	12-14
Petunia	XX	X		hardy	Oct.-Feb.	May-June	Oct.-Feb.	June	Sept.-Feb.	May	12-18
Phlox	XX			hardy	March-April	Aug.	March-April	Aug.	Feb.-March	July	8-14
Portulaca (Moss rose)	XX			tender	April-July	first frost	April-July	first frost	March-Aug.	first frost	10-12
Rudbeckia	XX			hardy	March-April	Aug.	March-April	Aug.	Feb.-March	July	15-18
Salvia	XX	X		tender	March 15-Aug.	when deteriorated	March 1-Aug.	when deteriorated	Feb. 15-Dec.	when deteriorated	8-12
Shasta daisy	XX	X		hardy	Oct.-Dec.	July	Oct.-Dec.	July	not recommended		12
Snapdragon	XX	X		hardy	Oct.-Feb.	June	Oct.-Feb.	May	Nov.-Feb.	April-May	10-15
Statice	XX			hardy	Feb. 15	June	Dec.-Jan.	June	Sept.-Jan.	May	8-10
Strawflower	XX			tender	March 15	Aug.	Feb.	July	Nov.-Feb.	June	12-14
Streptocarpus		XX	X	tender	March-April	June	March-April	June	Feb.-March	May	10
Sweet William	XX	X		hardy	March-April	Aug.	March-April	Aug.	Feb.-March	May	10-12
Thunbergia	XX	X		tender	March-May	first frost	March-May	first frost	Feb.-April	first frost	8-10
Torenia	XX	X		tender	March 15-June	leaf yellowing	March 1-June	leaf yellowing	Feb.-Oct.	leaf yellowing	12-18
Verbena	XX			hardy	March 1-May	when undesired	Feb. 15-May	when undesired	Feb.-April, Sept.-Nov.	when undesired	12
Vinca (Catharanthus) (periwinkle)	XX	X		tender	March-July	when undesired	Feb. 15-July	when undesired	all year	when undesired	12
Zinnia	XX			tender	March-June	when deteriorated	March-June	when deteriorated	Feb.-March, Aug.-Sept.	when deteriorated	12-15

Several plants in this table are perennials but may be grown as annuals.

‡Exposure: X = acceptable performance; XX = optimum performance.

North Florida — Pensacola to Jacksonville and south to Ocala.
Central Florida — Leesburg south to Punta Gorda and Fort Pierce.
South Florida — Stuart to Fort Myers and south to Homestead.

Marigold (*Tagetes*)

9

Perennials — permanent, repeat performers

Bleeding heart
(Dicentra spectabilis)

RELIABLE PERENNIALS provide seasonal color with minimal effort. These permanent plantings are the repeat performers of the landscape and are especially appropriate for the low-maintenance garden. Started from seeds, cuttings or divisions, perennials are perpetual. They lend seasonal flushes of foliage and flowers to the garden.

Many relocated gardeners leave behind their favorite perennials and are surprised to discover the attractive Southern alternatives.

A walk through a well-planned perennial garden can be exciting. Some plantings will be in full bloom, some will be just beginning to bud, while others display their colorful foliage.

Many gardeners choose to mix perennials with annuals. Perennials provide permanent and attractive backdrops for splashes of annual color. A few perennials in front of shrubbery or bordering a patio add seasonal color.

A perennial flower garden needs special preparation. Where soils are sandy add a 6-inch or more layer of organic matter such as peat moss, compost or stable manure with hay or sawdust.

A 25-pound bag of composted cow manure will cover 100 square feet of garden. Bone meal is also often scattered across the bed to supply nitrogen and slowly released phosphorus. Finally, most gardeners add a 6-6-6 or similar fertilizer. Use one to two pounds for each 100 square feet of bed area. The garden should then be thoroughly tilled.

Fumigation ensures a pest-free garden. The chemical application controls soil pests including nematodes, insects, diseases and weeds. Vapam is the only fumigant available for home use. Maximum effectiveness is obtained when the fumigation includes use of a plastic cover for seven days.

Bulbs — best kept Florida secret

Begin your perennial collection with flowering bulbs. The warm-season species that flourish spring through fall are among the best kept secrets of Florida gardening.

Horticulturists use the term bulb to describe a number of underground plant portions that store food and regenerate the species. Showy flowers from bulbs accent garden walks, perennial beds and naturalistic displays set among trees and shrubs.

In the spring bell-shaped red, pink and white amaryllis dispel the gloom of winter. The towering spikes, each with several blooms, rise just before the foliage. Amaryllis grouped in beds or scattered throughout the yard add more than a month of color to the Florida landscape.

Daylilies bring color to the landscape in early April. The golden-yellow varieties are normally the first to flower. During the next three months varieties in shades of orange, pink, red and bronze brighten yards. Daylilies are heat tolerant if they receive sufficient moisture.

Fairy lilies emerge from dormant flower beds at the start of the rainy season. These members of the amaryllis family give months of color when naturalized across the landscape, massed in perennial beds or grouped in border plantings. For white, pink and rose-red blooms select from the *Zephyranthes, Cooperia* and *Habranthus* genera.

In late spring the blood lily produces a brilliant red sphere of lacy florets. This plant can be grown in the perennial flower bed, but many gardeners believe better flowering plants are produced if grown in containers. The blood lily's flower precedes the leaves, which grow throughout the warm months.

The African lily or *Agapanthus africanus* produces bright blue or white inflorescences. During late spring or summer funnel-shaped blossoms appear as parts of large heads atop tall stems. African lilies can be planted in beds or large containers.

Crinum lilies start the summer season with a show of flowers and continue to produce sporadic blossoms throughout the year. Crinums range in color from white to deep rose.

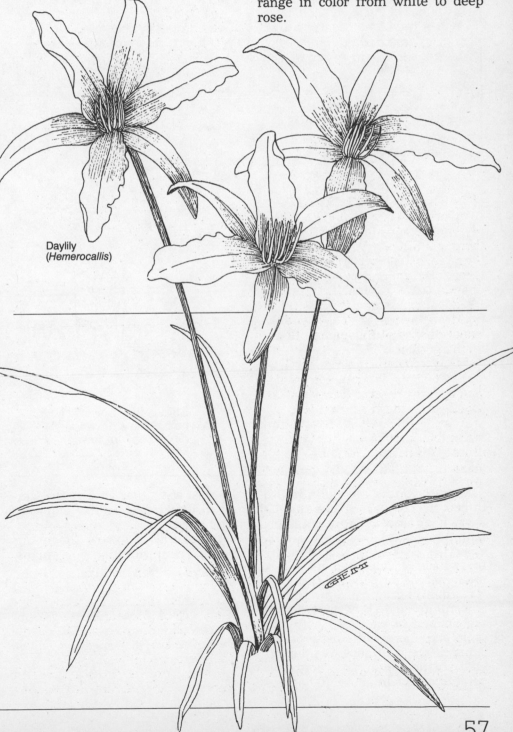

Daylily
(*Hemerocallis*)

Starting from cuttings

Maturing new growth makes excellent cuttings to begin a perennial hedge or indoor plant. For maximum success take only 4- to 6-inch cuttings from the tips of new growth. Avoid longer shoots because they suffer stress during propagation and require extra time to root.

Collect cuttings during the early morning when the stems and leaves are full of moisture. Protect them from drying by covering with layers of wet newspaper or by soaking in a pail of water. Strip leaves from the lower half of the stem and dip an inch or two of the basal end in a rooting powder. Stick the cuttings in pots or shallow trays filled with moist sand or vermiculite to root.

Cuttings are normally inserted two to three inches into the rooting medium. Try to place a node — the area where leaves were once present — below the medium level. Often plants root from these nodal zones. Cuttings can be placed fairly close together, preferably with the leaves just touching. A 6-inch flower pot will hold six or more carefully spaced stems.

Mist the cuttings with water several times a day until rooting begins. Keep the cuttings in a humid, bright area protected from full sun.

Rooting may take two weeks for succulent plants and 10 to 12 weeks for woody shrubs. From time to time fluff away the rooting medium and take a peek. When a small, well-branched root system has formed the young plants are ready for potting.

Use a potting mixture free from pests for the young plants. Place the potted ornamentals in filtered shade for several days to recover from transplant shock.

Shrubs and ground covers should be grown to a garden-center size before being placed on display under more stressful conditions. During this development period, water and fertilize to encourage growth.

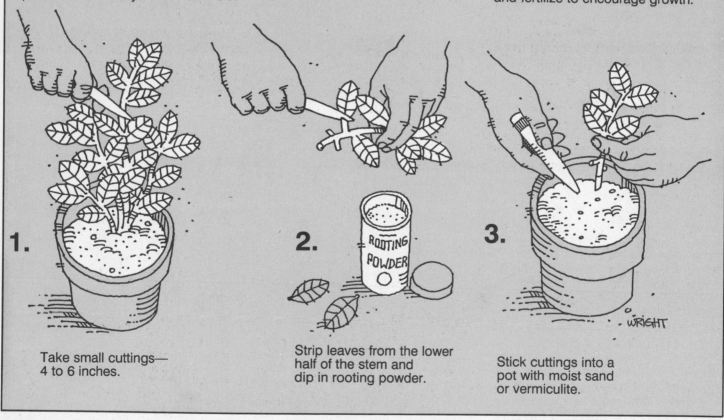

1. Take small cuttings—4 to 6 inches.

2. Strip leaves from the lower half of the stem and dip in rooting powder.

3. Stick cuttings into a pot with moist sand or vermiculite.

Many crinums are hybrids produced by crosses within the 100 known species. Their fragrant, trumpet-shaped flowers resemble amaryllis or Easter lilies. The hybrids have a wide color range and often include striped varieties.

Gardeners grow caladiums for the colorful foliage. Emerging leaves are striped or blotched with red, pink, green and white patterns. Caladiums are cold sensitive and tubers should be stored where temperatures remain above 70 degrees.

In most areas they survive the winter in the ground without appreciable injury.

Other easy-to-grow flowering bulbs recommended for spring through fall color include canna lily, gloriosa lily, gladiolus, hurricane lily, marica, moraea and society garlic.

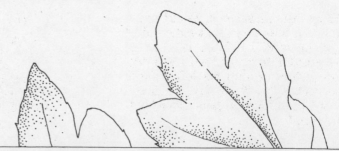

New plants by division

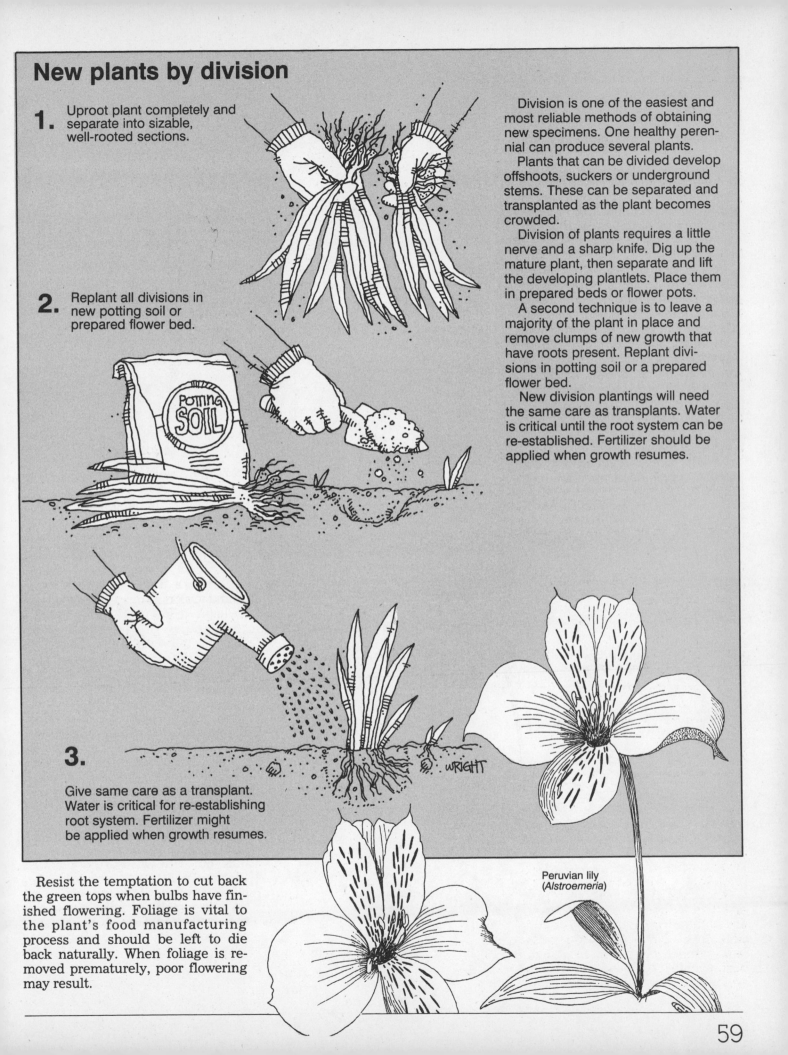

1. Uproot plant completely and separate into sizable, well-rooted sections.

2. Replant all divisions in new potting soil or prepared flower bed.

POTTING SOIL

3. Give same care as a transplant. Water is critical for re-establishing root system. Fertilizer might be applied when growth resumes.

WRIGHT

Division is one of the easiest and most reliable methods of obtaining new specimens. One healthy perennial can produce several plants.

Plants that can be divided develop offshoots, suckers or underground stems. These can be separated and transplanted as the plant becomes crowded.

Division of plants requires a little nerve and a sharp knife. Dig up the mature plant, then separate and lift the developing plantlets. Place them in prepared beds or flower pots.

A second technique is to leave a majority of the plant in place and remove clumps of new growth that have roots present. Replant divisions in potting soil or a prepared flower bed.

New division plantings will need the same care as transplants. Water is critical until the root system can be re-established. Fertilizer should be applied when growth resumes.

Peruvian lily
(*Alstroemeria*)

Resist the temptation to cut back the green tops when bulbs have finished flowering. Foliage is vital to the plant's food manufacturing process and should be left to die back naturally. When foliage is removed prematurely, poor flowering may result.

Herbaceous perennials

Herbaceous perennials include a wide variety of showy flowers. Among the most reliable are sprawling garden chrysanthemums, which flower fall through spring. Pinch stems and buds once or twice before mid-August to increase bushiness and produce mounds of fall color.

Gaillardia, also called blanket flower, will cover a corner of the garden with yellow to orangish-red flowers summer through fall. Blue sage produces upright flower spikes that bloom March through October. Another good blue is the Stokes' aster, a native treat for late spring.

The penta produces flamboyant color in a large bush. This warm-season bloomer offers red, pink, white or lilac flowers.

The daisy bush, *Gamolepis*, is a 2- to 3-foot-tall perennial with yellow blooms. Its blossoms open around 4 p.m.

Chrysanthemum

Gerbera daisy
(*Gerbera jamesonii*)

Gerbera daisies bloom year-round. Colors range from deep reds, brilliant yellows and sunny oranges to the purest of whites. The plants may be tall with single blooms or compact with double blossoms. Gerberas like full sun or partial shade and perform best in spring and fall.

Some varieties of Shasta daisy grow in North and Central Florida. Flowers appear in late spring and are big with snow-white outer petals and bright yellow centers. Cutting the flowers encourages plant growth and the plants can be divided frequently.

Popular perennials include coreopsis, gazania, ruellia, shrimp plant and verbena. Roses, too, are perennials but with woody stems that in Florida seldom suffer winter decline. Growing tall and vigorous, they take a little extra gardening time and should be given the special attention outlined on Page 62.

Plan the perennial garden to provide splashes of color. Group plants for eye-catching displays. Grouping also simplifies maintenance. Add rocks, statues or a fountain to create interest when perennials are not in flower.

Mulch aids in weed control and helps seal in moisture. However, new plantings may need daily watering until the roots are well established. After that, water needs may be met with a once or twice weekly soaking.

Most perennials are not heavy feeders. Apply a 6-6-6 or similar fertilizer once every six to eight weeks during the warm growing seasons. Scatter one to two pounds over each 100 square feet of bed area and water.

Remove spent flower blossoms to prolong the blooming of perennials. Springtime grooming chores include removal of stem and foliage decline from the deciduous or winter damaged species.

Every two or three years vigorous varieties will need thinning. Divide the plants immediately after flowering or before spring growth begins.

Dahlia

Easy-to-grow Florida bulbs

Name	Planting depth	Season of color	Light level	Flower color	Cultural notes
African lily	tip below soil surface	summer	sun to partial shade	blue or white	Also called Agapanthus. Requires plenty of moisture. Divide every 2-3 years.
Amaryllis	tip at soil level	spring	partial shade	white to red	Divide every 2-3 years. Red blotch disease, grasshoppers major pests.
Blood lily	tip just above soil	summer	partial shade	red	Keep soil fairly dry fall, winter.
Caladium	2 inches	summer to fall	sun to partial shade	insignificant (grown for foliage)	Fertilize every 2-3 weeks during growth. Tubers can be left in ground.
Canna	2 inches	summer	sun to partial shade	red, orange, yellow	Fertilize monthly. Dig and separate annually. Leafroller major pest.
Crinum	neck above ground	spring to summer	sun to partial shade	white to rose	Bulbs grow large. Mulch is recommended. Red blotch disease major problem.
Daylily	4 inches	spring to early summer	sun to partial shade	many colors	Divide as clumps enlarge. Evergreen varieties do well locally.
Fairy lily	1-2 inches	spring to fall	sun to partial shade	white, yellow, pink, red	Dig and divide when crowded. Blooms as rainy season arrives.
Gloriosa lily	4 inches	spring through summer	sun to partial shade	crimson with yellow, orange	Best trellised. Divide as plantings enlarge. All portions poisonous.
Gladiolus	3 inches	warm seasons	sun	many colors	Let tops grow until they die back. Immediate digging, separating is suggested, but often left in the ground.
Hurricane lily	3-4 inches	early fall	sun to light shade	yellow, red, pink	Should be dug and divided when crowded.
Marica	just below soil surface	spring, summer	partial shade	white with yellow, blue	Also called walking iris. New plants form at end of flower stem.
Moraea	2 inches	spring, summer	sun	white with blue	Divide clumps as needed. Flowers last only two days.
Society garlic	2 inches	warm months	sun	purple	Has garlic odor that may be objectionable. Divide when crowded.

The rose — America's favorite perennial

Florida's favorite roses require special root stocks. For year-round vigorous growth choose roses grafted onto fortuniana or Dr. Huey root stocks. Roses can be planted throughout the year, but the best seasons are spring and fall.

Soil preparation is the basis of rose culture. Improve the bed before planting by incorporating liberal amounts of peat moss, compost or manure and a phosphorus source such as bone meal or superphosphate.

Position the rosebush in the ground so the soil line is the same as it was in the container or field. Add the prepared soil around the root ball or bare root system. Add plenty of water to make the soil soupy, then lightly pack the soil.

Roses are heavy feeders and need a balanced fertilizer. Once a month use 6-6-6 at the rate of one pound per 100-square-foot bed. Water frequently to maintain moist soil and add mulch to deter weeds.

Give plants a major pruning in early February or when the dormant buds just begin to swell. Established plants will need to be cut back by a half to a third each spring.

The gardener who wants lots of flowers should strive for a plant with three to five vigorous canes originating from the graft union near the ground. Weak stringy shoots can be pruned out. Reduce the number of side shoots on these main stems or the plant will produce only small flowers.

All cuts should be made to just above a bud.

Black spot is a year-round problem and a major reason to spray home plantings. Plants affected will drop their diseased leaves, leading to weak stems, fewer flowers and a poor root system that eventually rots.

A few diseases can be pruned out of the plant. Among them is dieback, which occurs when a fungus enters a cut or other wound. Prune several inches back into healthy wood and apply a fungicide to prevent further spread.

Most insects can be controlled as they appear. Rose growers should learn to identify pests and inspect plants weekly. Aphids feed in succulent new growth, mites cluster on the underside of leaves and thrips hide in opening flower buds. A weekly spray will give the control needed.

Spray in the morning after the dew dries or in the late afternoon as the sun sets. Add a wetting agent, often sold as a spreader sticker. These products ensure pesticide adhesion. Apply insecticides in liquid rather than dust form to guarantee uniform and thorough coverage.

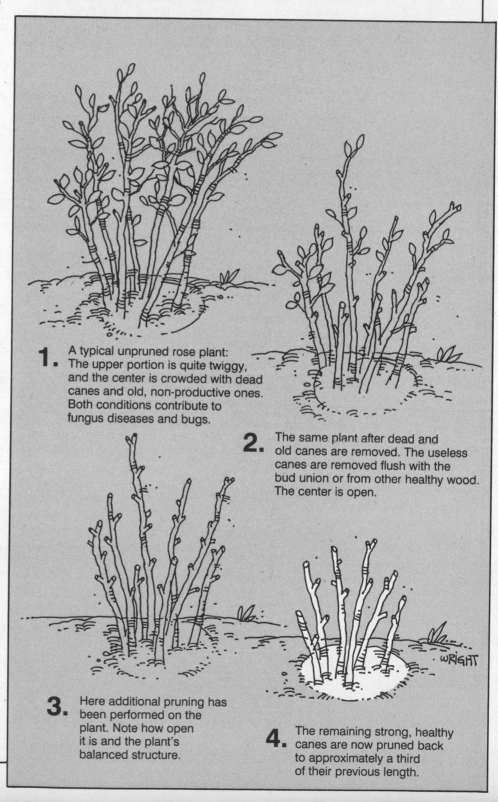

1. A typical unpruned rose plant: The upper portion is quite twiggy, and the center is crowded with dead canes and old, non-productive ones. Both conditions contribute to fungus diseases and bugs.

2. The same plant after dead and old canes are removed. The useless canes are removed flush with the bud union or from other healthy wood. The center is open.

3. Here additional pruning has been performed on the plant. Note how open it is and the plant's balanced structure.

4. The remaining strong, healthy canes are now pruned back to approximately a third of their previous length.

How to plant a rose

1. From your prepared mix, form a bed of soil in the hole. The soil bed should be high enough so that the bud union (where canes join the stalk) is just above ground level when the soil settles.

2. Set the plant in the hole. Position the plant at the same depth as it was growing in the container.

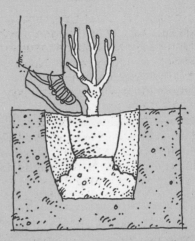

3. Work soil around the root ball and firm with your hands, taking care not to damage roots. Keep alternating the process until you can safely firm the soil with your foot to within 2 inches of the top of the hole.

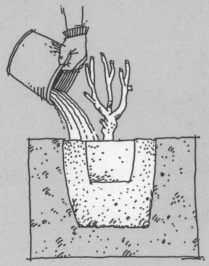

4. Fill the remainder of the hole with water (it will require 2-3 gallons) and allow to soak in. Check the bud union again for proper level and fill the hole with soil.

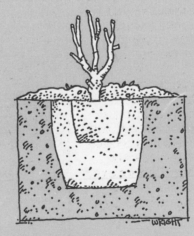

5. Add a mulch layer to conserve moisture. When vigorous growth starts, apply plant food according to the manufacturer's instructions.

Perennials

Name	Growth habit	Common height	Flower color/ season	Light conditions	Soil type	Salt spray tolerance	Cold hardy*	Method of propagation	Use/comments
African iris (Dietes spp.)	clumping	2 feet	white, yellow/ year-round	sun, partial shade	wide range	no	yes	division	background, bedding
Blackberry lily (Belamcanda chinesis)	upright	3 feet	orange/ June-Oct.	sun	wide range	no	yes	seed, division	background plantings, Iris-like foliage
Blue sage (Salvia farinacea)	upright	2 feet	blue/ March-Oct.	sun, partial shade	fertile, moist	no	yes	seed, division, cuttings	background, bedding
Butterfly weed (Asclepias tuberosa)	erect, slightly spreading	1-3 feet	orange-red/ May-Sept.	sun, partial shade	well drained	no	no	division, seed	bedding, attracts butterflies, bees, hummingbirds
Cardinal's guard (Pachystachys coccinea)	upright, multi-stemmed	4-6 feet	scarlet/ late summer	shade	well drained	no	no	cuttings, division	background plantings
Chrysanthemum (Chrysanthemum x morifolium)	spreading	1-2 feet	multicolors/ fall-spring	sun	fertile, well drained	no	yes	cuttings, division	pinch once or twice until Aug. 15 to induce bushiness
Coreopsis (Coreopsis lanceolata)	semi-compact	10-30 inches	yellow/ April-July	sun	well drained	yes	yes	seed	bedding, edging, cut flower
Daisy bush (Gamolepis chrysanthemoides)	erect, bushy	3 feet	yellow/ year-round	sun, partial shade	wide range	yes	no	cuttings	background or bedding
Daylily (Hemerocallis spp.)	clumping	1-2 feet	multicolors/ March-June	sun, partial shade	wide range	yes	yes	division, seed	background or border plantings
False dragonhead (Physostegia virginiana)	upright	2-3 feet	white, pink, lilac/fall	sun, shade	wide range	no	no	seed	border, cut flower
Four-o'clock (Mirabilis jalapa)	erect, bushy	4 feet	red, yellow, white/Aug.-Oct.	sun, partial shade	wide range	no	no	seed	background and border plantings
Gaillardia, blanket flower (Gaillardia spp. and hybrids)	compact	1-2 feet	yellow, orange/ summer-fall	sun	well drained	yes	yes	seed, division	border plantings, cut flower
Gazania (Gazania spp. and hybrids)	compact	6-12 inches	yellow, orange, white/spring-fall	sun, partial shade	fertile, well drained	yes	yes	seed, division	bedding, edging, cut flower
Gerbera daisy (Gerbera jamesonii)	clumping	12-18 inches	multicolored/ year-round	sun, partial shade	fertile, well drained	yes	yes	division, seed	bedding, cut flower, keep crowns above ground
Gloriosa daisy (Rudbeckia hirta)	clumping	2-3 feet	yellow, gold, bronze/ summer-fall	sun, partial shade	fertile, moist	no	no	seed, division	border planting, cut flower, very prone to fungus diseases
Golden shrimp plant (Pachystachys lutea)	upright	3-6 feet	yellow/ warm months	partial shade	wide range	no	no	cuttings	background
Jacobinia (Justicia carnea)	erect, bushy	2-4 feet	rose/ warm months	shade, partial shade	fertile, moist	no	no	cuttings	background or border plantings
Liatrus, blazing star (Liatrus spicata)	upright	2-3 feet	white, purple/ late summer	sun, partial shade	wide range	no	yes	division, seed	border, cut flower
Penta (Pentas lanceolata)	sprawling shrub	4 feet	red, pink, white, lilac/ warm months	sun, partial shade	well drained	no	no	cuttings	background plantings, cut flower
Ruellia (Ruellia brittoniana)	erect, bushy	2-3 feet	blue/ May-Nov.	sun, partial shade	well drained	yes	no	seed, cuttings	background, bedding
Shrimp plant (Justicia brandegeana)	sprawling	4-6 feet	reddish-brown/ spring-summer	sun, partial shade	wide range	no	no	cuttings, division	mass plantings, background
Shasta daisy (Chrysanthemum x superbum)	clumping	1-2 feet	white/ late spring	sun	fertile, moist	no	yes	division, seed	border, bedding, cut flower
Verbena (Verbena x hybrida)	sprawling ground cover	6-8 inches	red, pink, white, lavender/ March-Oct.	sun, partial shade	fertile, moist	no	yes	cuttings, seed	border, bedding
Stokes aster (Stokesia laevis)	clumping	1 foot	lavender-blue/ summer	sun, partial shade	well drained	no	yes	division	border, bedding, cut flower, native to Florida
Yarrow (Achillea spp.)	spreading	1-2 feet	yellow, rose, white/May-June	sun	well drained	no	yes	division	bedding

*Cold hardy — NO indicates the plant is killed to the ground by frost or freeze, but recovers quickly.

10

Go native for less maintenance

GO NATIVE AND LET NAture tend the garden. If your property is large, try landscaping near the home and leaving the periphery to nature.

The term *native* often reminds gardeners of wild scrublands, the original habitat of Florida plants. However, many have been domesticated and are as close as your garden center.

It may be a surprise to find many native trees and shrubs already growing in your landscape. Many gardeners believe these are recent discoveries, but the backbone of the home landscape always has been the native oaks, sweet gums, red

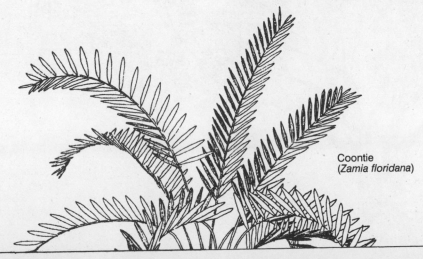

Coontie
(*Zamia floridana*)

maples and slash pines. Common native shrubs, vines and ground covers include wax myrtles, Spanish bayonets, yaupon hollies, coonties, Carolina yellow jasmines and sword ferns.

Nature has tested and selected plants best suited to Florida. Each has been subjected to pests, weather and soil conditions common to the state. Only the fittest have survived.

Do not assume that because a plant grows in the wild it automatically is suited to your landscape. Native plants must be selected for your section of the state and its specific soil conditions. Relocated native plants will require time and care to mature.

When beginning a native plant collection, remember many of Florida's rapidly dwindling wild trees, shrubs and ground covers are protected by law. Before digging any plants from another's land it's common courtesy to ask permission.

To gather plants protected by law — including orchids, bromeliads, Florida yew, wild azaleas and many palms — you need written permission from the landowner. Under no circumstances can sea oats or sea grapes be removed from beach areas, where they help control erosion.

Protect yourself by obtaining copies of the native plant laws. Write to Florida Department of Agriculture, Division of Plant Industry, P.O. Box 1269, Gainesville, Fla. 32601.

Fortunately, many nurseries are now propagating native plants and many of the harder-to-find specimens are available commercially.

Home gardeners are often disappointed by their native transplants. A big oak snatched from the woodlands turns yellow, drops leaves and dies from shock. In the wild, plant roots meander. They are not condensed into a ball as when grown in a container or dug from a nursery row. When a plant is gathered from the wild a major portion of the root system may be left behind.

Large trees and shrubs are particularly difficult to move. Big root systems end up with little soil attached. For a big plant this is disastrous. Consider moving 3- to 4-foot-tall plants or, with some preparation, plants to a maximum of 7 feet. Herbaceous plants, wildflowers and ground covers are much easier to move but even here think small.

If you are set on moving a large plant, start months ahead by condensing the root system. With a large intact root ball the plant is more likely to survive. Start at least 90 days before moving. Decide how big a root ball to gather with the plant. Think of what can be easily lifted and transported. A root ball 24 inches in diameter and 18 inches deep is about maximum size because it usually weighs more than 100 pounds. However, this size is needed for a tree with a trunk

measuring 2 inches in diameter. To determine the diameter measure the trunk at a point 6 inches above the soil.

Begin root pruning by digging straight down into the ground without digging under the plant. More than half of the roots are usually severed but those that remain still give support. Simple downward cuts with a shovel will do. Some gardeners like to trench 12 inches deep around the plant and backfill the trench with peat or compost. Either root prune around the tree in one day or root prune a third of the circumference at monthly intervals.

The plant needs extra care during the root pruning period because its ability to help itself is much restricted. Above all, keep the root ball area moist so roots will grow rapidly.

Live oak
(Quercus
virginiana)

Do-it-yourself digging

Neighborhood freebies make great landscape additions but without special care it's easy to spoil transplants. Part of a successful relocation is keeping the root ball intact. A few small shrubs and trees can take bare-root transplants, but often when the tiny root hairs are destroyed the plant is lost.

Gardeners planning to dig plants from the wild should either select a small, 3- to 4-foot specimen or prepare the root ball before the move using a technique called root pruning.

Root pruning is simply a method of condensing the plant's root ball by making several downward cuts to sever the roots. This should be done a month or more before the transplanting. For plants such as wild dogwoods, oaks and maples, root pruning is essential to ensure a successful transplant.

The root ball can be determined in several ways. You can move a foot out from the trunk for each inch of diameter or make the ball half of the spread of the plant.

Thoroughly moisten the soil in the digging site a day or two before the move. Begin digging by removing soil from the ball. Do not put pressure on the root ball. If roots interfere with the digging, cut them with hand pruners. Florida sandy soils fall apart easily and extra care is needed during the dig.

When the ball is well shaped and digging has reached a point below the major roots, usually 15 to 18 inches, begin removing soil from under the plant. Be careful to hand cut thick roots as the digging continues.

When digging is completed wrap the root ball in burlap or similar cloth. Even in a short move, wrapping is important because it helps bind the roots and soil before the plant is lifted.

Balled and burlapped plants can be heavy. Several workers, carts and even a hoist may be required to lift a large plant and ball that weighs more than 100 pounds. Avoid lifting or pulling on the trunk. That will cause the soil to fall from the roots and turn a successful transplant into a disappointment.

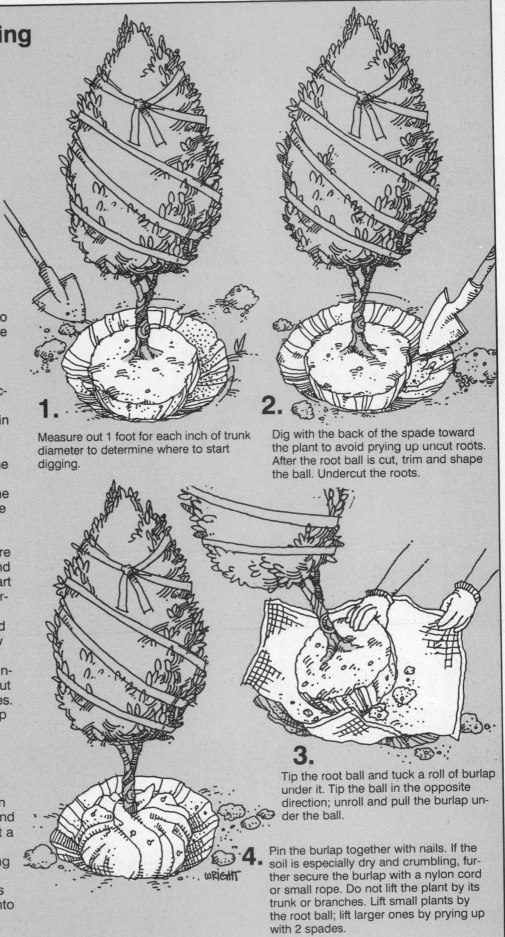

1. Measure out 1 foot for each inch of trunk diameter to determine where to start digging.

2. Dig with the back of the spade toward the plant to avoid prying up uncut roots. After the root ball is cut, trim and shape the ball. Undercut the roots.

3. Tip the root ball and tuck a roll of burlap under it. Tip the ball in the opposite direction; unroll and pull the burlap under the ball.

4. Pin the burlap together with nails. If the soil is especially dry and crumbling, further secure the burlap with a nylon cord or small rope. Do not lift the plant by its trunk or branches. Lift small plants by the root ball; lift larger ones by prying up with 2 spades.

Cabbage palmetto
(*Sabal palmetto*)

Saw palmetto
(*Serenoa repens*)

The cool dormant season of winter is the best time to move sizable native plants. Stress is less and roots can grow into the surrounding soil without having to support new leaf growth. By spring the plants should flush with green foliage and survive as well as nursery-grown specimens. Follow all transplant procedures suggested for trees and shrubs in Chapter 5.

A native plant taken from the wild may need better maintenance than one bought from a nursery. Greater transplant shock means more attention should be paid to water and nutrient needs. Failure to keep the soil moist could mean its few remaining roots dry out, killing the plant. Water every two to three days for at least a month. Mist new foliage with water during the heat of the day.

Begin feeding about four to six weeks after planting. A light scattering of 6-6-6 fertilizer is all that is needed under the spread of the planting. Continue this care for six months or until the plant is exhibiting normal, healthy growth.

A gardener may want to start a wildflower collection for a bog setting or a sandy, dry-land garden. Joining a native plant society and reading Florida wildflower books will help you discover just what to plant. Once established these plants will survive on their own. Expect seasonal plant decline, flushes of growth during the rainy season and animal life attracted to your native plants. Discover the continual subtle changes of a native garden.

Native Florida plants for home landscapes

Ground covers

Common/scientific name	Section of state to which adapted[1]	Native habitat	Height[2]	Foliage[3]	Flower & fruit color[4]/season[4]	Light[5]	Soil[6]	Salt spray tolerance[7]	Landscape uses[8]
Dichondra (Dichondra carolinensis)	S	hammocks over entire state	2 inches	(E)	inconspicuous	sun	moist	+	edging, mass
Gopher apple (Licania michauxii)	NCS	pinelands and sand dunes over entire state	3-12 inches	(E)	white flower/spring; pink fruit/summer	sun	dry	+	coastal locations
Partridgeberry (Mitchella repens)	NC	moist acid sites of North, Central Florida	1-2 inches	(E)	white flower/spring	shade	moist, acid	+	edging, mass
Railroad vine (Ipomoea pes-caprae)	CS	sandy shores	4 inches	(E)	pinkish lavender flower/summer	sun	well drained	+	coastal locations
Sword fern (Nephrolepis exaltata)	CS	moist hammocks	18-36 inches	(E)	none	partial shade, shade	moist	−	mass, hanging basket

Vines

Common/scientific name	Section of state to which adapted[1]	Native habitat	Height[2]	Foliage[3]	Flower & fruit color[4]/season[4]	Light[5]	Soil[6]	Salt spray tolerance[7]	Landscape uses[8]
Carolina yellow jasmine (Gelsemium sempervirens)	NC	woodland south to Osceola County	20 feet	(SEV)	yellow flower/spring	sun, partial shade	average	−	trellis, fence
Southern honeysuckle (Lonicera sempervirens)	NC	pine flatwoods of northwest Florida	20 feet	(D)	red flower/summer	sun, partial shade	any except light sands	−	screen
Trumpet creeper (Campsis radicans)	NC	throughout North and Central Florida, except on alkaline soils	50 feet	(D)	orange flower/spring, summer	sun	any except alkaline	−	screen
Virginia creeper (Parthenocissus quinquefolia)	N	pine flatwoods over entire state	30 feet	(SEV)	inconspicuous	sun	average	?	fence, on trees

Small shrubs

Common/scientific name	Section of state to which adapted[1]	Native habitat	Height[2]	Foliage[3]	Flower & fruit color[4]/season[4]	Light[5]	Soil[6]	Salt spray tolerance[7]	Landscape uses[8]
Adam's-needle (Yucca smalliana)	NCS	flatwoods of northwest Florida	4 feet	(E)	white flower/summer	shade	any	+	rock gardens, background
Coontie (Zamia floridana)	NCS	pinelands, flatwoods of North, Central Florida	3 feet	(E)	orange seed/winter	sun to shade	any if well drained	+	border
Eastern coralbean (Erythrina herbacea)	NCS	hammocks over entire state	4 feet	(D)	red/spring; red seeds/fall	partial shade	average	−	in front of large shrubs

Medium shrubs

Common/scientific name	Section of state to which adapted[1]	Native habitat	Height[2]	Foliage[3]	Flower & fruit color[4]/season[4]	Light[5]	Soil[6]	Salt spray tolerance[7]	Landscape uses[8]
American beautybush (Callicarpa americana)	NC	hammocks and rich woodlands of North, Central Florida	8 feet	(D)	purple flower/spring; purple fruit/fall	partial shade	well drained	−	mass
Fetterbush (Lyonia lucida)	NC	entire state	6 feet	(E)	white/flower spring	partial shade	average	?	screen
Firebush (Hamelia patens)	CS	throughout Central and South Florida	10 feet	(E)	red flower/fall; black fruit/all year	sun, partial shade	average	+	foundation, base screen

Common/scientific name	Section of state to which adapted[1]	Native habitat	Height[2]	Foliage[3]	Flower & fruit color/season[4]	Light[5]	Soil[6]	Salt spray tolerance[7]	Landscape uses[8]
Gallberry (Ilex glabra)	NCS	flatwoods over entire state	10 feet	(E)	black fruit/winter	sun, partial shade	acid, wet	+	trimmed hedges, foundation
Inkberry (Scaevola plumieri)	S	coasts of South Florida	6 feet	(E)	white flower/spring, summer	sun	dry	+	coastal locations
Oak-leaf hydrangea (Hydrangea quercifolia)	N	flatwoods and swamps of northwest Florida	6 feet	(D)	white flower/summer	partial shade	acid, well drained	—	mass
Sea lavender (Tournefortia gnophalodes)	S	beaches and sand dunes	6 feet	(E)	white flower/all year; black fruit/all year	sun	sandy	+	coastal locations
Strawberry bush (Euonymus americana)	N	rich woodlands of North Florida	8 feet	(D)	pink fruit/summer	sun, partial shade	average	?	foundation
Swamp hibiscus (Hibiscus coccineus)	CS	swamps of Central and South Florida	10 feet	(E)	red flower/summer	sun, partial shade	moist to wet	?	specimen[9]
Sweet pepperbush (Clethra alnifolia)	N	hammocks of northwest Florida	10 feet	(D)	white to pink flower/summer	partial shade	acid, well drained	?	natural areas, small tree
Sweet shrub (Calycanthus floridus)	N	rich woodland soils	10 feet	(D)	red to brown flower/spring	sun, partial shade	well drained, fertile	?	natural areas
Walter viburnum (Viburnum obovatum)	NC	south to Sarasota County	8 feet	(SEV)	white flower/spring; black fruit/summer	sun, partial shade	average	?	foundation, base
Wild coffee (Psychotria nervosa)	S	hammocks of South Florida	8 feet	(E)	white flower/spring; red fruit/summer	partial shade, shade	average	?	hedge, border

Large shrubs

Common/scientific name	Section of state to which adapted[1]	Native habitat	Height[2]	Foliage[3]	Flower & fruit color/season[4]	Light[5]	Soil[6]	Salt spray tolerance[7]	Landscape uses[8]
Bay cedar (Suriana maritima)	S	coasts of South Florida	20 feet	(D)	yellow flower/spring	sun	dry	+	coastal locations
Blueberry (Vaccinium spp.)	NC	south to Manatee County	3-15 feet	(E)	white flower/spring; black fruit/summer	partial shade, shade	acid, well drained	?	informal plantings
Cocoplum (Chrysobalanus icaco)	CS	throughout South Florida	20 feet	(E)	white flower/spring	sun	average wet or dry	+	screen, clipped specimens
Devilwood (Osmanthus americanus)	NC	south to Marion County	20-45 feet	(E)	white flower/winter	sun, partial shade	average	—	specimen, foundation
Eugenia (Eugenia spp.)	CS	most of South Florida	20 feet	(E)	white flower/summer; reddish fruit/fall	sun	average	—	clipped hedge
Florida anise (Illicium floridanum)	NC	West Florida	20 feet	(E)	red to purple flower/spring	partial shade	average	—	specimen, mass
Golden-dewdrop (Duranta repens)	CS	Everglades and Keys	18 feet	(E)	blue flower/spring, summer; yellow fruit/summer, fall	sun, partial shade	average	—	background, screen

Common/scientific name	Section of state to which adapted[1]	Native habitat	Height[2]	Foliage[3]	Flower & fruit color[4]/season[4]	Light[5]	Soil[6]	Salt spray tolerance[7]	Landscape uses[8]
Large gallberry (Ilex coriacea)	NCS	flatwoods of northwest Florida	10 feet	(SEV)	black fruit/fall	partial shade	fertile, well drained	?	specimen, informal hedge
Marlberry (Ardisia escallonioides)	S	coastal hammocks of South Florida	20 feet	(E)	white flower/all year; black fruit	partial shade, shade	moist	+	screen, specimen
Mountain laurel (Kalmia latifolia)	N	West Florida	20 feet	(E)	pink to white flower/spring	partial shade, shade	acid, well drained	?	specimen, informal hedge
Native azaleas (Rhododendron spp.)	N	moist, acid soils of northwest Florida	8-20 feet	(D)	pink to white flower/spring	shade, partial shade	moist, acid, well drained	—	mass
Scrub holly (Ilex opaca arenicola)	NC	scrub of Central Florida	15 feet	(E)	red fruit/fall	partial shade	dry	?	informal hedge
Silver bush (Sophora tomentosa)	S	sand dunes and coastal hammocks of South Florida	15 feet	(E)	yellow flower/all year	sun	dry	+	coastal locations
Southern wax myrtle (Myrica cerifera)	NCS	over entire state	20-30	(SEV)	gray fruit/summer	sun, partial shade	wet or dry	?	specimen, informal hedge
Spanish bayonet (Yucca aloifolia)	NCS	sandy soils over entire state	20-25 feet	(E)	white flower/spring	sun to shade	any if well drained	+	barriers, enclosures
Varnish leaf (Dodonaea viscosa)	S	inland woods, hammocks throughout South Florida	15 feet	(E)	yellow flower/summer, fall	sun, partial shade	dry	+	informal plantings, hedges

Small trees

Common/scientific name	Section of state to which adapted[1]	Native habitat	Height[2]	Foliage[3]	Flower & fruit color[4]/season[4]	Light[5]	Soil[6]	Salt spray tolerance[7]	Landscape uses[8]
American cherry laurel (Prunus caroliniana)	NC	hammocks and rich woods of North Florida	30-40 feet	(E)	white flower/spring; black fruit/summer	partial shade, shade	fertile	—	clipped hedge, screen
American hornbeam (Carpinus caroliniana)	NC	low areas south to Lake County	30 feet	(D)	inconspicuous	shade	average	?	shaded areas
Bontia (Bontia daphnoides)	S	Keys	30 feet	(E)	yellow flower/spring	sun	average or dry	+	foundation, specimen
Chickasaw plum (Prunus angustifolia)	NC	hammocks and fence rows of North, Central Florida	25 feet	(D)	white flower/spring; red to yellow fruit/summer	partial shade	average	?	specimen
Cinnamon-bark (Canella winterana)	S	woodlands of South Florida	30 feet	(E)	purple flower/fall; red fruit/spring	partial shade, shade	average, well drained	?	specimen
Devil's-walking stick (Aralia spinosa)	NC	low areas of North and Central Florida	15 feet	(D)	white flower/summer; black fruit/fall	partial shade	average	?	exotic specimen
Downey serviceberry (Amelanchier arborea)	N	woods and swamps of West Florida	25 feet	(D)	white flower/spring	partial shade	wet	?	specimen, early bloom
Flowering dogwood (Cornus floirda)	N	moist woodlands south to Orange County	30 feet	(D)	greenish with white bracts/spring	partial shade	fertile, well drained	—	specimen
Fringe-tree (Chionanthus virginicus)	NC	low woodland areas south to Manatee County	25 feet	(D)	white flower/spring	partial shade	moist	?	specimen

71

Common/scientific name	Section of state to which adapted[1]	Native habitat	Height[2]	Foliage[3]	Flower & fruit color[4]/season[4]	Light[5]	Soil[6]	Salt spray tolerance[7]	Landscape uses[8]
Geiger tree (*Cordia sebestena*)	S	Dade County and Keys	25 feet	(E)	orange flower/all year	sun	alkaline	+	specimen
Lignum-vitae (*Guaiacum sanctum*)	S	rare in Keys	25 feet	(E)	blue flower/spring; orange fruit/summer	sun	average	+	specimen
Mahoe (*Hibiscus tiliaceus*)	S	sand dunes South Florida	35 feet	(SEV)	yellow flower/all year	shade	sand, well drained	+	coastal locations
Monkey apple (*Clusia rosea*)	S	Keys	30 feet	(E)	white to pink flower/summer; green fruit/summer, fall	sun	average to poor	+	specimen, patio
Myrtle dahoon holly (*Ilex cassine myrtifolia*)	NCS	moist to wet soils over North, Central Florida	25 feet	(E)	red to yellow fruit/fall	partial shade	moist	?	specimen
Redbud (*Cercis canadensis*)	NC	fertile woods south to Marion County	30 feet	(D)	purple flower/winter	sun, partial shade	average	?	specimen
Sand live oak (*Quercus geminata*)	NC	dunes, scrub and south to Everglades	30 feet	(E)	inconspicuous	sun	well drained	+	coastal locations
Satin leaf (*Chrysophyllum oliviforme*)	S	coastal hammocks Brevard County and south	30 feet	(E)	inconspicuous	sun	average	+	specimen, patio
Sea grape (*Coccoloba uvifera*)	CS	coastal hammocks, dunes and beaches	15-25 feet	(E)	inconspicuous	sun	sand	+	espalier, screen, hedge
Shining sumac (*Rhus copallina*)	NCS	over entire state	25 feet	(D)	red fruit/summer	sun	well drained to dry	?	screen, specimen
Southern crab apple (*Malus angustifolia*)	N	West Florida to Taylor County	25 feet	(D)	pink flower/spring; green fruit/summer	sun	fertile	—	specimen
Southern red cedar (*Juniperus silicicola*)	NCS	limestone areas south to Sarasota County	25 feet	(E)	blue fruit/winter	sun, partial shade	average to alkaline	+	specimen
Southern wax myrtle (*Myrica cerifera*)	NCS	entire state	20-30 feet	(SEV)	gray fruit/summer	sun, partial shade	wet or dry	+	screens, clipped hedges
Yaupon holly (*Ilex vomitoria*)	NC	hammocks and stream banks of North, Central Florida	25 feet	(E)	red fruit/winter	partial shade, shade	average	+	clipped hedge, screen

Large trees

Common/scientific name	Section of state to which adapted[1]	Native habitat	Height[2]	Foliage[3]	Flower & fruit color[4]/season[4]	Light[5]	Soil[6]	Salt spray tolerance[7]	Landscape uses[8]
American holly (*Ilex opaca*)	NC	fertile woods, hammocks to Orange County	50-100 feet	(E)	red fruit/winter	sun, partial shade	fertile, well drained	+	specimen
Bald cypress (*Taxodium distichum*)	NCS	swamps throughout Florida, except Keys	150 feet	(D)	inconspicuous	sun, shade	wet, acid	+	shade, specimen, street
Black olive (*Bucida buceras*)	S	rare in Florida Keys	50 feet	(E)	black fruit/summer	sun, partial shade	alkaline	+	specimen, windbreak
Buttonwood (*Conocarpus erectus*)	S	coasts, Brevard and Levy counties south	50 feet	(E)	inconspicuous	sun, partial shade	wet, dry	+	coastal locations

Common/ scientific name	Section of state to which adapted[1]	Native habitat	Height[2]	Foliage[3]	Flower & fruit color/season[4]	Light[5]	Soil[6]	Salt spray tolerance[7]	Landscape uses[8]
Dahoon holly (Ilex cassine)	NCS	swamps over entire state	40 feet	(E)	red fruit/ winter	partial shade	wet	+	specimen
Devilwood (Osmanthus americanus)	NC	fertile woods south to Marion County	20-45 feet	(E)	white flower/ winter	sun, partial shade	fertile	−	specimen
Eastern cottonwood (Populus deltoides)	NC	swamps and rivers	80 feet	(D)	inconspicuous	sun	moist	?	windbreak
Florida basswood (Tilia caroliniana)	NCS	hammocks south to Orange County	60 feet	(D)	inconspicuous	partial shade	average	?	street
Florida boxwood (Schaefferia frutescens)	S	hammocks of Dade and Monroe counties	40 feet	(E)	red fruit/ winter	partial shade	moist	?	specimen
Florida torreya (Torreya taxifolia)	N	inland on moist sites	50 feet	(E)	inconspicuous	partial shade	average	?	specimen
Gumbo-limbo (Bursera simaruba)	S	coast of South Florida	60 feet	(D)	red fruit/ summer	sun	average, alkaline	+	specimen
Laurel oak (Quercus laurifolia)	NCS	entire state to Everglades	75 feet	(SEV)	inconspicuous	sun, partial shade	average	−	shade
Live oak (Quercus virginiana)	NCS	entire state	70 feet	(E)	inconspicuous	sun, partial shade	average, alkaline	+	shade, framing
Loblolly bay (Gordonia lasianthus)	NC	flatwoods, bays, hammocks	70 feet	(E)	white flower/ spring	partial shade	fertile, moist	−	specimen
Longleaf pine (Pinus palustris)	NC	flatwoods and sand hills	120 feet	(E)	inconspicuous	sun	any	+	shade, windbreak
Mahogany (Swietenia mahagoni)	S	hammocks of South Florida and Keys	50 feet	(E)	inconspicuous	sun, partial shade	acid, alkaline	+	street
Pigeon plum (Coccoloba diversifolia)	S	Brevard County to Keys	70 feet	(E) (E)	red fruit/ winter	sun	sand	+	specimen
Red maple (Acer rubrum)	NCS	moist to wet sites	80 feet	(D)	red flower, fruit/winter	sun, partial shade	fertile, moist	−	specimen
River birch (Betula nigra)	NC	stream banks south to Alachua County	60 feet	(D)	inconspicuous	sun, partial shade	moist	−	specimen
Sand pine (Pinus clausa)	NCS	dunes and scrub	70 feet	(E)	inconspicuous	sun	sand	+	coastal locations
Shumard oak (Quercus shumardii)	NC	well drained soils with underlying limestone, south through Marion County	100 feet	(D)	inconspicuous	sun	fertile, well drained	−	street specimen
Slash pine (Pinus elliottii)	NCS	entire state	100 feet	(E)	inconspicuous	sun	any	+	shade, windbreaks
Southern magnolia (Magnolia grandiflora)	NC	fertile woods south to Desoto County	100 feet	(E)	white flower/ spring	sun	fertile	+	street, specimen, framing
Spruce pine (Pinus glabra)	NC	fertile, moist	100 feet	(E)	inconspicuous	sun	fertile, moist	?	shade
Sweet bay (Magnolia virginiana)	NCS	flatwoods, bays, swamps	75 feet	(E)	white flower/ spring	partial shade	fertile, wet	−	specimen

Common/scientific name	Section of state to which adapted[1]	Native habitat	Height[2]	Foliage[3]	Flower & fruit color[4]/season[4]	Light[5]	Soil[6]	Salt spray tolerance[7]	Landscape uses[8]
Sweet gum (*Liquidambar styraciflua*)	NCS	south to Brevard County	100 feet	(D)	inconspicuous	sun, partial shade	average	+	shade, specimen
Tulip tree (*Liriodendron tulipifera*)	NC	woods and swamps to Orange County	100 feet	(D)	orange flower/ spring	sun, partial shade	moist	—	street
Water oak (*Quercus nigra*)	NCS	entire state to Orange County	75 feet	(D)	inconspicuous	sun	average	—	street
Winged elm (*Ulmus alata*)	NC	throughout North Florida	50 feet	(D)	inconspicuous	sun	average	—	specimen

Palms

Common/scientific name	Section of state to which adapted[1]	Native habitat	Height[2]	Foliage[3]	Flower & fruit color[4]/season[4]	Light[5]	Soil[6]	Salt spray tolerance[7]	Landscape uses[8]
Cabbage palm (*Sabal palmetto*)	NCS	entire state	90 feet	(E)	inconspicuous	sun, shade	any	+	specimen, coastal locations
Florida royal palm (*Roystonea elata*)	S	south and southwest portion of mainland	100 feet	(E)	inconspicuous	sun, partial shade	moist, rich	+	street, specimen, framing
Florida silver palm (*Coccothrinax argentata*)	S	Broward County through Keys	25 feet	(E)	inconspicuous	sun, partial shade	sandy, well drained	+	specimen, tropical effect
Florida thatch palm (*Thrinax radiata*)	S	South Florida	36 feet	(E)	inconspicuous	sun, partial shade	any	+	street, specimen
Key thatch palm (*Thrinax morrisii*)	S	lower end of mainland and Keys	30 feet	(E)	inconspicuous	sun, partial shade	any	+	street, specimen
Needle palm (*Rhapidophyllum hystrix*)	NC	Central and North Florida	6 feet	(E)	inconspicuous	partial shade	fertile, moist	+	specimen, foundation
Saw cabbage palm (*Acoelorrhaphe wrightii*)	CS	Collier County and Everglades National Park	30 feet	(E)	inconspicuous	sun, partial shade	variable	+	street, specimen
Saw palmetto (*Serenoa repens*)	NCS	entire state	4 feet	(E)	inconspicuous	sun, partial shade	variable	+	natural areas

Abbreviations, designations and terms used in table:
1. Section of state to which adapted:
   - a. N, North Florida — Pensacola to Jacksonville and south to Ocala.
   - b. C, Central Florida — Leesburg south to Punta Gorda and Fort Pierce.
   - c. S, South Florida — Stuart to Fort Myers and south to Homestead.
   - d. NCS, entire state.
2. Potential height of mature plant.
3. Type of foliage:
   - E — evergreen.
   - SEV — semi-evergreen.
   - D — deciduous.
4. Maximum flower and fruit color by season.
5. Light requirements.
6. Soil requirements:
   - average — average, most ordinary garden soils.
   - any — tolerant of a wide range.
   - other soil types as listed.
7. Salt spray tolerance:
   - +, tolerant, exact degree of tolerance unknown for most native plants.
   - —, not tolerant.
   - ?, tolerance unknown.
8. Only the most common possibilities for landscape use listed.
9. A plant that may be used alone for accent because of unusual shape or foliage or flower color, for instance.

11

Salt tolerance — not just important along the coast

FINDING QUALITY WATER IS a problem facing all Florida residents. By law statewide water management districts regulate all water usage.

Although the problems of obtaining fresh water appear to be coastal, some inland residents are drilling salty wells. Salty water previously capped by overlying fresh water is now moving closer to the soil surface. In coastal areas, freshwater sources for irrigation and drinking are drying up.

Although wells continue to supply vast quantities of water, the underlying aquifer has become tainted with salty seawater and is now objectionable to both people and plants.

After light, water is the most limiting factor in plant growth. Whether obtained from a pond, well or city, usable irrigation water must contain a minimal amount of soluble chloride or sulfate salts of sodium, potassium, calcium and magnesium.

Water tastes salty when it contains approximately 500 parts per million (ppm) soluble salts — a level too high for good orchid growth.

Years of drought, fluctuating rainfall and pumping for home and farm use have reduced the level of quality water in Florida's underground aquifer. As water is drawn out of the ground faster than rainfalls can replenish, seawater begins to intrude.

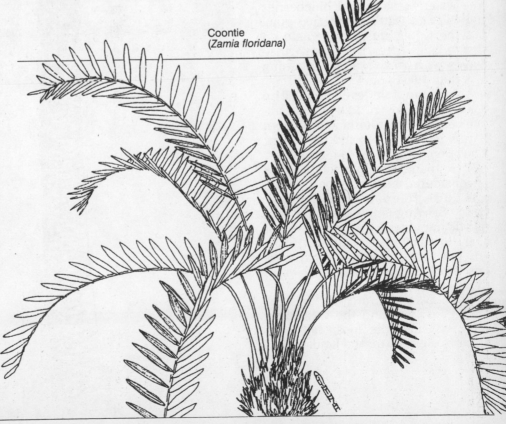

Coontie
(*Zamia floridana*)

Underground seepage of 32,000 ppm of seawater inland has now reached many home wells, mixing with the supply of fresh water. Because of this intrusion some coastal residents are pumping water that contains more than 5,000 ppm soluble salts. Coastal cities were first to recognize this problem and often rushed inland, seeking water from counties where the wells could still be established in the freshwater aquifer.

While most inland residents still enjoy liberal use of relatively fresh water, coastal dwellers must make do with salty supplies. The first question is how salty is the well water being used for home irrigation? This can be answered by most Cooperative Extension Service offices along the coast. Agents determine levels of soluble salt in water samples and recommend water use.

Salt damage to plants is very obvious. Early symptoms may be wilt, caused by root injuries, or a foliage burn. Eventually the plant turns yellow, browns and dies.

Water containing less than 1,000 ppm soluble salts generally is suitable for landscape and in-home plant culture. Only a few ornamentals, such as orchids, require salt-free water. Azaleas and blueberries can tolerate water with 1,500 ppm, but the water must not remain on the foliage. After irrigation, rinse leaves with fresh water containing less than 1,000 ppm.

A medium salt level is 1,000 to 2,000 ppm. A low of 1,200 ppm damages most succulents; 1,500 ppm harms foliage plants and bahia turf; 2,000 ppm is harmful to marigolds.

More than 2,000 ppm soluble salts is considered high but some plants are quite tolerant. The cabbage palm, St. Augustine turf and wax myrtle are vigorous growers even at 4,000 to 5,000 ppm. Also salt tolerant are roses, purslane, snapdragons, stock, beets and vegetables in the cabbage family.

When plantings are within sight of the seashore and the well turns salty, consider the most salt-tolerant ornamentals for the landscape.

Canary Island date palm
(*Phoenix canariensis*)

Where the salt level in irrigation water is too high for even salt-tolerant plants, it is time to add fresh water. Cut the parts per million almost in half by irrigating with equal parts salty well water and fresh water from a city source. Where the irrigation water is at 2,000 ppm, irrigate with a half-inch well water and a half-inch of city-supplied water. The dilution will give a final result of the 1,000 ppm tolerated by most plants. Make sure city water is used last in order to wash salt deposits off the foliage. If possible, water at night to gain the rinising effects of relatively fresh-water dews.

Even salty soil can be planted. A few good rains or irrigation with fresh water washes salts out of the root zone. When the soil has been rinsed, follow good preparation procedures and plant. Pay close attention to fertilizer sources. Natural organic products are low in salts. Sludges and manures are preferable to chemically formulated products.

Residents who want to grow the highly salt-sensitive ornamentals should use containers for azaleas, bird-of-paradise, Florida heather, crossandra and gardenia. Irrigate only with city water. In a few areas of Florida, treated wastewater can be purchased for special irrigation purposes. This relatively salt-free water source allows economical irrigation for salt-sensitive plants.

Along the seacoast, salt water and salty air are blamed for a lot of plant damage that is really caused by the wind. Being whippped and desiccated by seacoast winds can injure even the most salt-tolerant plants. Unless the plantings are extremely durable, expect winds to be at least enemy No. 2 to the home gardener. Wind-resistant trees, shrubs, dunes and other physical barriers help create a microclimate where sensitive ornamentals can be cultivated.

Lady palm
(*Rhapis*)

Salt-tolerant plants for Florida

Trees

Common/ scientific name	Range in Florida	Approximate height
Australian pine (Casuarina equisetifolia)	C,S	60 feet
Black olive (Bucida buceras)	S	40 feet
Bontia (Bontia daphnoides)	S	30 feet
Cajeput tree (Melaleuca quinquenervia)	C,S	50 feet
Frangipani (Plumeria spp.)	S	15 feet
Geiger tree (Cordia sebestena)	S	30 feet
Japanese pagoda tree (Sophora japonica)	S	60 feet
Live oak (Quercus virginiana)	N,C,S	60 feet
Mahogany (Swietenia mahogani)	S	40 feet
Ochrosia (Ochrosia elliptica)	S	20 feet
Pigeon plum (Coccoloba laurifolia)	S	70 feet
Pitch apple (Clusia rosea)	S	30 feet
Sapodilla (Manilkara zapota)	S	35 feet
Satin leaf (Chrysophyllum oliviforme)	S	30 feet
Sea hibiscus (Hibiscus tiliaceus)	C,S	35 feet
Seaside mahoe (Thespesia populnea)	S	35 feet
Silver button-bush (Conocarpus erectus)	S	60 feet
Tabebuia (Tabebuia argentea)	C,S	variable
Tropical almond (Terminalia catappa)	S	30 feet

Palms

Bottle palm (Hyophorbe spp.)	S	15 feet
Brittle thatch palm (Thrinax morrisil)	S	15 feet
Cabbage palm (Sabal palmetto)	N,C,S	60 feet
Canary Island date palm (Phoenix canariensis)	C,S	60 feet
Coconut (Cocoa nucifera)	S	80 feet
Hurricane palm (Dictyosperma album)	S	40 feet
Lady palm (Rhapis)	C,S	10 feet
Saw palmetto (Serenoa repens)	N,C,S	10 feet
Senegal date palm (Phoenix reclinata)	C,S	25 feet
Silver palm (Coccothrinax argentata)	S	20 feet
Washingtonia palm (Washingtonia spp.)	N,C,S	80 feet

Shrubs

Adam's-needle (Yucca smalliana)	N,C,S	4 feet
African milk bush (Synadenium grantii)	S	8 feet
Bay cedar (Suriana maritima)	S	20 feet
Crown-of-thorns (Euphorbia milii)	C,S	3 feet
Inkberry (Scaevola plumieri)	S	6 feet
Lantana (Lantana camara)	N,C,S	10 feet
Marlberry (Ardisia escallonoides)	S	20 feet
Milkstripe euphorbia (Euphorbia lactea)	S	15 feet
Natal plum (Carissa grandiflora)	C,S	10 feet
Oleander (Nerium oleander)	N,C,S	20 feet
Pittosporum (Pittosporum tobira)	N,C,S	15 feet
Sea grape (Coccoloba uvifera)	C,S	25 feet
Silver thorn (Elaeagnus pungens)	N,C	20 feet
Southern wax myrtle (Myrica cerifera)	N,C,S	25 feet
Yaupon (Ilex vomitoria)	N,C	25 feet

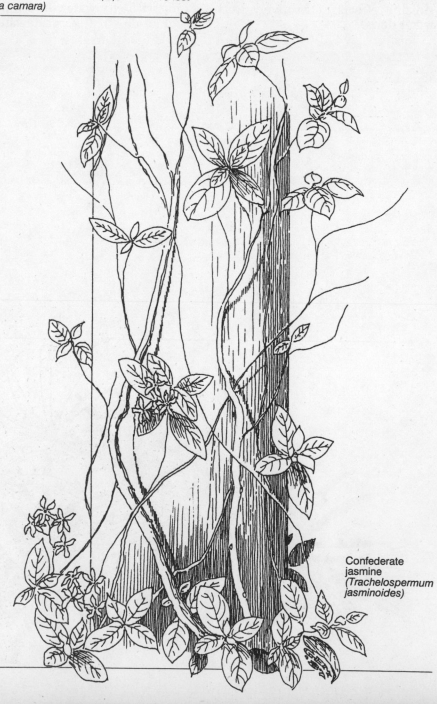

Confederate jasmine (Trachelospermum jasminoides)

Ground covers

Plant	Region	Height
Caltrops (*Tribulus terrestris*)	S	12 inches
Confederate jasmine (*Trachelospermum jasminoides*)	N,C,S	variable
Coontie (*Zamia integrifolia*)	N,C	24 inches
Creeping fig (*Ficus pumila*)	N,C,S	12 inches
Dichondra (*Dichondra carolinensis*)	N,C,S	2 inches
English ivy (*Hedera helix*)	N,C,S	4-6 inches
Fig-marigold (*Glottiphyllum depressum*)	S	6 inches
Hottentot fig (*Carpobrotus edulis*)	C,S	6 inches
Lily turf (*Ophiopogon japonicus*)	N,C,S	18 inches
Lirope (*Lirope spicata*)	N,C,S	18 inches
Purslane (*Portulaca spp.*)	N,C,S	6 inches
Running strawberry bush (*Euonymus fortunei*)	S	10 inches
Virginia creeper (*Parthenocissus quinquefolia*)	N,C,S	variable
Wedelia (*Wedelia trilobata*)	C,S	6-12 inches
Weeping lantana (*Lantana montevidensis*)	C,S	18-24 inches

Vines

Plant	Region	Height
Algerian ivy (*Hedera canariensis*)	N,C,S	variable
Bougainvillea (*Bougainvillea spp.*)	C,S	variable
Cape honeysuckle (*Tecomaria capensis*)	C,S	variable
Confederate jasmine (*Trachelospermum jasminoides*)	N,C,S	variable
Night blooming cereus (*Hylocereus undatus*)	C,S	variable
Rubber vine (*Cryptostegia grandiflora*)	S	variable

N — North Florida
C — Central Florida
S — South Florida

Live oak
(*Quercus virginiana*)

12

Harvest fruit from an edible landscape

HARVEST THE FRUITS OF your labors from dooryard plantings of trees, shrubs and vines. Most will double as attractive ornamentals while providing crops for year-round consumption.

Citrus is the most popular fruit among Florida's home gardeners. Picking an orange, grapefruit, tangelo or tangerine fresh from the tree is one of the joys of living in the Sunshine State.

From time to time, major freezes have dampened the enthusiasm of both professional and home citrus growers, but severely freeze-damaged trees generally are replaced with new ones that provide years of bountiful harvests. Citrus trees need minimal care, making them the easiest fruit trees to cultivate.

Gardeners also may enjoy many deciduous fruits. Reliably hardy, they may even need cold to flower and bear the harvest. Such deciduous fruits as grapes, apples, peaches and pears worth producing will take a little more care than citrus.

Because most residents will not have a large area to devote to production, fruiting plants should be considered as part of the decorative landscape. Grapes can be trained to form a hedge or to scale an arbor.

Pears, peaches and apples may serve as accent or background plantings or be espaliered to border a patio or planting bed. Figs or blueberries can be grown as hedges or in a shrub grouping and citrus makes great view barriers.

Except for relatively carefree citrus, most fruit trees and bushes require continuing attention. A neglected planting may yield meager harvests or become an eyesore in the landscape. Regular pest control, fertilizing and pruning schedules will have to be followed closely to produce successful crops.

Fruit plantings need a sunny location with plenty of space to grow. A garden spot may appear ample, but remember trees and vines normally spread out rapidly. Crowded plantings limit production, hinder good management and make picking difficult.

First determine the type of fruit you want to grow in your landscape. Next study the characteristics of the available varieties of that fruit. The primary consideration is adaptability to the Florida climate. Also important are nematode resistance, insect and disease resistance and overall fruit quality. These are the factors taken into consideration by

Cooperative Extension Service recommendations. Florida-tested varieties will ensure the best chance for success.

Many types of fruit trees and shrubs are self-pollinating. Others need a different pollinator to ensure a good crop. Some varieties of muscadine grapes, for instance, bear only female flowers and in order to fruit need another variety of grape planted nearby. Apple, blueberry, pecan and some citrus plantings benefit if different varieties are planted together.

When planting citrus and other fruits, follow the planting procedures recommended for trees and shrubs in Chapter 5. Most fruit plantings can be mulched but citrus is an exception. Citrus requires good air circulation and water drainage at the base of the tree. Mulching citrus, especially near the trunk, encourages a disease called foot rot.

Citrus trees fall prey to few damaging pests. As a result, most home growers do not need to spray their trees with pesticides to produce healthy plants with desirable fruit. However, some surface blemishes on the fruit and dark surface discoloration on the foliage will have to

Figuring citrus fertilizer needs

Calculate the fertilizer your citrus tree needs each February, June and October by measuring trunk circumference at 6 inches above the ground. Weigh out a half pound of citrus food per inch of trunk diameter. When the normal size of the tree has been reduced by cold, injury or decline, reduce the application rate proportionately.

There is no need to be fussy when it comes to picking a fertilizer — either a citrus special or 6-6-6 will do. Minor nutrients are included in most citrus fertilizers but they really are not necessary unless deficiency symptoms appear.

Be sure the fertilizer is evenly distributed under the tree. Start a few inches out from the tree trunk and uniformly scatter the measured fertilizer out past the drip line. Where the lawn can be injured by fertilizer make holes 2 feet apart and several inches below the lawn to receive the fertilizer. As an extra precaution, fertilize when the grass is dry and wash all fertilizer into the soil to avoid burning.

Improper fertilizing can result in considerable leaf drop. The cause may be too much fertilizer but is often a response to poor distribution. Suprisingly, most trees recover after such harsh treatment if the soil is kept moist. Using too much fertilizer or one with a high nitrogen content is likely to produce lush growth, thick skins and coarse, dry fruits.

1. Measure circumference of the tree 6 inches above the ground. Then weigh out ½ pound of fertilizer for each inch of trunk circumference.

Holes 2 feet apart

2. Start fertilizing a few inches out from the trunk. Uniformly scatter the measured fertilizer out past the drip line. Where turf could be damaged by high fertilizer rates, make holes 2 feet apart and several inches below the turf to receive the fertilizer.

be tolerated.

Established citrus trees need regular watering for good fruit. Poor watering can cause fruit to split or become dry and ricey during the fall months. Water home plantings once or twice a week and feed the trees three times a year. The result is almost assuredly a bumper crop.

Grapes and other popular fruits

After citrus, grapes are the home gardener's most foolproof crop. During the growing season, muscadine grapes produce vigorous vines that can conceal a fence or cover an arbor or trellis while giving good production. They have only a few pests and little spraying is required.

Some residents dislike the thick, tough muscadine skins. Most savor the flavor of the juicy pulp then discard the skins and seeds. These grapes are picked individually from large clusters during July and August.

Florida grape growers have another option — bunch grapes that fruit in June and July. Credit goes to the Institute of Food and Agricultural Sciences Research Center near Leesburg for developing the grape varieties with better quality and improved taste. One hit with home growers is the bunch grape Conquistador, which brings the long sought-after Concord taste south. Another, Orlando Seedless, is Florida's first seedless variety.

Bunch grapes are good producers but require a spray program to guarantee harvest. Diseases are a major concern with this crop. Protect both fruits and foliage by applying a fungicide every 10 to 14 days during spring and early summer.

Keep all grape vines productive with fertilizer applications in February, June and September. Winter pruning is also important, although the techniques differ for bunch and muscadine varieties. Consult a County Extension Service guide to southern grape culture.

Edible landscape

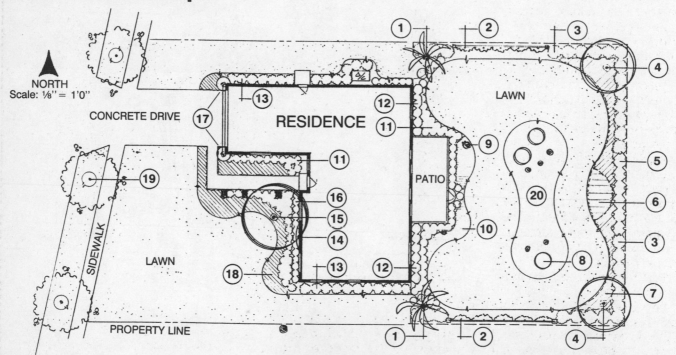

1. Banana tree
2. Grapes on vertical lattice work
3. Blueberry bushes
4. Peach tree
5. Feijoa shrubs
6. Herb garden
7. Pineapple (ground cover)
8. Fig shrub
9. Existing trees
10. Sweet potato (ground cover)
11. Natal plum
12. Mint shrub
13. Surinam cherry
14. Pear (espalier)
15. Apple tree
16. Dwarf pyracantha
17. Kumquat
18. Creeping blackberry
19. Citrus trees
20. Mulched activity area

Simple budding techniques for home grafters

Grafting unites the best portions of two plants. Usually home growers and commercial producers are attempting to place a desirable fruity variety on a vigorous, Florida pest-resistant root system. Just for fun home growers may also wish to make a cocktail tree — the growing of several varieties on one plant.

Classic grafting techniques were often difficult for weekend gardeners. Recent methods have reduced budding to a few simple cuts that ensure good grafts for both home and commercial propagators.

Securing budwood — a bud on a stem — is the first step to a good graft. Buds found at the base of each true leaf can grow new branches. Grafters like to collect stems with several buds present. Such stems are called budsticks. A budstick is obtained from maturing limbs, usually a few months old.

All budwood is treated similarly. Cut an 8- to 10-inch length of limb from a parent tree. Trim off the leaves, leaving short stems intact. Place the budwood in a plastic bag, mist with water and seal. If the buds cannot be used the same day, store in the refrigerator.

Successful budding requires clean, smooth cuts. This is not the chore for the serrated kitchen knife. Some gardeners use razor blades and Exacto knives, but the professionals prefer a special budding knife available from local hardware stores and garden centers.

Produce a chip bud (see illustration) by first removing a thin slice of wood from the rooted plant portion or stock onto which you wish to graft. Cut down the stem of the stock about an inch, slicing under the bark and just penetrating the wood. Make a second cut at the base of the first, forming a notch and removing the flap of plant tissue. A thin slice of tissue with bud present is then cut from the budwood to match the cut on the stock. When this bud is positioned on the stock, the edges of the bud tissue and stock should touch. When wrapped in place, union between these matched plant portions will occur rapidly.

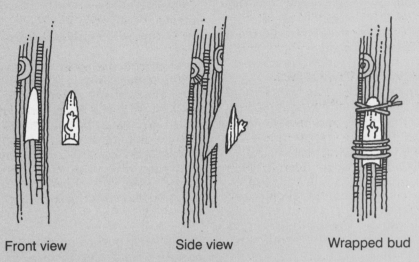

Front view   Side view   Wrapped bud

1. Chip bud is fitted down under flap of tissue on plant stock.

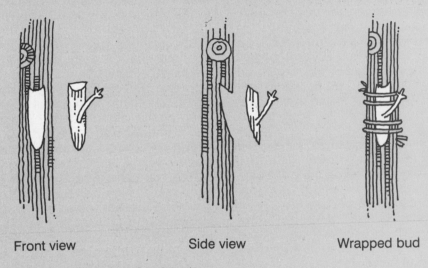

Front view   Side view   Wrapped bud

2. Hanging bud is fitted under flap of tissue on plant stock.

Making a hanging bud is almost the reverse of the chip bud. The first cut on the stock is upward, about an inch long just under the bark, penetrating the wood. Then move down about an eighth-inch on the flap and sever it from the stock, leaving just a little tissue to bind a new bud in place. Cut the budwood in a similar manner, but trim the top to a slight wedge that will slip under the flap left on the stock, thus hanging the bud.

Wrap the inserted budwood with strips of rubber, plastic, raffia or non-sticky plastic tape. Use a plastic bag to make economical wrap, cutting strips a half-inch wide and 10- to 12-inches long. Wrap snugly enough to keep the bud in place and water free.

After about three weeks unwrap the bud. If all is bright green, you've been successful. In another week or so the new bud will sprout into growth. Reluctant budwood can be encouraged to sprout by lopping off the top of the plant just above the graft.

Juicy, ripe peaches also can be grown in Central Florida. Trees should produce a fruit or two the first year and a good crop the second. Peaches need lots of pruning during January to keep trees within bounds and to produce bigger fruit.

Early-fruiting peach varieties often escape the Florida pests. Begin fertilizing during late winter and continue with monthly applications while the fruit is forming. Also, make sure established trees are watered once or twice a week.

Peach trees need a spray program. Obtain a fruit tree spray, which contains an insecticide and fungicide. Apply about twice a month during the fruiting period and monthly for the remaining warm season.

Florida apples will be the first on the east coast of the United States to ripen, maturing during June and July. During the first year or two after planting, a tree will produce only about 5 to 10 apples, but future production will soar to more than 150 apples a year. Harvest apples early: Anna, when it has just a red blush; Dorsett Golden, when yellowish green. At these stages the flavor is best and the fruit is not mealy.

Apples need continual care. Feed lightly once a month from late winter through fall using a 6-6-6, 10-10-10 or similar product. A fruit tree spray also is important. Apply at least once a month while fruit and foliage are present. Prune apple trees in January before the trees are in full flower.

Pears have been only fair producers for Central Florida, but yield well in the north. Many people object to their gritty texture. The pears are somewhat improved if picked slightly green and left to ripen in the home. Stone cells —

small, gritty fruit portions — disappear when the pears are canned. A new variety, Flordahome, promises problem-free fruit. This variety is adapted for Central Florida and can be eaten when picked from the tree.

A bacterial disease known as fireblight is the scourge of pear production along the east coast of the United States. Affected limbs quickly die back and must be pruned periodically. It is a major problem locally and is only partially controlled with seasonal sprays of a copper fungicide. Pear trees also are slow to produce. Expect the first fruit four to five years after planting.

Blueberry bushes often are planted with a few fruits clustered on the shrubs. They are only a sample of the bountiful harvest to come.

Blueberry bushes grow tall and wide with glossy blue-green foliage in the warm season that turns yellow to orange during the fall. Highbush varieties ripen in May and grow to about 6 feet. Rabbiteye blueberries grow taller, often reaching 16 to 18 feet; berries ripen during June. Many people plant blueberry bushes as ornamental hedges and prune annually after harvest.

Cultural conditions for blueberries are very specific. Check the soil before you plant. The pH must be between 4.5 and 5.2 for plants to prosper. Keep the soil acid by fertilizing with an azalea-camellia product in February, June and September. Plantings also should be mulched. Gardeners may have to share the berries with wildlife. To ensure your pick of the harvest, cover the bushes with nets when the fruit begins to ripen.

Fruits for the home

Fruit	Varieties	Months ripe
Apple	Anna	June
	Dorsett Golden	June
Blackberry	Brazos	May
	Flordagrand 1	April-May
	Oklawaha 1	April-May
Blueberry	Briteblue 2	June
	Southland 2	June
	Tifblue 2	June
	Bluegem 3	June
	Delite 3	June
	Woodward 3	June
	Flordablue	Late April
	Sharpblue	Late April
Fig	Brown Turkey	July-fall
	Celeste	July to August
	Magnolia	July to August
Grape — bunch	Blue Lake	July
	Conquistador	July
	Daytona	July
	Lake Emerald	July
	Orlando Seedless	July
	Stover	July
	Suwanee	July
Grape — Muscadine	Cowart	August
	Dixie	through
	Southland	early
	Triumph	September
	Welder	
Nectarine	Sunred	mid May
Pear	Flordahome	June
	Hood	July
	Pineapple	July
Peach	Early Amber	early May
	Flordagold	mid May
	Flordaprince	early May
	Flordasun	early May
	Flordabelle	late May
	Floradawon	early May
	McRed	mid May
Persimmon	Fuyu	Sept.-Oct.
	Hachiya	Sept.-Oct.
	Hanafuyu	Sept.-Oct.
	Hayakume	Sept.-Oct.
	O'Gosho	Sept.-Oct.
	Saijo	Sept.-Oct.
	Tamopan	Oct.-Nov.
	Tanenashi	Sept.-Oct.

1 — Varieties with the same numbers must be planted together.
2, 3 — Plant two or more varieties with same number.

Expect blackberry canes to run rampant but to provide a lot of fruit. The biggest problem is keeping the new shoots contained. A 10-foot hedge of berries will supply enough fruit for pie and preserves, plus all you can eat while picking. In Florida, blackberries need a yearly pruning to renew the canes. Cut back all growth to the ground immediately after harvest.

Gardeners can add figs to the patio and garden. A fig tree planted in a wooden tub makes an excellent foliage plant for a sunny location. Fig trees planted in the ground grow as tall shrubs with attractive deep green foliage. Figs are susceptible to nematodes, so many gardeners plant them near a walk or the foundation of a home where these pests are less likely to be prevalent. Add a heavy mulch to promote root growth. Fig trees fruit late spring through summer the first year and require only normal shrub care.

Tropical fruit in subtropical climate

Although most of Florida has a subtropical climate there are some areas where tropical fruits can be grown.

Most years South Florida achieves good fruit production. Tropical crops extend up the coast to Tampa on the west and Merritt Island on the east. These regions are warmed by Gulf of Mexico and Atlantic Ocean breezes that temper the flow of cold from the north. Inland and northern residents, however, can expect gusts of cold each winter that limit success with tropical fruits.

Where temperatures often sink below freezing, cultivate a backyard fruit selection by choosing varieties that survive the mid- to high 20s. Those with exotic tastes can grow the jaboticaba, cherry of the Rio Grande, grumichama and pitomba, all of which can be eaten fresh or used in jellies. Many gardeners also enjoy the carambola, a yellow desert fruit with deep ridges.

In areas where winters are warm for two or more consecutive years, fruit can be expected from the papaya, guava, banana, passion fruit and lychee.

Extremely cold-sensitive fruits can be cultivated in large tubs that hold 15 to 25 gallons of soil. Give this technique a try with the carambola, mango, lychee and small bushy tropicals. When cold warnings are sounded, tip the plants on their sides and cover; slide the containers under the canopy of a tree, or pull them into a heated enclosure for maximum protection.

Well-drained, homemade soil mixes are ideal for tropical plantings. Use equal parts peat moss and perlite, plus a tablespoon of dolomitic lime for each gallon of soil prepared. Position the new plant at the same depth it was growing in its original container to prevent root and crown rots.

Researchers are learning that many fruiting trees do not have to be kept tall. Even in grove conditions, avocados and mangos now are pruned to around 15 feet, facilitating maintenance and harvest. Work regularly with the trees to develop broad-spreading plants of about 12 feet. Don't be afraid to prune or nip out growing tips to encourage branching or direct growth.

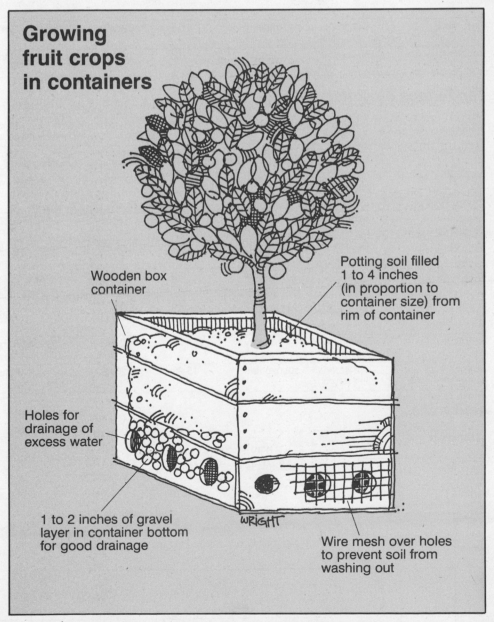

Growing fruit crops in containers

Wooden box container

Potting soil filled 1 to 4 inches (in proportion to container size) from rim of container

Holes for drainage of excess water

1 to 2 inches of gravel layer in container bottom for good drainage

WRIGHT

Wire mesh over holes to prevent soil from washing out

Home growers guide to Florida citrus

Oranges

Type/variety	Season of maturity	Hardiness	Seed per fruit	Average diameter (inches)	Comments
Hamlin	October-January	very hardy	0-6	2¾-3	Popular early juice orange. Ripens before danger of freeze.
Navel	October-January	hardy	0-6	3-3½	Good fruit to juice or section and eat. Often shy bearer but fruit are large.
Parson Brown	October-January	medium	10-20	2½-2¾	Originated from seedling planted by Rev. N.L. Brown in 1865. Juice quality rated poor.
Pineapple	December-February	susceptible	15-25	2¾-3	Juice quality, color are excellent. Fruits will not store on tree.
Valencia	March-June	hardy	0-6	2¾-3	Leading variety of sweet orange in Florida and world. Standard of excellence for eating and juicing.

Grapefruit

Type/variety	Season of maturity	Hardiness	Seed per fruit	Average diameter (inches)	Comments
Duncan	November-May	medium	30-70	3½-5	White fleshed. Oldest grapefruit variety. Considered by many to have superior taste. Good for sectioning.
Marsh	November-May	medium	0-6	3½-4½	Most widely grown grapefruit throughout the world. White fleshed. Sugar and acid content slightly lower than seedy varieties.
Pink Marsh	December-May	medium	0-6	3¾-4½	Similar to Marsh but pink fleshed. Color does fade as as season progresses. Also called Thompson.
Redblush	November-May	medium	0-6	3½-4½	Name describes pink blush in peel, but variety is also called Ruby Red. Flesh color is crimson.

Tangerines & hybrids

Type/variety	Season of maturity	Hardiness	Seed per fruit	Average diameter (inches)	Comments
Dancy	December-January	hardy	6-20	2¼-2½	Easy to peel, popular tangerine for the holidays. Trees tend to be alternate bearing (heavy crop one year, light the next).
Minneola	December-January	hardy	7-12	3-3½	Tangelo with such sweet taste many know it as Honeybell. Fruit often has a pronounced neck.
Murcott	January-March	hardy	10-20	2¾	Very sweet, late-season fruit often called Honey tangerine but is most likely a hybrid. Trees very susceptible to scab fungus.
Orlando	November-January	hardy	0-35	2¾-3	Tangelo that is resultant cross of Duncan grapefruit and Dancy tangerine. Leaves cup shaped. A heavy feeder.
Ponkan	December-January	hardy	3-7	2¾-3½	Fruit is delicious but will not ship. A tangerine that peels easily and has alternate bearing habit.
Robinson	October-December	hardy	1-20	2½-2¾	Tangerine that needs cross-pollination of tangelo or Temple to be good producer. Susceptible to limb, twig dieback.
Satsuma	September-November	very hardy	0-6	2¼-2½	One of first to ripen home grown fruits. Placed in tangerine group, the fruits are often edible when green. Stores poorly on tree.
Sunburst	November-December	hardy	1-20	2½-3	Hybrid that needs cross-pollination of tangelo or Temple to be good producer. Bright color; sweet taste.
Temple	January-March	susceptible	15-20	2¼-3	Peelable, sweet and very juicy fruit. Grow in protected location. Susceptible to scab.

Acid fruits

Type/variety	Season of maturity	Hardiness	Seed per fruit	Average diameter (inches)	Comments
Calamondin	year-round	very hardy	6-10	1-1½	Tree is small, upright, suitable for container growth. Heavy producer of small, acid fruits.
Key lime	year-round	susceptible	12-20	1-1½	Small tree that can be container grown to protect from cold. Highly aromatic. Also called Mexican Lime.
Kumquat	fall	very hardy	6-10	¾-1	Small tree with few thorns. Varieties for Florida include Morumi, Meiwa, Nagami.
Lemon	July-December	susceptible	1-6	2-2½	Can be grown in container for cold protection. Number of varieties exist including Bearss, Eureka, Lisbon, Villafranca.
Persian lime	June-September	susceptible	0	1¾-2½	A lime hybrid. The commercial lime of Florida. Can be grown in container to protect from cold.

13

Planning a year-round vegetable garden

HOME VEGETABLE GROWers in Florida farm all four seasons. The climate is ideal for warm-season gardens in spring and fall, cool-growing crops in winter and a few heat-tolerant survivors in summer.

Plant the vegetables the family will enjoy most. Surveys suggest corn, potatoes and tomatoes will be a hit at the dinner table. Losers include eggplant, turnips, Brussels sprouts and squash. Unless a vegetable has been a family favorite it will probably not be eaten.

In urban areas where postage-stamp-size gardens are common, it is probably a good idea to grow only as much as the family will eat fresh. With all the work and potential costs involved, canning and freezing of small quantities often is not profitable. Sharing surplus with neighbors or even trading for different vegetables can be fun.

No plot of land is too small for a garden. Many growers have discovered ways to maximize production. Square-foot gardening is a system in which every inch of the garden plot is closely planted with compatible crops. Gardeners using the French intensive method scatter seeds instead of sowing single rows.

For the really cramped, there is gardening in containers, a very productive method for growing high-yield crops.

Regardless of the method, a gardener's first step is to improve the soil.

Gardeners who cannot adjust to farming in sand may want to improve their soil with liberal additions of organic matter. Incorporate compost, peat, manure, leaves and old hay with Florida sand. Improved soils offer better water retention, more plant nutrients and a uniform root temperature. Try to locate economical sources for organic materials; otherwise your profits from the garden could be consumed in this one stage of soil preparation.

Don't plant a new garden before reviewing the problems of the previous season. Weeds, root rots, nematodes and similar pests can survive in the soil until another season.

Check the roots of recent crops as they are cleared from the land. If they are abnormally swollen, the nematode, a small parasitic worm, will surely be a pest of future plantings. Mole crickets, cutworms and some diseases can also persist. For problems like these, soil solarization or fumigation with Vapam is the next step before planting. Allow for a month or more of preparation time when these special treatments are required.

Nematode control before you plant

Nematodes, the villains of the vegetable patch, are getting the hotfoot treatment from backyard farmers. These farmers are using solar power to bake nematodes and other garden pests out of the soil.

Microscopic nematodes cannot be seen by the unaided eye but gardeners can easily detect the damage. At first the plants appear in need of fertilizer and may show signs of wilt, but the real damage is observed when roots are checked. Affected vegetable roots are abnormally swollen, often twisted and gnarled by the root knot nematode. The crippled root systems are unable to absorb water and nutrients needed for growth and production and the plants often become dwarfed and non-productive.

Soil solarization is a worthy alternative to chemical treatment. The best time of the year to employ this technique is the summer. First rake and till the soil until the earth is smooth, without clods or root fragments. Water it well because moisture will help conduct the heat deep into the ground. Cover the garden area with a clear plastic tarpaulin and seal the edges into the earth with soil.

The benefits of soil solarization can only be obtained by careful maintenance of the plastic. Use clear polyethylene that lets the sun through to strike the moist soil and heat the earth. Black plastic becomes hot above the soil and does not work as well. The entire garden area, including paths, should be covered. Keep the plastic in place until the garden is ready to plant.

If the cover is left undisturbed four weeks or more, temperatures in the soil will reach more than 120 degrees to a depth of about a foot. When the soil gets that hot for that long the nematodes die.

When a gardening season is fast approaching there may not be enough time for biological control. Also, most techniques depend on summertime treatment and nematodes are at work year-round. In these instances, chemical fumigation offers the most practical approach to nematode control. Currently only Vapam is labeled for home garden application. It is effective when incorporated into the soil but requires almost a month of treatment time before planting.

The most economical fumigation technique is in-the-row treatment. This involves placing the fumigant in a 6-inch-deep trench where the crop is to be planted. After the fumigant is applied, the row should be filled and the soil surface watered well to seal in the chemical. A plastic covering is then applied and the edges are sealed with a covering of soil to guarantee good pest control. Keep the soil covered for seven days and then let it air out for at least 14 days before planting begins.

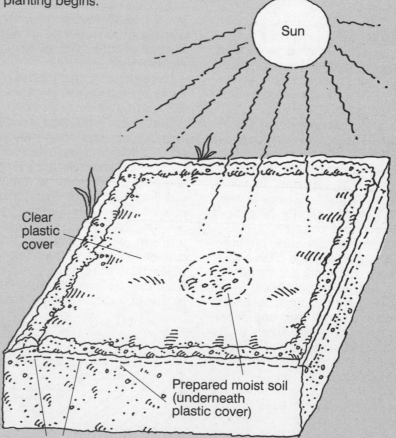

Sun

Clear plastic cover

Prepared moist soil (underneath plastic cover)

Edges of cover buried in shallow soil to hold them down

Fertilizing can be accomplished in many ways, but the simplest is to make an application to the prepared land just before planting. Scatter 1 to 2 pounds of a 6-6-6 fertilizer over each 100 square feet of garden or down 100 feet of garden row. Some gardeners work the fertilizer a few inches into the soil, but normally it is sufficiently incorporated into the soil during the planting process.

Water and fertilizer are the keys to a successful home garden, especially in sandy soil. Water after planting and continue watering almost daily to keep the surface soil moist while seeds are germinating. Half an hour is usually enough to wet the upper 3 to 4 inches. When the plants emerge, water every two to three days.

Stretch the time between waterings as much as possible — just so the crops do not severely wilt. This technique encourages plants to develop deep roots and conserve moisture. Mulching with compost, hay, leaves or newspaper is very valuable in Florida gardens.

Sowing seeds, setting transplants

Seeds can be sown in rows, hills or scattered across prepared planting sites. Follow label instructions or gardening charts regarding spacing. Careful sowing will prevent the extra work of thinning when the seedlings begin to grow. Most seeds, when properly planted and watered, germinate within a week or two. Carrots, beets and a few other fine seeds may need extra encouragement. Here is where the gardener can be innovative.

Get difficult seeds up and growing with the old-board trick. Dig a trench to the depth suggested on the seed packet. Wet the trench and sow the seeds. Cover the seeds with soil or vermiculite. (Vermiculite makes it easier to see the row.) Finally, place an old board over the row. Under its cover the seeds will stay warm and moist until they germinate. Peek under the board every few days and when sprouts just begin to poke through the soil prop up the board with bricks to admit some light and air. After two or three days, remove the board and

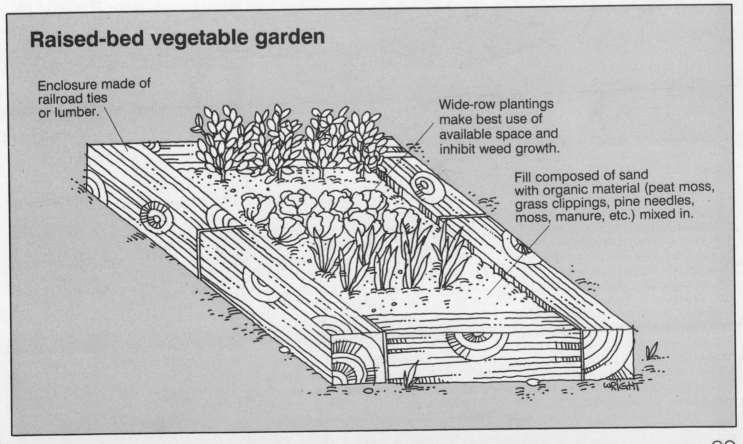

Raised-bed vegetable garden

Enclosure made of railroad ties or lumber.

Wide-row plantings make best use of available space and inhibit weed growth.

Fill composed of sand with organic material (peat moss, grass clippings, pine needles, moss, manure, etc.) mixed in.

WRIGHT

Insects that damage vegetable crops

Name	Description	Damage	Control
Aphids	Tiny, green to black, soft bodied, cluster on underside of leaves. Suck sap from leaves.	Curl and distort leaves. Stunt plants.	diazinon, malathion, insecticidal soap
Beetles	Numerous types. May be striped, spotted or solid colored. Usually less than ½ inch in size.	Holes in leaves, stems, flowers and fruits.	diazinon, Sevin
Cutworms	Dull gray, brown or black, striped or spotted; up to 1¼ inches long. Curl up tightly when disturbed.	Cut off plants at, above, or below surface. Some feed on underground portions of plants.	diazinon in soil prior to planting
Flea beetles	Black, brown or striped; jumping; about 1/16-inch long.	Severely damage young plants. Leaves look as if they had been shot full of holes.	Sevin, rotenone
Fruitworms, caterpillars	Green, brown or pink. May be striped along side or back; up to 1¾ inches long.	Eat holes in stems, leaves, buds and fruits.	Bacillus thuringiensis, Sevin, rotenone
Leaf miners	Larva: yellow, ⅛-inch long; live in leaves; make long, winding trails or tunnels.	Feed on leaves.	dimethoate
Mole crickets	Light brown; large, beady eyes; short, stout front legs and shovellike feet; to 1½ inches long.	Make burrows in soil and uproot young plants.	diazinon in soil prior to planting
Slugs	Not insects, but snails without shells.	Eat lower plant leaves. Damage seedlings.	methaldehyde baits
Spider mites	Tiny, red or greenish-red. Found on underside of leaves.	Yellow specks and fine webs on leaves. Plants and fruits are stunted.	diazinon, insecticidal soap, Kelthane, malathion

NOTE: Make sure products suggested can be used with your vegetable crops. Observe all label information.

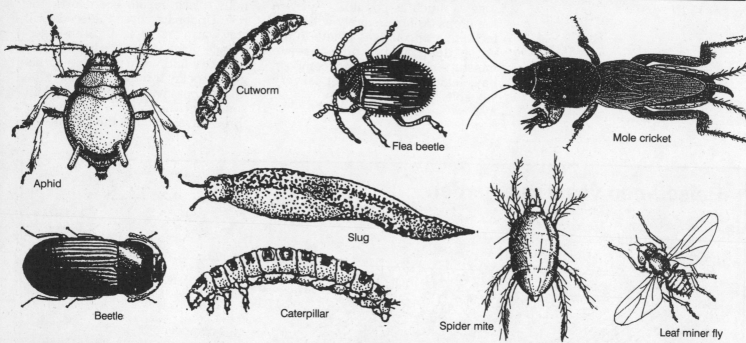

Aphid • Cutworm • Flea beetle • Mole cricket • Beetle • Slug • Caterpillar • Spider mite • Leaf miner fly

watch the seedlings grow.

Use only strong, stocky and vigorous transplants. Avoid disturbing roots when transplanting. Where seedlings are to be removed from boxes or flats, block out the soil around each plant by cutting it into squares. If transplants are obtained in individual plant containers or market packets, moisten the soil and gently tap out the young vegetable plants.

Transplant when conditions are most favorable. Planting after a rain, on a cloudy day or in late afternoon will help minimize shock. Where possible, shade plants with a palmetto fan, bush or board for two to four days after transplanting.

When planting, do not compress the soil too tightly around the roots. Gently pour water into the hole to settle the soil around the roots. Cover the moistened area around each new transplant with dry soil or a mulch to reduce evaporation.

A starter fertilizer solution helps get the transplants off to a quick start. Buy special starter solutions or make one by dissolving 1 to 2 tablespoons of a 6-6-6 fertilizer in a gallon of water. Pour half a pint of the solution into the hole while planting.

Stake or trellis such tall growing or vining vegetables as beans, cucumbers, squash, tomatoes and small melons. Keeping them off the ground helps prevent rot and makes insects easier to see. Harvesting and spraying also are easier if tall plants are trellised toward the center of the garden. This permits ready access to each side of the planting.

Tomato rings produce bumper crop

A sunny 7-foot circular plot can supply the family and a few neighbors with tomatoes for an entire season. This is the claim of gardeners who construct Japanese tomato rings, which are said to yield minimum harvests of 200 pounds.

The production technique combines the best of organic and inorganic gardening with only a few tomato plants to give high yields.

To prepare the garden site you will need two 50-pound bags of cow manure and a 6-cubic-foot bale of peat moss. Spade in one bag of cow manure and a half bale of peat moss. Have a sample of the soil tested to assure the proper pH and add lime or sulfur as needed.

In garden areas where nematodes have been a problem or are suspected, treat the soil before planting with a fumigant available from local garden centers. Consult the product's label for application instructions.

When preliminary soil preparation is completed, begin construction of a strong supportive wire ring. Form a 5- to 6-foot-high circle from 14 feet of heavy gauge fencing. Concrete reinforcement wire available from building supply stores is ideal because it has holes large enough for the gardener to easily reach through to pull weeds or pick tomatoes.

Add a second inner ring of finer mesh wire to contain the enriched soil. Hardware cloth 24 inches wide and 14 feet long is often used, but any screening material will work.

Construct the tomato ring in the center of the prepared planting site, leaving a foot or more of improved soil around the outer edge. Mix the remaining cow manure and peat moss and place inside the tomato ring.

Before planting, form a depression in the center of the peat moss-manure mix and add 10 pounds of a 6-6-6 fertilizer. Use a product that has a portion of its nitrogen in a water-insoluble form and contains minor nutrients.

Select tomatoes for planting from the tall-growing varieties that give a continuous harvest. Good producers for the Florida garden include Better Boy, Champion, Cherry, Floradel, Manalucie, Park's Whopper and Tropic. Evenly space four or five plants around the ring and tie the stems to the wire frame. Continue tying and supporting the vines as new growth is produced throughout the season.

The enriched soil will supply most of the nutrient needs for the growing plants. However, many gardeners like to boost growth even further with liquid or granular feedings. Where additional vigor is desired use either a 20-20-20 soluble fertilizer at the rate of a tablespoon to a gallon of water or a teaspoon of 6-6-6 per plant applied over the spread of the root system every two weeks. Water to keep the soil moist and control pest problems.

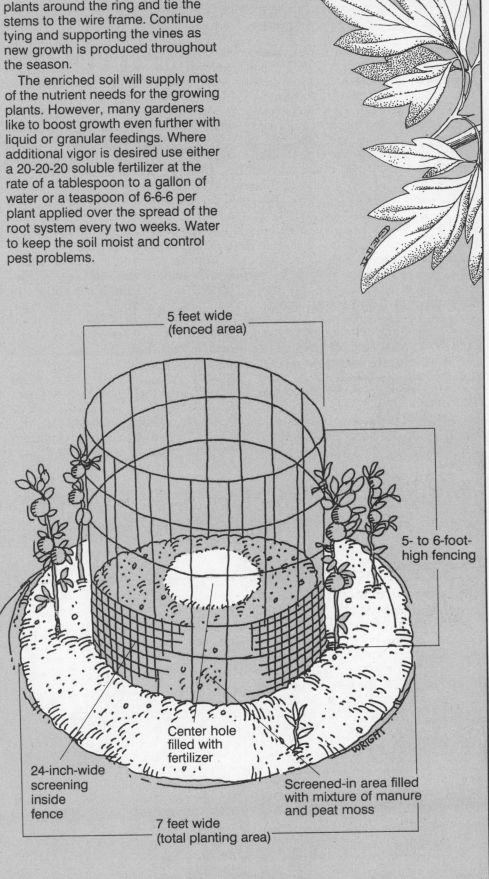

5 feet wide
(fenced area)

5- to 6-foot-high fencing

Center hole filled with fertilizer

24-inch-wide screening inside fence

Screened-in area filled with mixture of manure and peat moss

7 feet wide
(total planting area)

Weeds can become prolific if a gardener is not present to remove them from the vegetable patch. Many can be prevented by fumigating with Vapam before planting. With this product, weeds are virtually eliminated for one or more seasons providing the soil is not seriously disturbed between plantings.

Mulches are great aids in preventing weeds. Organic materials such as wood chips, grass clippings, old hay and compost are a few possibilities. Perforated black plastic and landscape fabrics also can be used. Resourceful gardeners have also used layers of newspaper, cardboard and old rags to prevent weeds.

Fertilizer keeps the crops growing. The sandier the soils, the more frequently nutrients should be added. During early growth fertilize every two to three weeks. Apply a light sprinkling of 1 pound of 6-6-6 per 100 square feet of garden. As plantings mature and near production, reduce the frequency of applications to a three- to four-week schedule. The addition of liberal quantites of organic matter to a sandy soil reduces the need for such frequent fertilizer applications.

Beating the heat with tropicals

Gardeners are most familiar with the temperate climate crops. Plan to raise these northern favorites during the warm and cool seasons. When the weather turns hot and humid many crops shrivel in the garden. Lesser-known, more tropical vegetables can fill these voids.

Some tropical vegetables run rampant in the garden before producing a harvest. The heart-leaf vining yam climbs rapidly up an arbor, fence or nearby tree. Wild yams are a familiar sight in Central Florida, but only the garden varieties are edible, growing tubers that average 3 to 8 pounds.

Yams are a 10- to 11-month crop and gardeners will have to wait until December for the season's harvest. Plantings begin in March with portions of the large tubers spaced about 3 feet apart. Then all they need is a place to climb to produce

a new crop ready to peel, boil and enjoy.

Another vining crop for the summer garden is the boniato, commonly called the Cuban sweet potato. This is a relative of the common garden sweet potato but it is more rounded and red-skinned. The crop is propagated from a cut-up potato or whole potato grown in a sandy soil to produce young plants called slips. Cuttings can also be made from vigorous vines by removing 8 to 10 inches of tip growth.

Space the boniatos, either plants or cut potato pieces, 12 inches apart in rows. It takes about 150 days before gardeners can dig under the vines for the plump potatoes.

The very tropical looking tanier grows leaves resembling big elephant ears and produces edible tubers. Also known as cocoyam, yautia and malanga, they grow more than 5 feet high, sending up many leaf blades from the base. Start a tanier crop early from tubers; production takes 9 to 10 months. Give it rich, moist soil for the best yield. Serve the tubers baked, mashed or fried just like potatoes. The dasheen is a similar crop also found in tropical gardens.

Gardeners wouldn't think of eating the ornamental hibiscus, but one tropical species, the roselle, is a favorite of many West Indies residents. The plant, also called sorrel, is an annual that grows 5 to 7 feet tall and produces lobed leaves that are sometimes used for greens. The main edible part is the calyx, a fleshy flower portion, that remains after the showy yellow bloom drops. The calyx is bright red and encases the developing seed. When separated from the seed, it is used in preserves, jelly, juice and a cranberry-like sauce.

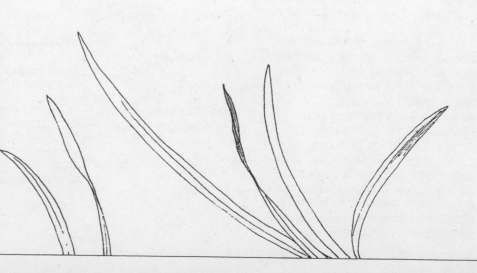

Roselle usually is started from seeds sown during the spring, but can also be propagated from cuttings. Plants flower by fall and the soft, plump edible calyx is harvested and separated from the seed in early winter.

The drought-tolerant but cold-sensitive pigeon pea is a special challenge. It is one crop that may not produce a harvest before frost. Plants last five years in the tropics but in Central Florida may produce only one crop. Seeds sown in spring grow into an 8-foot-tall bush. With some luck, they will flower by October to produce an early winter picking. The peas, fresh and dried, are used like the popular southern pea.

Additional tropical crops gardeners enjoy growing during the summer include the sweet cassava, the tapioca plant; calabaza, the Cuban pumpkin; and the banana. These are carefree crops that appear to need only water and hot weather. Add fertilizer before planting. If your soil is not quite up to par, scatter extra fertilizer under the plants every four to six weeks to ensure your harvest.

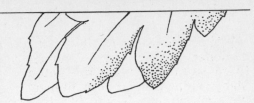

Vegetable planting guide

Warm weather crops

Crop	Varieties	Days from seed to maturity	Planting times											
			Aug.	Sept.	Oct.	Nov.	Dec.	Jan.	Feb.	March	April	May	June	July
Beans, lima	Henderson, Fordhook 242, Jackson Wonder, Concentrated, Dixie Butterpea	65-75		X						X	X	X		
Beans, pole	Dade, McCaslan, Kentucky Wonder 191, Blue Lake	60-65	X	X						X	X	X		
Beans, snap	Bush Blue Lake, Contender, Roma, Harvester, Miami, Cherokee (wax)	50-60		X						X	X	X		
Cantaloupe	Smith's Perfect, Samson Hybrid, Edisto 47, Planters Jumbo	75-90								X	X			
Corn, sweet	Silver Queen, Gold Cup, Iobelle, Bonanza, Florida Staysweet	80-85	X	X					X	X				
Cucumbers	Poinsett, Ashley, Gemini, SMR 18, Pixie, Galaxy	50-55	X	X						X	X			
Eggplant	Florida Market, Black Beauty, Long Tom, Ichiban	80-85	X	X						X	X			
Okra	Clemson Spineless, Perkins Long Green, Emerald, Dwarf Greenpod	50-55	X							X	X	X	X	X
Peas (southern)	Blackeye, Snapea, Mississippi Silver, Cream 40, Floricream, Zipper Cream	70-80	X	X						X	X	X	X	X
Pepper (sweet) *	Early Calwonder, Yolo Wonder, World Beater, Florida Giant	70-80	X	X						X	X			
Squash (summer)	Early Prolific Straightneck, Dixie Summer Crookneck, Cocozelle, Gold Bar, Patty Pan	55-65	X	X						X	X			
Squash (winter)	Sweet Mama, Table Queen, Butternut	95-105								X	X			
Tomatoes	Floradel, Tropic, Manalucie, Better Boy, Manapal, Cherry, Walter, Homestead, Fla. MH-1, Tropired, Floramerica, Flora-Dade	75-85	X	X						X	X			
Watermelon	Charleston Gray, Congo, Jubilee, Crimson Sweet, Dixielee, Tri-X 317, New Hampshire Midget, Sugar Baby	80-100	X							X				

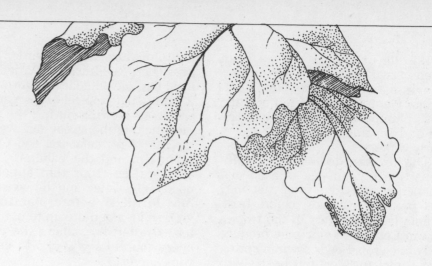

Vegetable planting guide

Cool weather crops

Crop	Varieties	Days from seed to maturity	Planting times											
			Aug.	Sept.	Oct.	Nov.	Dec.	Jan.	Feb.	March	April	May	June	July
Beets	Deroit Dark Red, Early Wonder	60-70			X	X	X	X	X					
Broccoli *	Early Green Sprouting, Waltham 29, Atlantic, Green Comet, Green Duke	60-70		X	X	X	X	X	X					
Cabbage *	Copenhagen Market, Marion Market, King Cole, Market Prize, Red Acre, Chieftan Savoy, Rio Verde	70-90		X	X	X	X	X						
Carrots	Imperator, Nantes, Chantenay, Gold Pak, Waltham Hicolor	70-90			X	X	X	X	X	X				
Cauliflower	Snowball Strains, Snowdrift, Snow Crown, Imperial 10-6	55-60			X	X	X	X	X					
Collards *	Georgia, Vates, Louisiana Sweet	50-60	X	X	X	X	X	X	X	X	X			
Lettuce	Minetto, Great Lakes, Fulton, Bibb, White Boston, Prize Head, Ruby, Salad Bowl, Parris Island Cos, Dark Green Cos	50-80			X	X	X	X	X	X				
Mustard	Southern Giant Curled, Florida Broad Leaf	40-45		X	X	X	X	X	X	X				
Onions	Excel, Texas Grano, Granex, White Granex, Tropicana Red, White Portugal, Evergreen, Shallots	100-130			X	X	X							
Parsley	Moss Curled, Perfection	90-95				X	X	X						
Peas	Wando, Green Arrows, Laxton's Progress, Sugar Snap	50-55			X	X	X	X	X					
Radish	Cherry Belle, Comet, Early Scarlet Globe, White Icicle, Sparkler, Red Prince, Champion	20-25			X	X	X	X	X	X				
Spinach	Virginia Savoy, Dixie Market, Hybrid 7, Bloomsdale Longstanding	40-45			X	X	X	X						
Turnips	Shogoin, Purple Top White Globe, Just Right	40-50			X	X			X	X				

* Usually transplanted. Days are from transplanting to maturity.

14

Pots and planters — gardening in small spaces

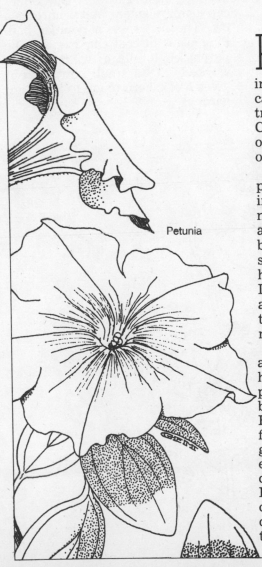

Petunia

POTS AND PLANTERS BRIM-ming with blooms and fancy foliage can turn outdoor living into a festival of color. Gardeners can carry the excitement to an entrance, porch or poolside setting. Containers also may provide the only spaces available for planting on a crowded patio or balcony.

Choose a container to fit the planting. Petunias adapt well to a 6-inch pot, but tall-growing tomatoes need at least 5 gallons of root space and a fruiting citrus tree survives best in a large tub. A confined root system dwarfs many plants and helps to keep growth in bounds. Limited growing space, however, also means restricted water and nutrient supplies and makes good maintenance a must.

Possibilities for plant containers are unlimited. They have only to hold soil and drain well. Typical planters are pots of clay or plastic, bushel baskets and paint buckets. Even old bathtubs have been used for growing flowers and food. Ingenious gardeners have constructed container gardens by lining sturdy fencing a foot high with plastic. Bags of potting soil also have been cut with an X and planted. Where decor is important, consider decorative clay pots, ceramic urns, fused stone and wooden planters.

Drainage is the most important feature of any pot. Holes should be plentiful. One big hole in the bottom of a small pot is usually adequate but a large container needs three or more holes in the bottom and along the sides. Good drainage also can be aided by a 1- to 2-inch layer of gravel or pebbles added to the bottom of each container at planting time.

Container gardens need loose, well-drained soil with good structure. Each planting may spend months or years in the container and the soil must be able to support growth by supplying air, water and nutrients to the root system. Ferns and cacti may need a special mixture to flourish, but for most vegetables, flowers and foliage a general potting soil purchased at the garden center or formulated at home will be adequate.

Color spots provide highlights

Containers let growers put the color where it is needed. Container gardens should attract the eye and give visitors an exciting view. A pot

with a single flower can provide enjoyment but a blend of several species creates the most colorful garden. Pick blossoms and foliage features that mix well together. Stage flowers of red, white and blue; yellow, orange and rust; or a selection of pastels against bright green foliage. Create a striking effect by combining pink and lavender blooms against silvery foliage.

Give the container garden height and gain planting space by mounding the soil in the middle. Position tall plants in the center, shorter plants toward the edges. One-sided gardens can be designed but the best attract attention from all directions.

Space plants close together with leaves touching for an immediate effect. Use 12 to 14 plants for a garden 15 inches in diameter; use up to 45 plants for a spectacular 36-inch display. Be sure to position the root balls at the same depth as they were growing in the pots.

A flower garden can be planned for survival at any light level. In full sun select from familiar annuals including ageratum, alyssum, celosia, dianthus, dusty miller, geraniums, marigolds, pansies and verbena. A few tolerant perennials include bush daisies, kalanchoe and osmanthus. Partial shade dwellers include begonias, caladiums, coleus, impatiens and streptocarpus. In dense shade ferns make a good showing.

Just a little planning provides color throughout the year. Follow an annual or perennial guide to ensure flowers when they are desired. Plant alyssum, begonia, browallia, periwinkle, impatiens and marigolds spring through summer.

When the cool fall and winter seasons return, replant with pansies, dianthus, johnny jump-ups, salvia and petunias or experiment with plants usually excluded from Florida in-ground gardens. Gardeners can give cyclamens and primroses a try. The primrose, a popular bedding plant in cool climates, can be purchased locally in winter. When worked into a small container it gives a Northern touch to Southern gardens.

Container garden

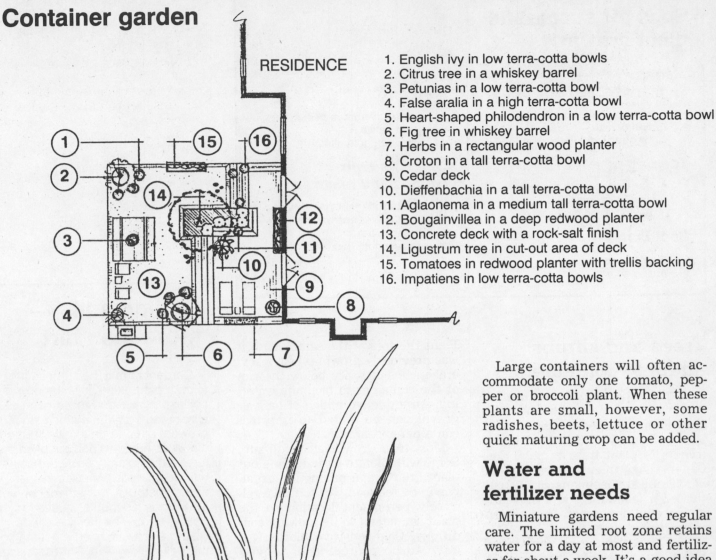

RESIDENCE

1. English ivy in low terra-cotta bowls
2. Citrus tree in a whiskey barrel
3. Petunias in a low terra-cotta bowl
4. False aralia in a high terra-cotta bowl
5. Heart-shaped philodendron in a low terra-cotta bowl
6. Fig tree in whiskey barrel
7. Herbs in a rectangular wood planter
8. Croton in a tall terra-cotta bowl
9. Cedar deck
10. Dieffenbachia in a tall terra-cotta bowl
11. Aglaonema in a medium tall terra-cotta bowl
12. Bougainvillea in a deep redwood planter
13. Concrete deck with a rock-salt finish
14. Ligustrum tree in cut-out area of deck
15. Tomatoes in redwood planter with trellis backing
16. Impatiens in low terra-cotta bowls

Vegetable gardens in miniature

The rules for good vegetable gardening never change, only the planting sites. Light is the most important factor to successful vegetable gardening. It is just as crucial when crops are cultivated in containers. Vegetables grow best in full sun. Root and fruiting crops such as carrots, beets, tomato, beans and corn must have light while leafy herbs, lettuce, collards and mustard greens can tolerate some shade.

Pot size regulates plant height and production. Six-inch containers are good for chives, basil, marjoram and other herbs. Ten-inch pots will yield crops of radishes, green onions and strawberries. Tomato, pep-

per, eggplant and squash plants should have the largest containers available.

Seeds for miniature versions of many vegetables have been introduced recently to maximize the use of space in the small garden. Look for varieties described as compact or suitable for pot or hanging basket culture.

The most difficult aspect of vegetable planting can be spacing the seeds. Crops can grow when a little cramped but production is likely to suffer. Even in pots, space smaller-growing onions, carrots, beets and radishes as suggested on the seed package. Space plants equally apart. Where crowding occurs, thin or harvest some plants early and leave the remaining crop to continue growing.

Large containers will often accommodate only one tomato, pepper or broccoli plant. When these plants are small, however, some radishes, beets, lettuce or other quick maturing crop can be added.

Water and fertilizer needs

Miniature gardens need regular care. The limited root zone retains water for a day at most and fertilizer for about a week. It's a good idea to check the soil twice a day; when it feels dry, water the plant thoroughly.

When growth is needed, feed frequently. Small vegetables and flowers can be fertilized at least once a week with a houseplant fertilizer. Mix a 20-20-20 analysis product at the rate of a tablespoon to a gallon of water and apply to moist soil to provide a good feeding. If extra growth is needed, dilute the same fertilizer by half and feed twice a week to maintain a constant supply of nutrients. As flowering and fruiting begin, reduce the feeding frequency to every other week.

The joy of growing vegetables is picking the results. From that point little additional maintenance is needed. Flower gardens will require some grooming to remain attractive. In a small garden it is not hard to pick the faded flowers. It is the best way to encourage new blooms.

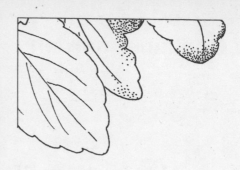

Soils for successful plant growth

General mix — vegetables, flowers, trees

- 2 quarts sphagnum peat moss
- 2 quarts perlite
- ½ tablespoon dolomitic lime

Seeding mix

- 2 quarts sphagnum peat moss
- 2 quarts fine vermiculite
- ½ tablespoon dolomitic lime

Cactus mix

- 1 quart general mix
- 3 quarts coarse sand

Fern mix

- 2 quarts sphagnum peat moss
- 1 quart perlite
- 1 teaspoon dolomitic lime

Gesneriad mix (violets and relatives)

- 2 quarts sphagnum peat moss
- 1 quart coarse vermiculite
- 1 quart perlite
- ½ tablespoon dolomitic lime

Trees and shrubs adapt to containers

Gardens too small for a full-sized tree may be able to accommodate a smaller one planted in a half barrel. Poor soils may also prompt homeowners to plant trees in pots. Containers make trees somewhat portable. Tropical specimens can be cultivated in containers and moved to a protected area when freeze warnings are sounded.

Most trees make an easy transition to container life. Tropical trees, large foliage plants and shrubs include the ficus, false aralia, palms and dracaena. A beginner's list of fruit trees includes avocado, banana, coffee, guava, papaya, pineapple, calamondin, key lime, kumquat, fig and mango. A fruit tree grown in a pot or tub is likely to produce less than the same tree planted in the ground, but with proper care should yield a number of quality fruit.

A container must be large enough to permit root and shoot development. In general the larger the plant normally would grow in the ground, the larger the container must be. A 25-gallon tub or barrel is usually the minimum size for productive tree growth.

Examine the root system of a new tree at planting time. If it is potbound, judiciously prune some of the large roots and loosen others to encourage growth into the new soil.

Plant the tree at the same depth it was previously growing. Leave several inches of space below the rim of the container to facilitate watering. An attractive mulch of bark or gravel can be added to improve container appearance.

Most trees grow best in full sun. Some will tolerate partial shade but plant growth and production usually will be reduced. Try to find a relatively permanent location so the plant can adjust to its growing conditions. Cold-sensitive plants will have to be protected or moved when temperatures drop.

Water container-grown trees and shrubs when the soil surface becomes dry to the touch. Water until moisture drips from the drainage holes.

Gardeners can use a visual approach to fertilizing. Trees with deep green foliage and good growth are being well fed. Use a houseplant product at the recommended rate every few weeks. This schedule may have to be adjusted during the warm growing season to maintain healthy plants.

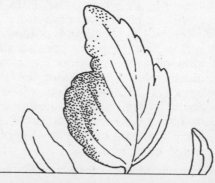

Potting soils — more than dirt

Gardeners may be surprised to learn most potting soils are now soilless. Native soils have been eliminated from the material home growers depend on to give support, dispense nutrients and supply moisture to their plants. Backyard soil harbors insects, weeds, diseases and nematodes. Its nutrient content also varies. Garden soil used for potting should be sterilized first.

Home growers need a potting soil that will be forgiving. Soilless blends are formulated to allow for overwatering or compaction. Ingredients include peat moss, perlite, vermiculite and sand.

Gardeners have often been told to add lime to home gardens and potting soils to reduce the soil acidity. Adjustment of pH is not as critical with the soilless mixtures, which release nutrients at a much lower acidity level than many true soils. Even an acid pH of 5.5 will support good plant growth in a soilless potting mix. Nevertheless, dolomitic lime or a similar product is added to every standard mix to adjust the pH to about 6 and to supply calcium and magnesium.

Gardeners who want to mix their own potting soil should be careful to keep the product free from contamination. Combine the ingredients on a concrete drive or in clean trash cans. Nematodes are a big problem in Florida and could be introduced with native soil.

15
Lawns — No. 1 ground cover

HOMEOWNERS LOVE LUSH green lawns. No one says lawn care is fun, but it consistently ranks No. 1 among outdoor gardening activities.

Florida has five varieties of grass, but none equals the fine textured bluegrass and fescues grown in cooler regions of the country. Coarse, long-bladed, durable St. Augustine and bahia varieties comprise more than 80 percent of Florida turfs. Their culture presents the fewest problems for home growers.

Each gardener must decide which type to cultivate. If there is no available irrigation the answer is fairly easy because bahia is the most drought tolerant. Coastal residents should choose St. Augustine because of its salt tolerance.

Centipede grass is often called the poor man's turf. All it really needs is water. This turf mimics St. Augustine and often invades lawns. It's ideal for the heavier soils of North Florida but in other areas it is susceptible to nematodes and ground pearls, a type of scale insect. Before planting centipede grass, check the soil for nematodes and fumigate if necessary.

Bermuda and zoysia grasses are the Florida lawns most reminiscent of northern fine-bladed turfs. Promotions have convinced many gardeners that zoysia is carefree, but only the growth is slow. Zoysia is tough and durable to traffic but susceptible to nematodes. Careful watering and feeding programs are required to keep Florida zoysia lawns green and growing.

Bermuda has similar problems with nematodes plus a demanding maintenance schedule. A fine, closely clipped Bermuda lawn requires mowing twice a week, feeding eight times a year and frequent pest control.

Check the Florida turf table to decide which species is suitable for your home lawn. In addition, survey the neighborhood to discover which turf grows the best in your area.

Properly establishing the new lawn

Spring and summer are the ideal times to establish a new lawn. Growth is enhanced by the seasonal rain and warm temperatures. Sod and plugs can be planted year-round but seeding and sprigging are best reserved for the warmer seasons.

Prepare the planting site before starting a new lawn or patching existing turf. Loosen the soil with a spade, rake or cultivator. This reduces soil compaction, eliminates weeds and restricts competition from roots. A pH test is advisable and 6-6-6 fertilizer may be worked into the prepared soil at the rate of 10 pounds per 1,000 square feet.

If re-establishing turf, investigate why the previous lawn declined. If there is evidence that nematodes have affected the turf, a treatment should be applied. Both fumigants and chemical drenches are available from local garden centers to help eliminate nematodes and other soil pests.

Seeding is an economical method of starting a new lawn. It is a practical way to establish bahia grass, but can also be used with centipede, Bermuda and zoysia turfs. April through September is the best time to seed because the weather is warm and rainfall generally is adequate.

A uniform distribution of seed across the prepared soil is necessary to obtain a good stand of grass. A spreader is recommended, but an acceptable job can be performed by careful hand seeding. For best coverage, apply half the seed in one direction and the remaining half at right angles to the first seeding. Very small seed like centipede and Bermuda can be mixed with soil or sand to ensure uniform distribution.

The seed must be covered after sowing. Top dressing with a quarter to half inch of soil is the best method, but the seed can also be incorporated into the ground by raking. Once covered, water lightly and if possible firm the soil with a roller.

Proper watering is the most critical step in establishing a lawn from seed. The soil should be kept moist until the grass has germinated and plants become established. If the surface of the soil is allowed to dry out at any time before roots develop, the lawn may be lost.

Gardeners can also stretch their dollars by plugging or sprigging a new lawn. Small portions of healthy turf quickly cover barren soil or invade weaker turf to produce a thick lawn in 8 to 10 weeks. Most St. Augustine varieties are marketed as plugs ready to plant. Bermuda, centipede and zoysia can also be started from small grass portions.

Many gardeners simply cut up pieces of sod to obtain sprigs.

Plant plugs in the prepared soil using a trowel or plugging device. Turf sections usually are set 6 to 12 inches apart, tamped or rolled and then watered. Successful establishment depends on continuing care.

New turf sections have a limited root system and need irrigation almost daily for the first week or two. When new runners begin to grow, watering can usually be reduced to every other day. As the lawn begins to knit together water as needed.

Although good site preparation will produce the fastest turf growth, it is not always necessary. Many gardeners have successfully changed grass types by plugging an existing lawn. This works well with weakened bahia, but is less successful where noxious weeds are present. In problem areas, apply glyphosate, a weedkiller, marketed as Kleenup, Roundup and Blot Out. The soil can be plugged two weeks after treatment.

Sodding produces an instant lawn but is expensive. It is recommended where immediate cover is desired. All turf types are available as sod.

Soil preparation is also required when establishing sod. After preparation, make sure the soil is moist before the first strip of sod is laid. The pieces of sod should be fitted together tightly. Fill in any cracks between sections with sand or clean topsoil.

Tamp or roll the sod to remove air pockets and ensure close contact between the turf and soil below. Water thoroughly to wet the sod and underlying soil. If the soil below the sod is allowed to dry, the roots will not penetrate below the original turf layer.

Gardeners laying more than a few pallets of sod should begin watering before the job is finished. Water for short intervals several times daily until the sod is established. Give the sod a tug; when it cannot be lifted, it is anchored into the soil. This usually takes about three weeks in Florida sands.

Then it's time to begin a normal watering program. If you can pinch the soil and it holds together, you don't need water.

Begin a normal turf care program when the seedlings or plugs are well established or sod is firmly anchored in the soil. Begin mowing as needed and fertilizing according to the turf chart on Page 103. Although insect or disease problems probably will not appear during the first few months, check frequently to be sure.

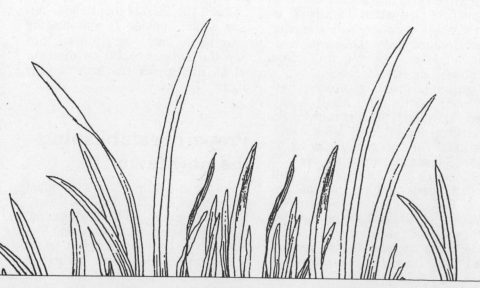

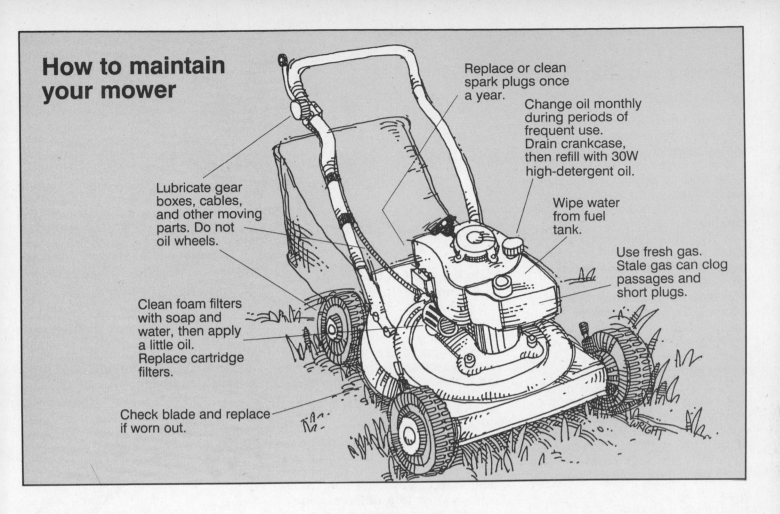

How to maintain your mower

Replace or clean spark plugs once a year.

Change oil monthly during periods of frequent use. Drain crankcase, then refill with 30W high-detergent oil.

Lubricate gear boxes, cables, and other moving parts. Do not oil wheels.

Wipe water from fuel tank.

Use fresh gas. Stale gas can clog passages and short plugs.

Clean foam filters with soap and water, then apply a little oil. Replace cartridge filters.

Check blade and replace if worn out.

Maintaining the turf

It's a tradition to keep lawns green by pouring on fertilizer. This intensifies turf color but also causes a surge of growth and the need for more frequent mowing. What gardeners really need is the color response without the growth. Besides making more work, insects prefer the lush, succulent new growth. Keeping the growth down also reduces thatch and a tendency for turf to grow well above the soil.

Turf needs complete fertilizer applications in March and September. These feedings build durable turf capable of surviving stresssful winter and early spring periods. An additional feeding can be made in May. Many products can be used but a 16-4-8 or similar product is preferred. Use the fertilizer at the rate of 6 pounds per 1,000 square feet.

During the summer keep the green without the growth with two evenly spaced iron applications. Apply during July or whenever the green begins to fade. A second application should be made four to six weeks after the first. Iron sulfate is available from most garden centers. Follow label instructions to obtain the re-greening.

Even with grass on a lean feeding schedule, weekly mowing will be required during the warm season. Bahia and St. Augustine should be maintained at a height of 3 to 4 inches. This usually is the highest setting on the mower. Remove no more than a third of the blade at a cutting. This means a turf cut at the 3-inch height should be mowed before it grows to 4 inches. Removing too much top growth at one time causes yellowing and sun scald.

Grass clippings generally should be left on the lawn as they return nutrients to the soil.

Check the lawnmower blade regularly. Weekly or monthly blade inspections are recommended. Grass that appears brown on the top could be the result of a dull blade. Keep it sharp to maintain a clean cut and avoid ragged ends that are unsightly and promote disease.

Water the turf when it wilts. There may be a few telltale spots in the lawn that dry first. Use these areas as gauges; when they start to wilt, it is time to water. Some gardeners use their footprints in the grass as an indication of when to water. If the crushed blades lay over instead of returning to the upright position, supply at least half an inch of water. A general rule to follow is: Water from irrigation or rainfall will be needed once or twice a week during the cool seasons and two or three times a week during the hot, dry seasons.

Rains that appear to arrive daily during the summer can still leave the lawn thirsty for water. During a hot day more than a quarter of an inch of moisture is lost from the turf. Sandy soil will hold only about half an inch of available moisture in the major root zone. In two days the available supply of water will be exhausted if not replenished. Daily sprinkles that wet the grass may do little to moisten the earth. Use a rain gauge to keep an accurate record or dig into the turf to determine moisture levels.

Become familiar with common pests

Bright green lawns provide comfortable living and free food for turf pests. Lawns harbor many insects, but only a few are really harmful. Take time to become familiar with pests common to your variety of turf before the growing season begins.

Mole crickets tunnel through bahia turf, feeding on and disrupting root growth. These pests won't go away on their own until the turf is destroyed. Gardeners will always notice a few mole crickets in the spring when the bugs seek out new feeding grounds. These fully mature crickets should be tolerated unless damage to turf is significant.

By May, however, mole crickets will be laying eggs that begin the new and ravenous generation. Gardeners can obtain the best control of this invasion May through late summer with baits or sprays specially labeled for mole crickets.

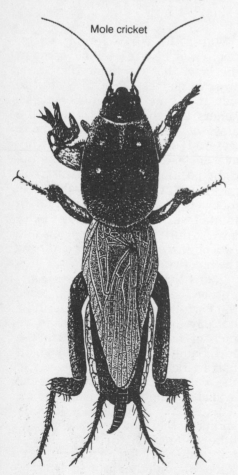

Mole cricket

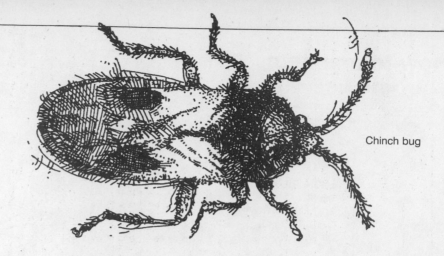

Chinch bug

Chinch bugs will be on the prowl in St. Augustine turf as soon as the weather warms. Expect the earliest damage by the end of March. Lawns ravaged by chinch bugs first turn yellow in the warmest locations. These small spots rapidly enlarge to big brown areas. Remember, if you give a chinch an inch it will take your yard.

Chinch bugs have been easy to control in the past, but a pesticide-resistant population is emerging. If one or two applications of the common insecticides don't affect these pests, switch to a different type of insecticide or contact a local pest-control professional.

Sod webworms retreat to South Florida for the winter, but each spring begin the migration back to Central and North Florida. They can arrive as early as the first week of July. Sod webworms chew grass blades, giving lawns a closely mowed look.

Webworms arrive as brown dingy moths which soon lay eggs. Control at this stage is futile — wait until the eggs hatch in about two weeks and spray the caterpillars. Webworms prefer St. Augustine turf but will also feed on other Florida grasses.

Insecticides should give good control of sod webworms but must be applied frequently. Eggs are often not controlled and the moths infiltrate from neighboring lawns to restart infestation. Summer is a difficult time to control the caterpillars. Rain washes pesticides off the grass, sunlight decomposes the chemicals and frequent mowing removes the insecticide. When infestations are heavy, expect to re-treat in just a few weeks. Additional caterpillars that may feed in home turf include the army worm and looper.

Nematodes are too small to be seen and must be detected in the lab. However, a declining turf with a stunted root system indicates that nematodes are present.

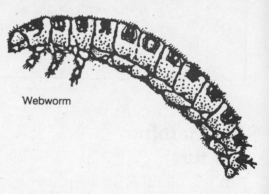

Webworm

Nematodes are frequently found in older established turf but may also be a problem after sodding. A nematode test is available through your County Extension Service.

Nematodes are often a problem in St. Augustine turf and control is limited to a few pesticides. The nematicide Sarolex is available for use by homeowners; Mocap is used by professionals.

Do-it-yourself pesticide application takes professional techniques. It's not a time for bare feet. Wear boots, rubber gloves and long sleeves. Goggles are also a good idea as the eyes are very susceptible to wind-blown spray. Respirators are optional for most home-use pesticides. Follow label instructions and you should be just as effective as the professional.

Florida grasses at a glance

Turf type	Shade tolerance	Irrigation	Establish	Fertilizer schedule	Mowing height	Insects	Diseases	Nematode problems	Varieties
St. Augustine	filtered	needed	sod, sprigs or plugs	March, May, July, Sept.	3-4 inches	chinch bugs, sod webworms	brown patch	buildup expected	Bitterblue, Floralawn, Floratine, Floratam, Gulfstar, Raleigh, Seville
Bahia	very light	suggested	seed or sod	March, May, July, Sept.	3-4 inches	mole crickets, caterpillars	few problems	damaging if present at planting	Argentine, Paraguay 22, Pensacola
Centipede	very light	needed	seed, sprigs or sod	March, July	1½-2 inches	ground pearls, caterpillars	brown patch	severe	Common
Bermuda	none	needed	sod or sprigs	Jan., March, April, June, July, Sept., Oct., Dec.	½-1 inch	caterpillars, mole crickets	dollar spot, brown patch	severe	Ormond, Tiflawn, Tifway
Zoysia	very light	needed	sod or plugs	March, April, June, Sept., Nov.	1-2 inches	hunting billbug, caterpillars	dollar spot, brown patch	severe	Meyer, Emerald

Insects that damage home turf

Insect	Description	Damage	Cultural controls	Chemical controls
Chinch bugs	Pinhead to 1/5 inch in length. Newly hatched are red with white bands. Adults are black with white wings.	Sucks juice from the grass. Only affects St. Augustine. Yellowish to brownish patches produced.	Reduce lawn fertilization to a minimum schedule. Control thatch in the lawn. Establish resistant Floratam variety.	Aspon, Baygon, diazinon, Dursban, Mavrik
Lawn caterpillars	Includes army worm, grass looper and sod webworm. All larva stages of moths. Sod webworms are the most prevalent, growing to ¾ inch in length and feeding only at night.	Grass blades chewed and eaten. Foliage almost completely stripped off in patches. Close-cropped areas soon become yellow to brown. All grasses susceptible.	Reduce lawn fertilization to a minimum schedule. Mow St. Augustine and bahia turf at 3- to 4-inch height. Check frequently for signs of early feeding.	Bacillus thuringiensis, diazinon, Dursban, Mavrik, Sevin
Mole crickets	Light- to dark-brown crickets living mainly in the soil. Young hatch in May; feed summer long becoming 1½-inch adults by spring.	Tunneling loosens soil, and disturbs grass roots. Some feed on grass roots. Turf yellows then turns brown leaving barren areas. Bahia and Bermuda turf most often affected.	Mow bahia at 3- to 4-inch height. Do not allow the turf to dry out excessively. Coarse textured varieties such as Argentine bahia appear more tolerant of infestations.	Sprays: Baygon, diazinon, Sarolex. Baits: Baygon, Dursban, malathion.

16

The tropical look
for a
temperate climate

F LORIDA GARDENERS CAN
create the illusion of a tropical
jungle but must cope with the
limitations of a temperate climate.
"Give me a tropical look — but I
don't want it to freeze," is a common request from Florida residents.

Florida borders the tropics, which
begin just north of Cuba at the
Tropic of Cancer. As a result of this
geographic location, many years
Florida landscapes escape the dev-
astating freezes typical of temperate zones. In mild years, the subtropical climate of Central and
South Florida means a variety of
tropical, subtropical and temperate
plants can be cultivated. Cold winters do eventually return, however,
and restrict plant growth.

In North and Central Florida it's
best not to give your entire yard the
jungle treatment. Just work with a
patio or small section of the landscape. Plant most of your tropicals
in pots that can be quickly ushered
indoors or given similar protection
when a freeze returns. In South
Florida these freeze precautions
generally are not necessary.

Gardeners need an overhead canopy to create the junglelike atmosphere of the tropics. A canopy retains moisture and fosters lush
growth underneath. Large trees,
such as oaks, trimmed to allow
some sun to penetrate, are ideal.

Where trees are not available, use
lattice or shade cloth to create a
canopy. Trees are preferable, however, and should be planted, even if
the effect will not be achieved for
many years.

Palms add a tropical look. The
majority will need full sun and can
be used to extend the overhead canopy. Some tolerate filtered sun,
while others grow well at the edge
of tree plantings. Clusters of winter-
hardy sabal palms can be planted
near the canopy, and lady palms
grow well in shade. Sagos and Florida coonties grow in shade to full
sun and help add a tropical look
with their palmlike foliage.

Cabbage palmetto
(*Sabal palmetto*)

Big leaf shrubs in understory plantings convey the feeling of lush vegetation. Choose a majority of hardy ornamentals, including the cast iron plant, anise, Indian hawthorn, fatsia and camellias. Then add exotic but cold-sensitive philodendrons, gingers, tree ferns and banana trees. Use just a few tropical plants in the background. Their beauty can be admired during the warm seasons, but the landscape won't be devastated should the temperature drop to freezing.

In the shadiest location, plant groupings of ferns and bromeliads. The sword fern grows quickly, becoming a ground cover with bright green foliage. Bromeliads, with their narrow to broad fleshy leaves, can grow in beds or be attached to trees. The foliage is unique and many flower during the warm seasons.

Bromeliad
(*Cryptanthus spp.*)

Bromeliads

Many members of the bromeliad family are almost carefree. Living as epiphytes attached to trees, cliffs and rocky hillsides, they have adapted to caring for themselves.

Spanish moss is the most widely distributed bromeliad and can be found from Virginia to Florida. It lives on rain, dew and bits of trapped organic matter.

A bromeliad that many have propagated is the pineapple. Tops, cut from fresh fruits, root rather easily.

Many bromeliads can be wired to tree limbs lined with sphagnum moss, while others can be mounted on tree fern, cork or bark slabs. Most, except for the truly epiphytic types, quickly adapt to pot or in-ground culture.

Porous and highly organic potting mixes should be prepared for bromeliads. A popular growing medium consists of equal parts peat moss, leaf mold and sand. Other organic sources frequently added include chopped osmunda, coconut husk, bark and tree fern fiber. Perlite can be substituted for sand. For in-ground culture simply mix organic matter with sandy Florida soil.

A beginning bromeliad collection should include some of the hardier members of the *Aechmea, Billbergia* and *Neoregelia* genera. Many can be grown both in full sun or partial shade. They also contain species that survive Florida winters and make excellent ground covers for low maintenance landscapes.

The collection may also include members of the *Cryptanthus, Dyckia, Guzmania* and *Nidularium* genera. Each has many species with attractive foliage and flowers for use in the homes, on patios and as semipermanent landscape plants.

Encourage growth with a liquid fertilizer applied to plantings once each month. Select any evenly balanced product that can be mixed with water and use it at half strength.

The vaselike cups of many bromeliads make watering extra easy. When rains and dews fail to keep the cups filled it's time to water. Periodically, empty the cups of potted plants to eliminate accumulated fertilizer and plant residues that may rot the foliage. Species without vases are watered just like houseplants.

Papyrus and other members of the sedge family, which feature umbrellalike foliage, grow best in full sun but tolerate shade. Try bamboo, but plan to keep it in bounds because it is a rapid grower.

Enhance the tropical look with potted foliage. Large scheffleras, ficus, neanthe bella palms, dieffenbachia, dracaena and many plants common to indoor culture can create the image of a tropical retreat.

Add color with flowering plants tied to the trees, swung from overhead limbs or planted in beds. Orchids are the queen of exotics and grow well in filtered sun. The wide variety of flower colors and sizes ranges from the big fleshy cattleya to the small and delicate epidendrums.

Big leaf caladiums offer a spectrum of foliage color for filtered to full sun locations. These remain attractive spring through summer and can be grown in beds or large planters. Use impatiens, begonias and coleus to create interesting pockets of annual color.

Carefully positioned rock outcroppings of small or large boulders can create the illusion of a mountain jungle. Use them to build ideal planting sites for ferns and bromeliads. Construct berms or ravines to form a varied terrain. Many gardeners add a water feature. A small waterfall or pond creates the moist, humid atmosphere of the tropics.

To complete the illusion of your backyard jungle, add tropical birds. Install outdoor lighting and your hideaway can become an airy escape for evening enjoyment. Lights also allow you to enjoy your oasis from indoors.

Cultivating a jungle takes work. It's a high maintenance garden because plant growth is rapid and requires periodic pruning to stay within bounds. Frequent watering and fertilizing are also necessary to maintain the lush vegetation.

Cold protection for tropical plantings

Florida gardeners should plan for cold-weather plant protection each winter. Many plants can be carried inside while others can be protected using makeshift shelters.

Winter covers give the best protection and are easy to construct. When freeze warnings are sounded, hammer long stakes into the ground to form four corners of a support. Then stretch plastic over the stakes, drape it to the ground and anchor it with soil or bricks. It will only take about half an hour to protect a prized queen sago, philodendron or hibiscus.

Bromeliad
(*Pinguin*)

Orchids

Orchids, once admired by many but cultivated by specialists, can now be grown at home. This queen of exotics was once collected only by gardeners sporting royal budgets. Breeders working to dispel the mystique of orchid culture now attract home hobbyists with durable, easy-to-grow varieties offered at affordable prices.

Collections often begin as gifts or as impulse purchases. Orchids can be hung under a tree or set on a carport, but extensive collections generally are kept in a shade house or greenhouse.

Most orchids should be kept out of the bright sun. They can withstand some morning sun but by afternoon will certainly require shade. Vanda orchids and their relatives are an exception and like high light. They can be grown under overhangs or in the filtered light of a screened enclosure.

The queen of the orchids is the cattleya. Its many hybrids are often associated with Easter and Mother's Day corsages. The flowers are large and showy. Gardeners with limited space can collect miniature versions.

The following species are recommended for a home collection:

● Ascocenda.

A hybrid formed from crossing a large *Vanda* and small *Ascocentrum* species. Plants are compact, free-flowering with a wide color range.

● Dendrobium.

A very diverse orchid genus. Some require cool weather to set blooms. Offers a wide color range. Plants are upright to arching in habit.

● Epidendrum.

Growth is variable but the reed-types are very popular, bearing long stems of small pastel flowers. Prolific roots along the stems make these species easy to propagate.

● Oncidium.

Also known as the dancing lady orchid. Easy to grow with dainty yellow and brown or white and brown flowers.

● Phalaenopsis.

Also known as the moth orchid. Produces long arching sprays with 10 to 20 blooms. Many hybrids and a wide color range are available.

● Vanda.

Many large growing species. Flowers are borne on sturdy upright stems, a dozen or more at a time. Many colors available.

Orchids must be grown in a medium that provides good drainage. Epiphytic orchids have special roots that absorb moisture in their outer velvety layers. They grow in chunky, porous mixes where most of the excess moisture drains through.

Growers can select from a wide variety of media for an epiphytic collection. Osmunda fiber, the aerial roots of a fern, was once a standard medium but is now relatively expensive and often difficult for the beginner to use.

Orchid
(*Vanda luzonica*)

Popular ingredients that now fill the pots separately or in blends include tree fern, fir bark, rock, horticultural charcoal, cork and coconut husk. Many growers also add styrofoam chips to the bottom of pots to ensure good drainage. For the beginner a tree fern and fir bark mix makes an almost foolproof medium and is available from most garden centers.

Overzealous gardeners often cause problems by overwatering orchids. One way to determine water need is to feel the medium and water when dry.

Another technique is to learn the difference in weight between a well-moistened plant and a dry one.

During the hot, dry season, orchids should be misted daily.

Obtain the best growth and increase flowering by fertilizing regularly. There are many formulas and techniques for fertilizing, but novices generally use an 18-18-18 or 20-20-20 analysis product. Follow label instructions when mixing and applying these products.

Tropical landscape

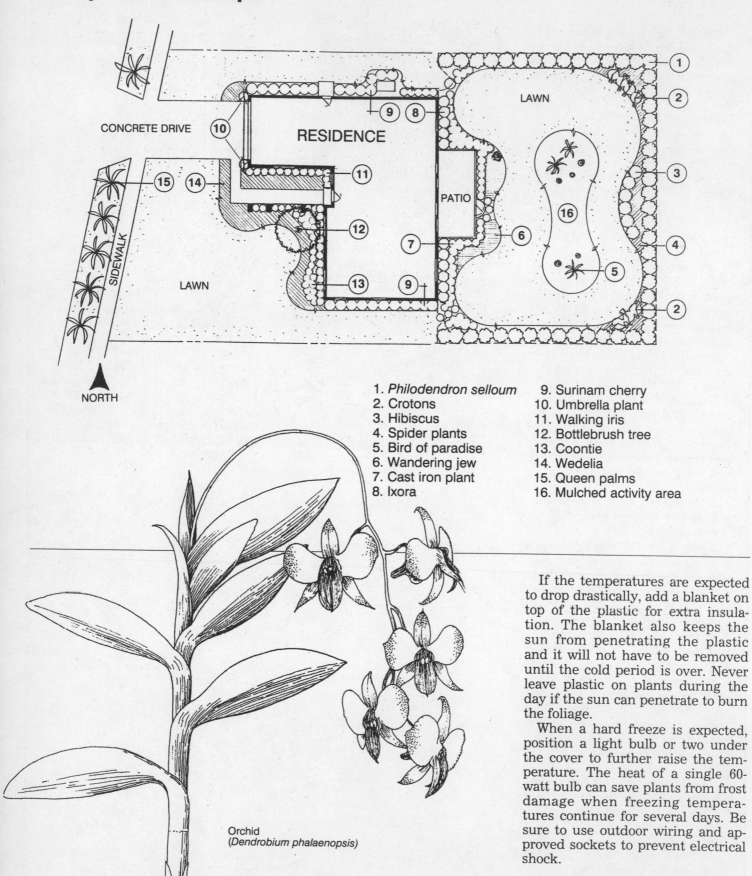

CONCRETE DRIVE

RESIDENCE

LAWN

PATIO

SIDEWALK

LAWN

NORTH

1. *Philodendron selloum*
2. Crotons
3. Hibiscus
4. Spider plants
5. Bird of paradise
6. Wandering jew
7. Cast iron plant
8. Ixora
9. Surinam cherry
10. Umbrella plant
11. Walking iris
12. Bottlebrush tree
13. Coontie
14. Wedelia
15. Queen palms
16. Mulched activity area

Orchid
(*Dendrobium phalaenopsis*)

If the temperatures are expected to drop drastically, add a blanket on top of the plastic for extra insulation. The blanket also keeps the sun from penetrating the plastic and it will not have to be removed until the cold period is over. Never leave plastic on plants during the day if the sun can penetrate to burn the foliage.

When a hard freeze is expected, position a light bulb or two under the cover to further raise the temperature. The heat of a single 60-watt bulb can save plants from frost damage when freezing temperatures continue for several days. Be sure to use outdoor wiring and approved sockets to prevent electrical shock.

Bamboos

Swaying with the gentle breezes, willowy bamboos awaken a resting garden. Listen to the whisper of rustling leaves or the tapping of reedy stems that strike a musical note. Through sight and sound bamboos bring excitement to the home landscape when clustered to form an impermeable barrier or an eye-catching focal point.

Once established, bamboos are tolerant of Florida growing conditions. Grow them in full sun or partial shade. They flourish in rich soil near the water but can tolerate the poor, dry garden sites.

Bamboos can be divided into two groups: running and clump forming.

The running varieties are the hardiest and most vigorous types. They quickly invade the garden, spreading by underground rhizomes from which new shoots, called culms, arise. These plants can be contained with 2-feet-deep concrete, fiberglass or metal barriers.

Clump-forming bamboos do not spread as rapidly, but send up new culms close to the base of the mother plant. Even though they do not sprout the vigorous rhizomes, the root system is extensive, reaching out many feet. Thus, the roots may compete with nearby plantings. Many clumping types are ornamental and of tropical or subtropical origin.

Bamboo, a member of the grass family, can be cultivated similar to the home turf. Use a high nitrogen fertilizer once each spring, summer and fall. Use a 16-4-8 or similar product at the same rate suggested for home turf where vigorous growth is desired. Use less to supply just a maintenance diet.

Water when the soil begins to dry. A mulch will help extend the time between waterings, which are usually twice a week during the hot, dry season.

Periodically thin out the dead stems and prune back all tall, floppy growth. Pests are rare, but scale is a problem that could eventually affect plantings.

A majority of bamboos are hardy throughout Central and South Florida. A few suffer leaf burn during extreme cold but send up new growth as warm weather returns.

Of the following collection the golden and black bamboos are the hardiest, surviving to near zero degrees.

● Alphonse Karr bamboo.

Grows to 35 feet. Mature canes turn yellow and sport a bright green stripe. A clump type.

● Beechey bamboo.

Can grow 40 feet tall producing 4-inch-diameter canes. A clump-forming species.

● Black bamboo.

A running type but slow growing, reaching a height of 4 to 8 feet. New stems emerge green but turn black the second year.

● Budda's belly bamboo.

Normally grows 15 to 35 feet tall. When grown in a container and given a restricted diet, sprouts can be maintained at 3 to 6 feet. Stems swell at the base to form the Budda's belly.

● Chinese goddess bamboo.

Grows 4 to 6 feet tall in ferny sprays or arching branches. A clump type.

● Golden bamboo.

Grows 6 to 10 feet, producing brilliant yellow canes. A running type.

● Oldham bamboo.

Grows 55 feet tall with an open habit. A clump-forming species with thick canes.

Despite their popularity, bamboos are not easily located for home planting. Check with local garden centers and neighbors for your first starts.

The quickest way to obtain new plants is through divisions. It's not easy however, because the stems are thick and woody. Be prepared for some hacking and sawing to obtain a small clump.

When starts are dug, trim culms back by about two-thirds. New plants will require about a year to become established in the planting site.

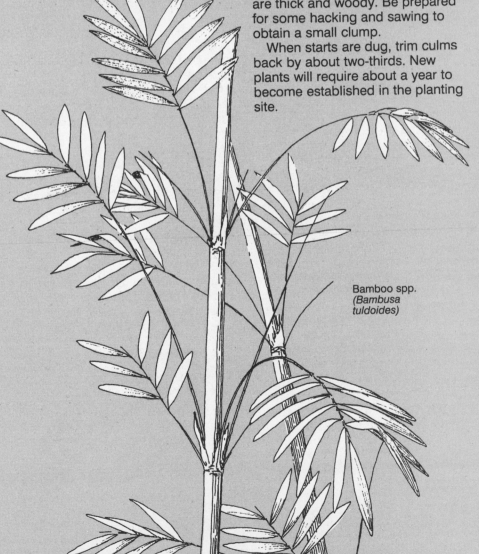

Bamboo spp.
(Bambusa tuldoides)

17

Garden critters — a few prevalent pests

BEAUTIFUL LANDSCAPES and productive gardens are often marred by Florida's prevalent pests. The caterpillars, aphids and mites are similar to those found in the North, but they are more numerous. Mild subtropical weather and lush plant growth create a favorable environment for insect life.

Vigilance is essential for successful gardening. Herbaceous flowers and vegetables are more likely to be attacked than mature trees and shrubs. Take daily walks through the garden to inspect plants and control insects by handpicking them from the plants. Spotting pests early is crucial. Regular surveys usually bring to light most turf, tree and shrub insect problems.

All flowers and vegetables require attention to grow and flourish. Florida weeds harbor many pests that can move to desirable plants. Keep weeds to a minimum to help control insects.

Detection by feeding habits

Chewing insects remove hunks of foliage or stems as they feed. The damage is easy to spot but the insects may be evasive.

Caterpillars, tiny at first, hide beneath foliage, curl up in leaves or burrow into the soil during daylight hours. Beetles and grasshoppers are migratory and by the time damage is spotted they have moved on.

Although not insects, slugs chew leaves only at night and creep under mulch, bricks and boards during the day.

Where chewing insects are suspected, check for other telltale signs. Most chewing insects leave behind excreta in the form of roundish pellets. Slugs form slime trails that can be traced across the

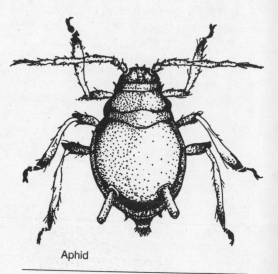

Aphid

foliage. Often, the pests are not far away and can be found by closely inspecting the leaves.

Foliage that is curled or matted together probably has been chewed by caterpillars. Dig into the soil to eliminate cutworms and check neighboring plants to find beetles. The devastation may be caused by just one large insect that can be handpicked and destroyed.

Piercing insects suck juices from the plants. Their work is not always detected until the plant is badly damaged. Some, such as aphids, feed only on new growth. Scales, whiteflies and mealybugs are not as fussy.

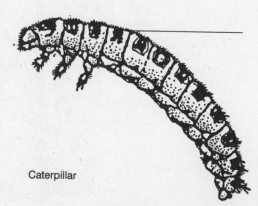

Caterpillar

Piercing-sucking insects can often be discovered by the damage on the foliage. Their feeding removes chlorophyll and leaves yellow pinpoint spots on the foliage. With continued feeding the spots grow and the foliage becomes yellow blotched and eventually browns. Turn the leaf over to find and eliminate these pests.

Mites, a spider relative with eight legs, are pests which use the piercing-sucking technique to feed. They are often not detected until plants are wrapped in a spiderlike web or the stem and foliage are covered with thousands of these tiny critters. Heavily infected plants probably will need to be destroyed.

Besides observing the plant damage, there are other methods of detecting piercing-sucking feeders. Skins which have been shed are often detectable on the foliage. The skin accumulations of mites look like ashes or dust. Aphid skins appear white, resembling the insects.

Many pests also produce excreta called honeydew that, together with sap from the plant wounds, is the food for the sooty mold fungus. When piercing-sucking insects are prevalent, plant foliage can turn black with the fungal growth. This is a good time to begin looking for scale, whiteflies and aphids.

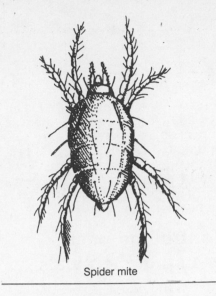
Spider mite

Natural control of garden pests

Pesticides are so handy, it is a common practice to reach for a chemical control when insects strike. Some products may eventually be needed, but many garden pests can be eliminated without resorting to toxic chemicals that kill both good and bad insects.

Before overreacting to an insect, make sure it is a pest. Praying mantises, ladybugs and assassin bugs are beneficial insects. The presence of these bugs in the garden may mean no other insect control will be needed. Learn to identify these garden helpers and let them continue to work.

Handpicking is always a good control. Sometimes just one cutworm or a few beetles are feeding on a crop. Quick action to destroy the pest could eliminate the problem. If a single limb has become a haven for caterpillars, remove that portion of the plant to

stop the infestation.

Lures and traps sometimes help with garden pests. One effective trap is the sticky board. Purchase it from a garden center or make your own. The lure, a bright yellow rectangle of rigid plastic, attracts whiteflies, leaf miners and other pests and traps them in a sticky substance. Homemade versions can be constructed using a 4-by-12-inch rectangle of bright yellow plastic coated with petroleum jelly. Place several in the garden near susceptible plants.

Simple mechanical barriers sometimes work to keep insects away. Cutworms love transplants but cannot climb paper cups or cardboard collars placed around the succulent stems. These barriers must be pressed into the soil and cover the stem a few inches above the ground to be effective.

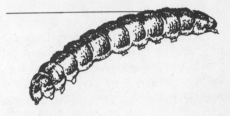
Cutworm

Florida gardeners can attempt biological controls that have worked in other regions of the nation. The techniques of releasing predators, planting trap crops and intermingling herbs to repel insects work well in some local gardens. However, pest populations increase so rapidly that these reliable methods for cooler climates often fail in subtropical gardens.

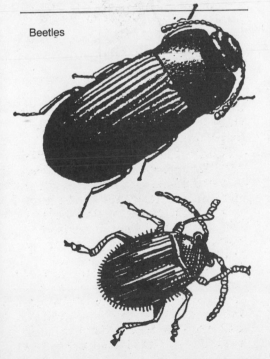
Beetles

Scale

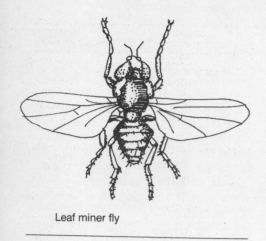

Leaf miner fly

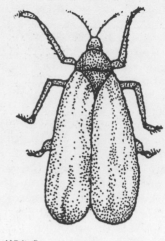

Whitefly

Also environmentally sound is insecticidal soap. Here, too, there is no residue and many pests are susceptible to the soap. Biological pesticides often permit a harvest shortly after spraying. Check the pesticide label to be sure when a crop can be picked and consumed.

Controlling pests by using chemicals

Man-made pesticides are the last resort for gardeners. If the plantings are extensive and biological controls are not working, judicious use of chemical pesticides can eliminate the insect problem. With certain susceptible fruit and vegetable plantings, a spray program may be needed at some stage. Many pests can be controlled with just one pesticide application. Getting to know the plant and its insects is the most important aspect of pest control.

Biologically acceptable pesticides have succeeded in Florida gardens. Many gardeners rely on pyrethrin and rotenone, naturally derived plant products, to keep the insects under control. These break down completely after a few days and do not harm non-target insects, man and animals.

A great control for caterpillars is the *Bacillus thuringiensis* preparation. Caterpillars react by ending feeding immediately and die within a few days.

Proper usage is the secret to good chemical pest control. Follow all label instructions and thoroughly treat the affected planting. Observe all precautions, including the protective clothing to be worn during pesticide application. When vegetables are treated always allow for the time that must elapse between the last spray and harvest.

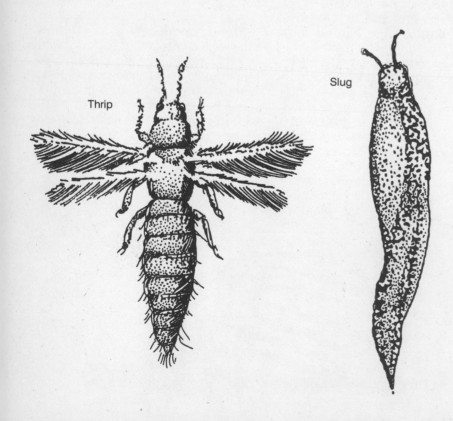

Thrip

Slug

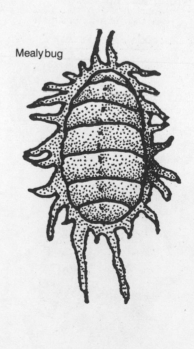

Mealybug

Common insect pests

Name	Description	Damage	Control — vegetables *	Control — ornamentals **
Aphids	Pear-shaped. Varying in color and may have wings. Cluster in new growth and under succulent leaves.	Suck juices. Cause new growth to curl and become distorted. Sooty mold may build up on leaf surfaces.	diazinon insecticidal soap malathion	diazinon insecticidal soap malathion Orthene
Beetles	Numerous types. May be striped, spotted or solid colored. Usually less than a half inch in size.	Holes in leaves, stems, flowers and fruits.	diazinon Sevin	diazinon Orthene Sevin
Caterpillars	Many green or brown but colors vary. May be striped along side or back. Less than an inch to several inches long.	Holes in stems, leaves, buds and fruits.	*Bacilius thuringiensis* diazinon Sevin Thiodan	*Bacillus thuringiensis* diazinon Orthene Sevin
Flea hoppers	Black with long legs; half inch in length	Suck juices from foilage. Produce yellow dotted leaf surface.	diazinon malathion	diazinon malathion Orthene
Leaf miners	Flylike adults rarely noticed by gardeners. Yellow larva tunnels between leaf surfaces.	Chew, tunnel in leaves forming twisting patterns. Reduce leaf efficiency.	dimethoate	dimethoate Orthene
Mealybugs	Soft-bodied. Covered with white, waxy powder. Some with long wax filaments from rear of body.	Suck juices. Plants weaken, decline rapidly. Leaves frequently wilt or drop.	seldom a problem	diazinon insecticidal soap malathion Orthene
Scales	Almost any color. Surrounded with a waxy covering that may be circular oval, oblong or pear-shaped. Can pop off covering to expose insect.	Suck juices. Cause yellowing of leaves and eventually decline.	seldom a problem	dimethoate ethion plus oil malathion plus oil Orthene
Slugs, snails	Slimy and elongate to shell covered. Brownish in color. Leaves slime trails.	Chew holes in leaves and flowers.	methaldehyde baits	Mesurol bait methaldehyde baits
Spider mites	Very small. May need hand lens to see. Often on underside of leaves. Have eight legs. Vary in color. May form webs.	Suck juices. Leaves become yellow dotted. Plants deteriorate and die.	insecticidal soap Kelthane	insecticidal soap Kelthane Vendex
Thrips	Small linear insects. Black or yellow in color.	Rasp leaves and flowers, then suck the juices. Plant portions curl and brown.	diazinon malathion	diazinon malathion Orthene
Whiteflies	White in color and resemble tiny moths. Swarm around plants when disturbed. Young are pale green in color; found on underside of leaves.	Suck juices. General weakening of plant. Often responsible for sooty mold buildup on leaves.	seldom a problem	diazinon malathion Orthene

* Use only products labeled for specific crop cultivated. Note time between last spray and harvest.

** Use only products labeled for plant to be sprayed.

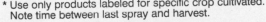

Flea hoppers

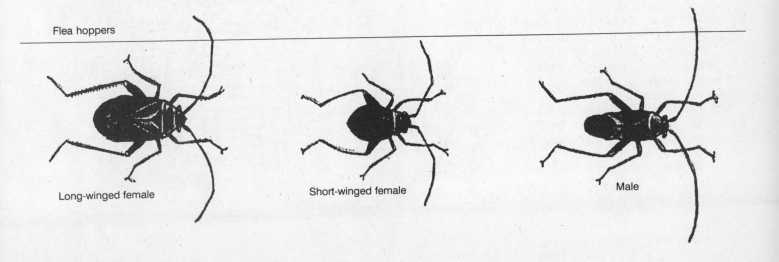

Long-winged female   Short-winged female   Male

18
The backyard menagerie

MANY ANIMALS SIMPLY meander into the lawn and garden looking for food. In their search for meals, moles raise the soil above the ground as they tunnel, and armadillos dig holes that are often a foot or more deep. Both are searching for grubs, earthworms and similar insects, their favorite foods. Their visits damage the landscape, making repair work for gardeners.

Gardeners can just ignore moles. They feed on harmful insects and aerate the soil. Moles move on when the food supply runs out. They are quite prevalent and many landscapes will have a few. They are active near the soil surface when the earth is moist and the weather is warm.

Armadillos live in deep burrows during the day and leave to feed in the evening. The burrows may be under bushes, stumps or rock piles. Armadillos were once feared because they can carry leprosy. However, there has been no leprosy associated with armadillos east of the Mississippi.

To chase away moles and armadillos, eliminate their food supply by applying the insecticide diazinon to lawns and around the border of gardens. Water the soil in the treated areas after applying insecticide. Allow about two weeks for the treatment to become effective. With insects in short supply, both pests will become discouraged and move on to more favorable feeding grounds.

Other controls for moles and armadillos are generally not effective.

Armadillo

Squirrel

Soda bottles buried so the wind whistles over the openings quickly lose their ability to frighten; buried objects designed to injure or discourage the animals are simply pushed aside. Methods that appear to work may coincide with an exhaustion of the local food supply.

Trapping moles is not for the fainthearted. Inserted into the active tunnels, traps spear or choke the rodents as they traverse the landscape. Armadillos can be lured into Hav-A-Hart live traps. Coax them into the traps with rotting fruit, including bananas, pears and grapes. When captured they can be released, unharmed, miles away from the home.

Another tunneling rodent likely to appear in Florida landscapes is the pocket gopher, also called a salamander. Looking like a large rat, he feeds on plant life including roots, tubers and bulbs. The animal prefers well-drained sands, upheaving mounds of soil as it tunnels a foot or more below the surface. Traps are the most effective control, but good results have also been obtained with poison peanuts placed in the tunnels. These rodenticide-treated peanuts are available from garden centers and hardware stores.

Coping with squirrels and rabbits

Almost everyone likes to watch squirrels as they jump from tree to tree. Although innocent looking, the squirrels may nest in the house and, if the food supply runs out, may become obnoxious and bite. Squirrels do chew on plants and have been observed defoliating elm trees, one twig at a time. They also bury food in the ground, digging holes in flower beds and later returning to sniff out the hidden supplies.

Prevent squirrel injury to buildings by sealing them out. Use screening, metal plates and other covers to prevent the entrance of squirrels into the home and storage buildings. If they are already present in the building, they can be driven out by scattering moth balls in their living area.

Outside shrubs and bulbs can be protected by sprays of nicotine sulfate and homemade preparations of epsom salts and other smelly disinfectants. Perhaps the best control is to capture the squirrels in live traps for removal to the wild.

Inquisitive rabbits are also pests that can cause widespread damage to gardens. As well as feeding on soft, succulent plants they also like to chew on tree and shrub bark. They may completely girdle a small plant and cause its death. Young trees and shrubs may be gnawed in two, but not eaten.

Rabbit

Chemical repellents are available to discourage rabbits from entering the yard and feeding on plants. Many gardeners report that the products are only temporarily effective. Home remedies of sprinkling blood meal on the soil around plants and spraying garlic or hot pepper extracts on the desirable plants can sometimes be successful.

One sure method of eliminating rabbits from the garden is to fence them out. The fence must be several feet high and completely covered or imbedded in the ground. Fencing or screening tree and shrub trunks and covering small crops are also good methods of preventing damage by rabbits.

Pocket gopher (salamander)

Woodpeckers, raccoons and other pests

Woodpeckers may visit the landscape. These beneficial birds are protected by law from trapping or other harm.

Woodpeckers feed on insects living in trees, fence posts, wood siding, window frames and wood piles. They chip and flake the wood away as they feed. Their search for food may leave shallow holes around the trunk of a tree that cause little or no harm.

Courting woodpeckers attract their mates through flight displays, calling and drumming. Most gardeners have heard their "a-rata-tat-tat" made on utility poles, rain gutters, vent caps, dead trees and wood siding. The tapping usually causes little damage but can be extremely annoying.

Nesting can cause a great deal of damage. Often woodpeckers will decide to nest where they have been feeding. The cavities they create for nests can be quite large, even hammered through sides of buildings into the insulation. Several cavities may be started until the woodpecker decides on an acceptable location.

Take prompt and persistent action to discourage vagrant woodpeckers. Remove dead trees and large dead limbs which they favor. Keep bird feeders designed for woodpeckers away from buildings.

It may be possible to frighten woodpeckers away. A dousing with water from a high-pressure hose

Woodpecker

can discourage visiting birds. Gardeners can also try startling woodpeckers by placing moving objects near them. Attach pie plates or 2- to 3-foot-long strips of aluminum foil to a length of string and place near the damage or tapping site. The birds can also be excluded from some problem sites with plastic and nylon screening or hardware cloth

— a type of wire screening.

The list of landscape varmints includes skunks, raccoons and opossums. These animals seldom cause major plant damage but gardeners should be wary of them. All can carry rabies, but the raccoon is most likely to be affected with the deadly disease. Raccoons also can carry roundworms that affect humans. It's best to view these visitors from a distance and leave trapping to a professional. Should the animals act tame, beware: It's the first sign of rabies.

Gardeners are also likely to encounter frogs, lizards and garden snakes. All are beneficial, as they feed on insects and cause no harm to plants.

Get to know poisonous snakes so an encounter can be avoided. The remainder of these visitors are harmless to man and best tolerated or scooted on their way to feed in other gardens.

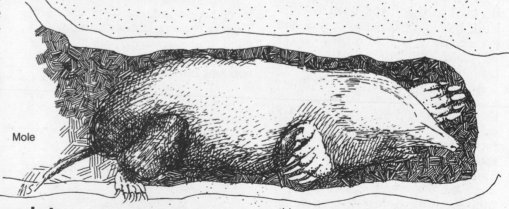

Mole

Common landscape varmints

Animal	Damage to landscape	Controls
Armadillos	Dig holes up to a foot deep and equally wide in the turf and ornamental plantings. May live in burrows within the landscape.	Control soil insect food supply with labeled insecticide. Lure into live trap for relocation.
Moles	Tunneling disturbs roots, produces uneven terrain, causes small plants and turf to decline.	Control soil insect food supply with labeled insecticide. Insert traps into tunnels.
Pocket gophers (salamanders)	Tunnel underground. Push up mounds of soil. Feed on roots, tubers and bulbs.	Poison peanuts placed in tunnels. Traps inserted into tunnels.
Rabbits	Feed on succulent plants. Nibble bark and limbs of small trees and shrubs.	Fence out of gardens. Use repellent sprays. Lure into live traps for relocation.
Squirrels	Dig holes in lawns, flower beds. Chew plant portions.	Lure into live trap for relocation. Repellent sprays.
Woodpeckers	Make small, usually harmless holes to large cavities for nesting in trees and buildings.	Frighten with water dousing or moving objects. Eliminate dead limbs, nesting sites. Wrap trunks with hardware cloth.

Appendix I

Resources you can use

GARDENING ENCOURAGES a never-ending education. With each plant grown a new adventure begins, bringing an abundance of beauty and new problems. It's impossible to cultivate a garden, design a landscape or manage turf without the knowledge and help of others.

In Florida there are many individuals readily available to assist with plant culture. Use these resources to obtain the firsthand information needed to grow an attractive and productive landscape.

Cooperative Extension Service

All of Florida's 67 counties have Cooperative Extension Service offices. In the past the service was known as the Agricultural Center or county agent's office. These educational centers dispense plant culture information disseminated by the Institute of Food and Agricultural Sciences at the University of Florida, Gainesville. Researchers, professors and extension agents work together to develop classes, bulletins and mass media programs to help gardeners.

Through the County Extension

Service problems can be diagnosed and soil samples can be tested. It's one of the first resources gardeners should call upon for help. Most services are tax supported and only small fees may be charged to cover laboratory tests, a few publications and instructional materials. Find your county agent's office and give it a call.

ALACHUA
2800 N.E. 39 Ave.
Gainesville 32609
(904) 377-0400

BAKER
P.O. Box 1018
Macclenny 32063
(904) 259-3520

BAY
2234 E. 15 St.
Panama City 32405
(904) 763-5456

BRADFORD
P.O. Drawer 1028
Starke 32091
(904) 964-6280

BREVARD
1125 W. King St.
Cocoa 32922
(305) 632-9505

Bamboo spp.
(Bambusa tuldoides)

BROWARD
3245 College Ave.
Davie 33314
(305) 475-8450

CALHOUN
340 E. Central Ave.
Blountstown 32424
(904) 674-8323

CHARLOTTE
6900 Florida St.
Punta Gorda 33950-5799
(813) 639-6255

CITRUS
3600 S. Florida Ave.
Inverness 32650
(904) 726-2141

CLAY
2463 State Road 16 W.
P.O. Box 278
Green Cove Springs 32043
(904) 284-6355

COLLIER
Court Plaza
2663 Airport Road
Suite D-103
Naples 33962
(813) 774-8370

COLUMBIA
P.O. Box 1587
Lake City 32056-1587
(904) 752-5384

DADE
18710 S.W. 288 St.
Homestead 33030
(305) 248-3311

DESOTO
P.O. Drawer 310
Arcadia 33821
(813) 494-0303

DIXIE
P.O. Box V
Cross City 32628
(904) 498-3330

DUVAL
1010 N. McDuff Ave.
Jacksonville 32205
(904) 384-2001

ESCAMBIA
P.O. Box 7154
Pensacola 32514
(904) 477-0953

FLAGLER
P.O. Box 308
Bunnell 32010
(904) 437-3122

FRANKLIN
P.O. Box 190
Apalachicola 32320
(904) 653-9337

GADSDEN
P.O. Box 820
Quincy 32351
(904) 627-6315

GILCHRIST
P.O. Box 157
Trenton 32693
(904) 463-2022

GLADES
P.O. Box 400
Moore Haven 33471
(813) 946-0244

GULF
Gulf County Courthouse
Port St. Joe 32456
(904) 229-6123

HAMILTON
P.O. Drawer K
Jasper 32052
(904) 792-1276

HARDEE
P.O. Box 1288
Wauchula 33873
(813) 773-2164

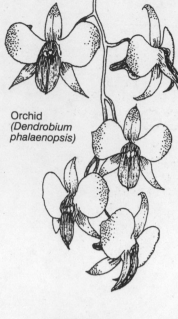

Orchid
(*Dendrobium phalaenopsis*)

HENDRY
P.O. Box 68
Labelle 33935
(813) 675-5261

HERNANDO
6460 W. Broad St.
Brooksville 33512
(904) 796-9421

HIGHLANDS
4509 W. George Blvd.
Sebring 33870
(813) 382-5248

HILLSBOROUGH
5339 State Road 579
Seffner 33584
(813) 621-5605

Orchid
(*Vanda luzonica*)

HOLMES
201 N. Oklahoma St.
Bonifay 32425
(904) 547-3602

INDIAN RIVER
2001 Ninth Ave.
Suite 303
Vero Beach 32960
(305) 567-8000

JACKSON
P.O. Drawer 698
Marianna 32446
(904) 482-2064

JEFFERSON
1246 N. Jefferson St.
Monticello 32334
(904) 997-3573

LAFAYETTE
Route 1, Box 15
Mayo 32066
(904) 294-1279

LAKE
1220 Duncan Drive
Tavares 32778
(904) 343-4101

LEE
3406 Palm Beach Blvd.
Fort Myers 33905
(813) 335-2421

LEON
615 Paul Russell Road
Tallahassee 32301
(904) 487-3003

LEVY
P.O. Box 219
Bronson 32621
(904) 486-2165

LIBERTY
P.O. Box 368
Bristol 32321
(904) 643-2229

MADISON
900 College Ave.
Madison 32340
(904) 973-4138

MANATEE
1303 17th St.
Palmetto 33561
(813) 722-4524

MARION
2232 N.E. Jacksonville Road
Ocala 32670
(904) 629-8067

MARTIN
2614 S.E. Dixie Highway
Stuart 33494
(305) 283-6760

MONROE
P.O. Box 2545
Key West 33045
(305) 294-4641

NASSAU
P.O. Box 489
Hilliard 32046
(904) 845-2121

OSCEOLA
1901 E. Vine St.
Kissimmee 32743
(305) 846-4181

PALM BEACH
531 N. Military Trail
West Palm Beach 33415-1395
(305) 683-1777

PASCO
1516 Highway 52 W.
Dade City 33525
(904) 521-4288

PINELLAS
12175 125th St. N.
Largo 33544
(813) 586-5477

SARASOTA
2900 Ringling Blvd.
Sarasota 33577
(813) 955-6239

SEMINOLE
4320 S. Orlando Drive
Sanford 32771
(305) 323-2500

ST. JOHNS
49 King St.
P.O. Drawer 270
St. Augustine 32804
(904) 824-8131

ST. LUCIE
8400 Picos Road
Suite 101
Fort Pierce 33451
(305) 464-2900

SUMTER
P.O. Box 218
Bushnell 33513
(904) 793-2728

Snapdragon
(*Antirrhinum*)

SUWANNEE
1302 11th St. S.W.
Live Oak 32060
(904) 362-2771

TAYLOR
P.O. 820
Perry 32347
(904) 584-4345

UNION
35 N.E. First St.
Lake Butler 32054
(904) 496-2321

VOLUSIA
3100 E. State Road 44
DeLand 32724
(904) 736-0624

WAKULLA
P.O. Box 40
Crawfordville 32327
(904) 926-3931

WALTON
900 N. Ninth St.
DeFuniak Springs 32433
(904) 892-5415

WASHINGTON
800 Highway 90 W.
Chipley 32428
(904) 638-0740

OKALAOOSA
P.O. Box 488
Crestview 32536
(904) 682-2711

OKEECHOBEE
501 N.W. Fifth Ave.
Okeechobee 33472
(813) 763-6469

ORANGE
2350 E. Michigan St.
Orlando 32806
(305) 897-4004

POLK
1702 U.S. Highway 17-98 S.
Bartow 33830
(813) 533-0765

PUTNAM
P.O. Drawer 918
Palatka 32078-0918
(904) 328-5181

SANTA ROSA
1099 Old Bagdad Highway
Room 116
Milton 32570
(904) 623-3868

Marigold
(*Tagetes*)

Plant societies

Enthusiastic gardeners have formed many societies to learn and share information about their favorite plants. Florida is rich with societies, each offering a wealth of knowledge to both the beginner and the expert.

Society members share cultural information, plants, field trips and good times. Many societies have lending libraries that members can use

Societies often do not have a permanent address. Contact your local extension service, library or botanical garden for an up-to-date listing of societies meeting in your area. Among the many societies in Florida are:

- African Violet Society
- Begonia Society
- Bonsai Club
- Bromeliad Society
- Camellia Society
- Caribbean Bamboo Society
- Fern Society
- Florida Native Plant Society
- Florida State Horticultural Society
- Heliconia Society
- Hemerocallis Society
- Herb Society
- Hibiscus Society
- Ikebana International
- Iris Society
- Orchid Society
- Palm Society
- Rose Society
- Wild Flower Society

Garden clubs

The many garden clubs of Florida meet to share plant knowledge, crafts, community projects and fellowship. Expect to find experienced gardeners at the clubs willing to share their knowledge. Many have libraries where reference books on a wide variety of subjects can be borrowed.

Large community garden clubs may be divided into smaller neighborhood circles. These small groups usually meet in members' homes. Many meet during the day but there are a few night owl clubs that serve working families.

Garden clubs from throughout the state belong to the Florida Federation of Garden Clubs, 1400 S. Denning Drive, Winter Park, Fla. 32789. Write to the Federation to obtain information about meetings in your area.

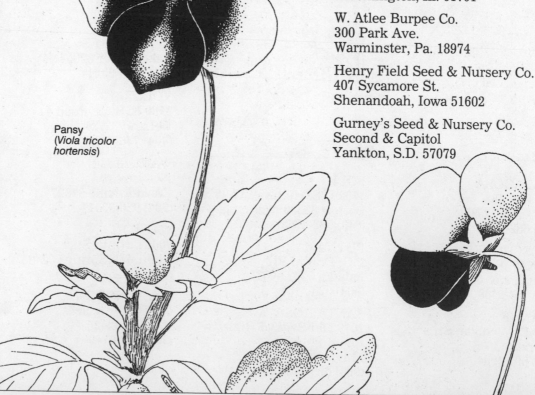

Pansy
(*Viola tricolor hortensis*)

Garden centers and seed companies

Every community has its nursery, plant store or garden center. Many of the supplies needed to cultivate a garden or landscape a house can be found locally. Plants for sale at garden centers are the right choices for Florida conditions. Garden centers are also staffed with knowledgeable individuals waiting to help with a problem or give advice on a new crop. Many will test soil and identify insects found in the landscape.

Seed companies are mail-order garden centers. Each year gardeners await the arrival of the catalogs so they can plan the new season's garden. Most catalogs serve as gardening guides with pictures and cultural information. Many companies offer transplants, trees, shrubs, pesticides and equipment as well as seeds.

Few gardeners would be caught without a stack of catalogs after the new year. Most are sent free, but some companies charge a small fee to cover the cost of printing. Some companies that offer mail-order sales are:

Burgess Seed & Plant Co.
905 Four Seasons Road
Bloomington, Ill. 61701

W. Atlee Burpee Co.
300 Park Ave.
Warminster, Pa. 18974

Henry Field Seed & Nursery Co.
407 Sycamore St.
Shenandoah, Iowa 51602

Gurney's Seed & Nursery Co.
Second & Capitol
Yankton, S.D. 57079

Harris Moran Seed Co.
3670 Buffalo Road
Rochester, N.Y. 14624

H.G. Hastings
P.O. Box 4274
Atlanta, Ga. 30302

Johnny's Selected Seeds
Foss Hill Road
Albion, Maine 04910

J.W. Jung Seed Co.
333 S. High St.
Randolph, Wis. 53957

Kilgore Seed Co.
1400 W. First St.
Sanford, Fla. 32771

Earl May Seed & Nursery Co.
208 N. Elm St.
Shenandoah, Iowa 51603

Mellinger
2310 W. South Range
North Lima, Ohio 44452

L.L. Olds Seed Co.
P.O. Box 7790
Madison, Wis. 53707

Geo. W. Park Seed Co.
Cokesbury Road
Greenwood, S.C. 29646

R.H. Shumway's
P.O. Box 1
Graniteville, S.C. 29829

Stokes Seeds
P.O. Box 548
Buffalo, N.Y. 14240

Thompson & Morgan
P.O. Box 1308
Jackson, N.J. 08527

Otis W. Twilley Seed Co.
P.O. Box 65
Trevose, Pa. 19047

The Urban Farmer
P.O. Box 444
Convent Station, N.J. 07961

Vermont Bean Seed Co.
Garden Land
Bomoseen, Vt. 05732

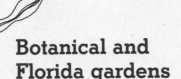

Bromeliad
(*Cryptanthus spp.*)

Botanical and Florida gardens

Experience the beauty of manicured landscapes, nature trails or plant collections by visiting the many Florida public gardens. Only a few botanical gardens are found within the state, but each community has its parks, trails and flower gardens available for visiting.

Botanical gardens offer an introduction to diverse collections of plants. Many specialize in certain genera or groups of plants for an area, and offer memberships. For a fee those who join receive newsletters, class information and discounts. In addition they can participate in field trips and plant exchanges.

Community parks and tourist attractions also offer great introductions to Florida's landscape plantings. Most are well planted, offering seasonal changes of flowers and new varieties to enjoy. Some have taken the extra effort to label plantings so gardeners will know what to request at their nursery.

It's often a great way to have fun and enjoy Florida plantings at their best. Visit the following to begin a tour of Florida horticulture:
- Audubon House and Gardens, Key West
- Bok Tower Gardens, Lake Wales
- Busch Gardens, Tampa
- Eden State Gardens and Mansion, Point Washington
- Fairchild Tropical Gardens, Coral Gables
- Flamingo Gardens, Fort Lauderdale
- Florida Cypress Gardens, Winter Haven
- Harry P. Leu Gardens, Orlando
- Hialeah Park, Hialeah
- Maclay State Gardens, Tallahassee
- Marie Selby Botanical Gardens, Sarasota
- Mead Gardens, Winter Park
- The Morikami Museum of Japanese Culture, Delray Beach
- The Oldest House Museum and Gardens, Key West

Cardboard palm
(*Zamia furfuraceae*)

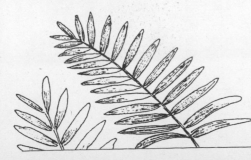

121

- Orchid Jungle, Homestead
- Ormond Beach Memorial, Ormond Beach
- Ravine State Gardens, Palatka
- Preston B. Bird and Mary Heinlein Redland Fruit and Spice Park, Homestead
- Sarasota Jungle Gardens, Sarasota
- Sea World of Florida, Orlando
- Sugar Mill Gardens, Port Orange
- Sunken Gardens of St. Petersburg, St. Petersburg
- Thomas A. Edison's Winter Home, Fort Myers
- Tiki Gardens and Shops, Indian Shores
- Vizcaya, Miami
- West Martello Garden Center, Key West
- Walt Disney World and Epcot Center, Lake Buena Vista

More help

Libraries are terrific resources for references on gardening. Learn how to grow a plant, build a greenhouse or make compost by drawing from the experience of horticulturists from around the world. Many books can be checked out, but larger and more costly editions will have to be used at the library.

Newspapers and magazines can keep gardeners up-to-date. Gardening techniques change rapidly. There are also new products, societies and pests. These, plus monthly plant care hints, are good reasons to check the gardening section of a newspaper or subscribe to a magazine devoted to gardening. A library is a good place to discover which magazine fits your horticultural needs.

Cabbage palmetto
(*Sabal palmetto*)

Appendix II

A month-by-month Florida gardening guide

Confederate jasmine (*Trachelospermum jasminoides*)

January

✔ Keep holiday plants attractive into the new year by providing bright light; water when the soil begins to dry.

✔ Complete cool-season vegetable plantings of beets, broccoli, cabbage, carrots, cauliflower, collards, lettuce, mustard, peas, potatoes, radishes and turnips.

✔ Flowers that brighten the winter landscape include alyssum, calendula, cleome, dianthus, gaillardia, lobelia, petunias, poppy and sweet pea.

✔ Remove spent blooms from annuals and fertilize every four to six weeks.

✔ Sow tomato, pepper and eggplant seeds by midmonth to have transplants by early March. Till soil, complete fumigation for spring garden.

✔ Prune apple, peach, grape and fig crops. Apply dormant spray before apple and peach trees flower.

✔ Regreen rye grass lawns with an application of 10 pounds of 6-6-6 fertilizer per 1,000 square feet.

✔ Transplant trees and shrubs during their dormant period. Remove large limbs and reshape trees.

February

✔ In midmonth, give trees and shrubs their first feeding of the new year. Prune shade and fruit trees. Complete transplanting bareroot trees and shrubs. Reshape hedges.

✔ Prune roses early and cut vigorous bushes back by a third to a half.

✔ Flowers to plant: alyssum, calendula, dianthus, gerberas, gaillardias, pansies, petunias and snapdragons.

✔ Vegetables to plant: beets, broccoli, collards, lettuce, peas, potatoes, radishes and turnips. Late-month crops include beans, cantaloupe, corn, cucumber, eggplant, pepper, squash, tomatoes and watermelons.

✔ Herbs to plant: basil, dill, sweet marjoram, chives, sage, thyme and mint.

✔ Turn fallen leaves into compost.

✔ Rake out crabgrass and apply a pre-emergence weed control in late February.

✔ Plant Florida varieties of apples, blackberries, blueberries, citrus, figs, grapes, peaches and pears.

March

✔ Prune cold-injured limbs back into healthy wood. Feed all trees and shrubs, using half the recommended rate for cold-damaged plants.

✔ Green up lawns with the first feeding of the year. Bahia lawns may need extra iron if yellowing occurs. Control lawn weeds with pre-emergence herbicides. A stiff raking will remove dead grass and speed regrowth.

✔ Finish fertilizing all trees and shrubs early in the month.

✔ Plant potted poinsettias in a sunny garden site and prune to 12 to 18 inches above the soil.

✔ Begin a spray program for apple, peach, pear and grape plants, using a product that contains both an insecticide and fungicide.

✔ Bulbs for spring planting: achimenes, amaryllis, begonias, caladiums, canna, crinum, gladioli and rainlilies.

✔ Plant corn, peppers, tomatoes and watermelons early. Warm-season crops to plant throughout March: beans, cantaloupe, cucumber, eggplant, okra, southern peas and squash.

✔ Flowers for spring planting: ageratum, balsam, celosia, cosmos, dahlia, four-o'clocks, marigolds, portulaca, torenia and zinnias.

Marigold
(*Tageta*)

Zinnia

April

✔ Complete fertilizing lawns. Attack broadleaf and grassy weeds while they're small and easy to control. Seed bare spots in bahia lawns. All sod grows well in April.

✔ Check lawnmower for proper height. Cut both St. Augustine and bahia grasses so blades are 3 to 4 inches high.

✔ Give newly planted trees and shrubs a light application of 6-6-6 or similar fertilizer.

✔ Replenish mulches to conserve moisture.

✔ Take winter-weary houseplants outdoors to a shady spot; water and fertilize.

✔ Spray roses weekly for black spot, mites and thrips.

✔ Prune azaleas when flowering is over.

✔ Perk up annual flower beds with warm-season replacements of ageratum, aster, balsam, celosia, cosmos, marigold, salvia, portulaca and zinnia plantings.

✔ Spring vegetables to plant: beans, cantaloupes, cucumbers, eggplants, okra, peppers, squash, southern peas and sweet potatoes.

May

✔ Fertilize flowers and vegetables lightly with a 6-6-6 product every three to four weeks.

✔ Give St. Augustine and bahia lawns a second fertilizer application. Boost shrubs with a late-spring fertilizing.

✔ Keep roses free of mites, thrips and black spot with weekly sprays.

✔ Plant caladium, canna and gladiolus bulbs for summer color.

✔ Annuals to plant: celosia, coleus, impatiens, marigolds, periwinkle, portulaca, salvia, torenia and zinnias.

✔ Vegetables to plant: collards, okra, southern peas, sweet potatoes and cherry tomatoes.

✔ Complete pruning of late-winter-spring flowering azaleas and camellias.

✔ Take tip cuttings to root in vermiculite.

✔ Check for chinch-bug and mole-cricket activity in lawns and treat as needed.

Daylily
(*Hemerocallis*)

124

Cardboard palm
(*Zamia furfuraceae*)

June

✔ Sow a bahia lawn and let Mother Nature do the watering.

✔ Give recovering citrus a second, light feeding. Fertilize shade trees.

✔ Begin to bait or spray for hatching mole crickets.

✔ Spray for black spot and mites on roses.

✔ Apply mulches to continue summer weed control.

✔ Only heat-tolerant okra, southern peas, sweet potatoes and cherry tomatoes will produce a summer crop.

✔ Summer flowers: celosia, coleus, impatiens, marigolds, periwinkle, portulaca, salvia, torenia and zinnias.

✔ Fertilize flowers and veggies every three to four weeks.

✔ Bake out nematodes by covering barren gardens for four to six weeks with clear plastic.

✔ Pinch back tips of new shrub growth to develop bushier plants.

✔ Find orchids a filtered-sun exposure and feed every two weeks.

✔ Divide and repot houseplants.

July

✔ Bait mole crickets in bahia and Bermuda lawns. Sod or seed lawns. Chewed grass blades indicate the presence of sod webworms.

✔ Blanket bare gardens with a layer of clear plastic to bake out nematodes before you replant — or fumigate.

✔ Spade and till the vegetable garden for mid-August planting.

✔ Sow tomato and pepper seeds by midmonth to have transplants by August.

✔ Add color to the landscape with coleus, impatiens, marigolds, torenia and periwinkle.

✔ Vegetables to plant include okra, southern peas and cherry tomatoes.

✔ Grow landscape replacements by rooting cuttings from favorite shrubs and foliage plants.

✔ Root 6- to 8-inch poinsettia cuttings to have potted plants by Christmas.

✔ Distorted and brown-speckled citrus foliage is damaged by a disease called melanose. Prune out dead wood and spray with a copper fungicide.

✔ Control black spot on roses with a weekly fungicide spray.

✔ Fertilize houseplants that are outdoors for the summer every two weeks.

August

✔ Heap on the organic matter and till the soil to prepare an early fall garden.

✔ Sow watermelon seed by the 10th, but delay planting bean, broccoli, celery, collard, corn, cucumber, eggplant, onion, pepper, squash and tomato crops until midmonth.

✔ Transplant tomato and pepper seedlings from July sowings to small containers.

✔ Bait now for mole crickets that surface to feed at night in bahia and Bermuda lawns. Chinch bugs are active in yellowing St. Augustine turf. Finish seeding bahia lawns.

✔ Eliminate black spot on roses with a weekly fungicide spray.

✔ Root poinsettia cuttings immediately to have plants in bloom for Christmas.

✔ It's too late to prune azaleas, but continue to cut back poinsettias and other shrubs.

✔ Feed grape vines as the harvest ends. Fertilize newly planted trees and shrubs lightly every six to eight weeks.

✔ Annual flowers to brighten the garden: celosia, coleus, impatiens, marigolds, periwinkle, purslane, salvia and torenia.

✔ Repot plants that are potbound.

✔ The rainy season is the best time to plant palms.

Cabbage palmetto
(*Sabal palmetto*)

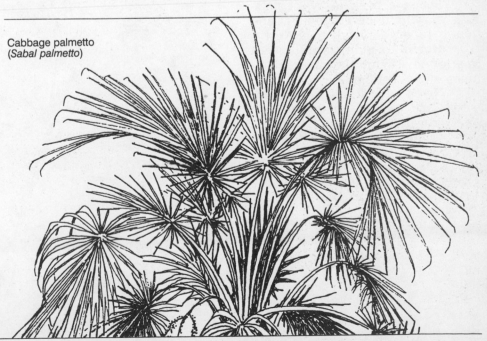

Bamboo spp.
*(Bambusa
tuldoides)*

September

✔ Complete the warm-season vegetable plantings of beans, cucumbers, eggplant, peppers, squash and tomatoes by midmonth. Save cool-season crops of broccoli, cabbage, celery, collards, onions and turnips for the end of the month.

✔ Regreen lawns with a complete fertilizer.

✔ Prune poinsettias by midmonth to keep them on schedule for holidays.

✔ Keep flower gardens from fading by planting amaranthus, coleus, cosmos, impatiens, marigolds, periwinkle, sunflower, torenia and verbena.

✔ Sneak a peck at sweet potatoes growing underground. Fat and plump tubers are ready to harvest.

✔ Herbs to plant: sage, sweet marjoram, thyme, lavender, rosemary and sweet fennel.

✔ Give final pruning to cold-sensitive hedges and ornamentals so new growth can mature by winter. Root-prune trees you plan to move this winter.

✔ Groom roses by removing old flowers, damaged limbs and spindly growth. Fertilize to encourage fall flowering.

✔ Hand pick and destroy caterpillars, or spray to control.

October

✔ Hurry to complete the seeding of permanent lawns. Sprigging, plugging and sodding can continue into the fall. Fertilizing of all turf should be completed early this month.

✔ Give citrus a final feeding early in the month using 6-6-6 or a specialty fertilizer.

✔ Prepare and plant strawberry beds.

✔ Vegetables to plant: beets, broccoli, cabbage, carrots, cauliflower, collards, kohlrabi, lettuce, mustard, onions, peas, radishes, spinach and turnips.

✔ Flowers to plant: alyssum, calendula, cleome, cornflower, dianthus, gaillardia, hollyhock, larkspur, lobelia, pansy, petunia, snapdragon, sweet pea and verbena.

✔ Check for pests on plants to be brought indoors; spray as needed.

✔ Position poinsettia, Christmas cactus and kalanchoe where they will receive no artificial light to have flowers for the holidays.

✔ Begin 12 weeks of refrigeration of tulip, narcissus, daffodil, crocus and hyacinth bulbs.

✔ Check roses, junipers, citrus and annual flowers for mites that build up when the rains stop.

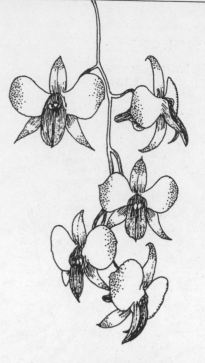

Orchid
(Dendrobium phalaenopsis)

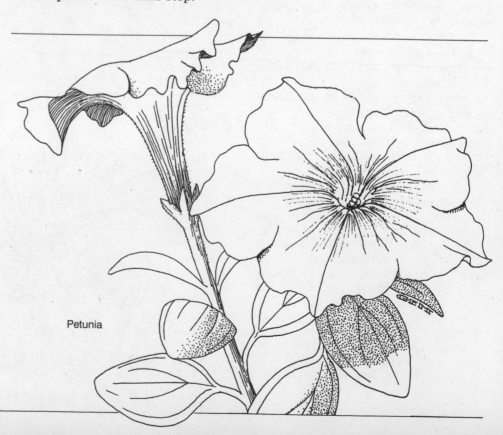

Petunia

November

✔ Fertilize roses monthly. Begin cutting blooms to reduce plant height.

✔ Flowers for fall include alyssum, calendula, cleome, cornflower, dianthus, gaillardia, hollyhocks, larkspur, lobelia, pansy, petunia, snapdragon, sweet pea and verbena.

✔ Vegetables for fall: beets, broccoli, cabbage, carrots, cauliflower, collards, kohlrabi, lettuce, mustard, onions, peas, radishes, spinach and turnips.

✔ Herbs for fall: anise, chives, coriander, dill, lavender, rosemary, sage, sweet fennel, sweet marjoram and thyme.

✔ Revive a sparse lawn with an overseeding of ryegrass.

✔ Continue to cut a growing lawn at the normal 3- to 4-inch height for bahia and St. Augustine. Control lawn weeds with a liquid herbicide.

✔ Caterpillars are voracious feeders during the cool months. Apply biological controls such as Dipel or Thuricide. Control scale insects with a low-toxicity oil spray.

✔ Move cold-sensitive foliage plants indoors before the temperatures dip below 55 F.

✔ Renew mulch to conserve moisture and prevent winter injury.

Live oak
(*Quercus virginiana*)

Orchid
(*Vanda luzonica*)

December

✔ Transplant trees and shrubs on cooler days.

✔ Be prepared with blankets, large boxes and trash cans to cover plants on frosty nights.

✔ Screen greenhouses and shade houses with plastic.

✔ Store fertilizers in a dry, cool place until spring.

✔ Reduce lawn irrigation to once or twice a week.

✔ Clean, oil and store garden equipment. Drain gas tanks and lubricate mower, edger and tiller engines.

✔ Flowers to plant: alyssum, calendula, dianthus, hollyhock, lobelia, pansy, petunia, snapdragon and verbena.

✔ Vegetables to plant: beets, broccoli, cabbage, carrots, cauliflower, collards, lettuce, mustard, onions, radishes, spinach and turnips.

✔ Make sure gift plants last through the holidays by displaying them in a bright, cool spot.

Crape myrtle
(*Lagerstroemia indica*)

Index

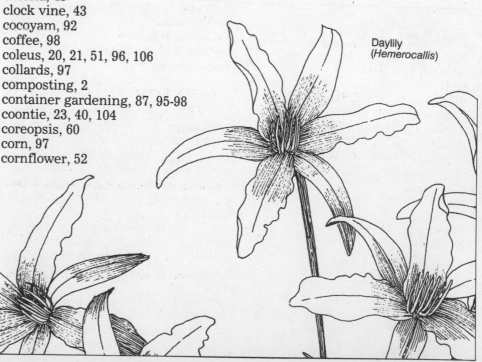

Daylily
(*Hemerocallis*)

Gerbera daisy
(*Gerbera jamesonii*))

Cardboard palm
(Zamia
furfuraceae)

List of plant illustrations